guardianstyle

David Marsh
and Amelia Hodsdon

guardianbooks

Published by Guardian Books 2010

First published in Great Britain in 2004 by
Guardian Books
Kings Place
90 York Way
London N1 9GU

www.guardianbooks.co.uk

A CIP catalogue record for this book is available from the British Library

ISBN: 978-0-85265-222-0

Produced by Artypeeps
Cover design by obroberts
Text design by Nicky Barneby

Printed and bound in Great Britain by Clays Ltd, St Ives PLC

Contents

Introduction

Forsweating all errors

Dedicated to the subeditors of the Guardian, Observer and
guardian.co.uk, past, present and (we hope) future.
"They also serve who do not sign their names"

This book is a statement of intent and an admission of failure.
Every day we aim to produce a perfect newspaper. We have
never succeeded yet, and we never will. It's doubtful that in the
200-plus years of newspaper history, anyone ever has. That isn't
going to stop us trying, although some days bring more
disappointment than others.

Take 15 July 2010, when a Guardian leading article began:
"The lower house of the French parliament passed a law on
Tuesday which, according to the interior ministry, would directly
effect fewer than 2,000 people ... " Beneath it, the second leading
article concluded: "The Treasury faces a tricky task in persuading
the rest of Whitehall not to cut investment even more deeply. But
unless it succeeds, a few years down the line, the coalition may
find that leaking school roofs become an emblem of all that is
wrong with its rule, just as they did for the Tories of old."

Did you spot the mistakes? That "effect" should of course be
affect, while the rogue comma after "a few years down the line"
blurs the point the writer is trying to make, namely that unless
the Treasury succeeds in its current task, leaking school roofs
may become an emblem of failure a few years down the line.

To be fair to our normally excellent leader writers and
subeditors, serious errors in leaders are rare. And if you think
things are bad now, they were much worse in the good old days.
Here is a verbatim extract from one of our attempts to cover
American politics in the 1960s:

*"Mr Nion was looking towards Washington, but the committee
was liiking at Mr Nixon. He would have to oick the candidate,
and if he oicked another man, eho lost, the party would be loth
to nominate for the Preidency a national leader whose
influence could not carry his own state in a state election. Yet, if*

*Mr Noxon ran himself and won, he would practiclly forsweat
the presidency; for, like allaspiring governors, he has been
bocal and bitter about men who use the governor's mansion as
a springboard int the White House."*

The "Grauniad" nickname, once well-earned, has been hard
to shake off, but on the whole we do better today - despite the
fact that we are processing many times the number of words in
a round-the-clock international operation that would astonish
the editors, writers, subeditors, compositors, proofreaders,
copyholders and typesetters who worked in Cross Street,
Manchester, a few decades ago. Typewriters, stubby pencils and
metal rulers have been replaced by computerisation and the
internet, opening up a new world of resources, although one
with its own set of pitfalls (see the "spellchecker" entry).

Guardian Style began life as a manual for journalists at the
Manchester Guardian, appearing in 1928 when the great CP
Scott was well into his sixth decade as editor. That first "Stylebook of the Manchester Guardian" was updated in 1950 and
subsequent editions followed at approximately 10-year
intervals, with an online style guide launched in 2000
(guardian.co.uk/styleguide).

Why bother with a book, you might ask, when the guide is
readily available, and widely used, online? Well, as one reader of
a previous edition pointed out, there are some places where you
just don't take your laptop: "A note of appreciation for the
stylebook, which I'm now reading for about the third time. Do
not take it the wrong way if I mention that it's an absolutely
perfect book to keep in the loo. Useful and amusing."

The three years since the last edition of Guardian Style have
been eventful - for Guardian News & Media, our owners, and for
our industry. Our move to a new building late in 2008 was
accompanied by the merger of Guardian and Observer
newspapers with the guardian.co.uk website, so that most
journalists now work across various formats, including digital,

which in many cases has required a different approach and new skills. This had implications for house style, as the Guardian and Observer had followed different versions over many years - it was no longer tenable to have separate styles when stories from either paper might run alongside one another on the website, read by millions of people who know us only through guardian.co.uk. The unifying process involved months of delicate negotiations as both papers were anxious not to sacrifice their distinctive character, but any disagreements were resolved amicably.

For the media as a whole, the past couple of years have seen a relentless acceleration in the growth of digital publishing, bringing amazing opportunities alongside doubts about the continued viability of the old print model. We now publish our material in every format from printed newspaper to iPhone app, from blogpost to podcast, from millions of words in our Data Store to 140-character tweets. The relationship between journalists and readers has been transformed by continual real-time feedback and interaction, now moving a stage further through the concept of mutualisation, which will create more of a joint enterprise as journalists work collaboratively with many other providers of information and expertise, including readers.

Participation from readers has, of course, been a feature of Guardian Style for years: many of the entries have been prompted by their comments, written in response to their queries (and occasionally rewritten in answer to their complaints).

The hundreds of entries may be broadly divided into the following categories: grammar and punctuation (which now have their own section); words easily confused, misused, misspelt, or all three; advice about how to write and edit well; factual information; and Guardian values - how what we write should reflect our traditions of tolerance and fairness.

What we have tried to avoid, unlike some style manuals, is to impose such a straitjacket that all our stories sound as if they were written by the same person - not much chance of that anyway, with writers as brilliant and distinctive as John Crace, Jonathan Freedland, Ben Goldacre, Simon Hattenstone, Simon Jenkins, Lucy Mangan, Zoe Williams and many others who have generously contributed to this book.

WP Crozier, himself an editor of the Guardian, recalled of CP Scott: "Since the paper was critical, independent, and in frequent opposition to popular opinion, he felt that everything should be done to make it clear to the average man and woman. It was to appeal to the intelligent rather than to the erudite. He tried to keep out of it the pedantic and obscure, pretence and ostentation. He liked plain English, holding that everything in a foreign language, living or dead, that crept into the paper could have been said as well or better in English ... He constantly asked the question 'What does it mean?' or 'What does he mean?"

Like Scott, we want the language we employ to be clear, contemporary and consistent, reflecting what we stand for and according respect to those we write about. And that is ultimately the purpose of this book: to help people to use English to communicate effectively.

David Marsh and Amelia Hodsdon
August 2010

David Marsh is production editor of the Guardian. Amelia Hodsdon is production editor of MediaGuardian. They blog at guardian.co.uk/mindyourlanguage, and tweet @guardianstyle. The authors would like to thank Rory Foster for his meticulous proofreading of Guardian Style

The Digested Read

John Crace

Welcome to the latest edition of Guardian Style, a book that will be as little read by Guardian journalists as the previous ones, if the number of inaccuracies in the paper are anything to go by. But for the rest of you who take an interest in the dustier reaches of the English language, I thought I'd use this space to highlight the changes the hacks are sure to ignore.

Grammar is the set of rules followed by speakers of a language, innit? By everyone except Guardian writers, that is, so I have pulled together all the dreary grammatical stuff on commas, colons and split infinitives to the front in the hope – rather than expectation – that just one member of staff bothers to have a look before putting their complimentary copy on eBay.

Over the years it has distressed me greatly to see that Guardian journalists consistently try to write foreign languages in a way that would be intelligible to native speakers. Quite simply this has to stop. Allowing the odd acute accent to prevent lame being read as lame is as far as I am prepared to go. It's time that Johnny Foreigner met us halfway. The day the Frogs stop calling the English Channel La Manche and call it La Manche Anglaise is the day I use a circumflex.

Occasionally, however, I do bow to public demand. In the last edition I arbitrarily changed aeroplane to airplane. This triggered the largest number of complaints I've ever had. Three. So after several years of lengthy deliberation, I have concluded aeroplane is indeed the correct usage.

it has also been said we go further than most in lowercasing words. this is because we are quite trendy and the designers say it looks better on the page. The only capitals that are therefore allowed are either those that aPPear for no good reason in the middle of words or when we want to deliberately annoy EE Cummings. By the way, much against my better judgment, I've been dragged screaming and kicking into the 20th century and forced to allow split infinitives in exceptional circumstances.

Talking of which, new technology gives me a real headache. No sooner have I worked out whether or not to hyphen email –

most definitely not! - than some Californian invents some newfangled thingy and I lose hours of sleep deciding whether a Blackberry is a BlackBerry. Someone has to worry about these things.

I've lost count of the number of times we fail to differentiate between goths and Goths. Am I the only one to spot that one of them has a capital letter? But as long as our writers continue to get it wrong, I will continue to point out the error of their ways. Because I'm that type of person and I haven't got much else to do. I also intend to make sure we address Nick Clegg's wife correctly. Her name is Miriam González Durántez. Do not call her Miriam Clegg or Mrs Clegg. Though Mrs C is obviously fine.

These are just a few of the excitements you will find inside. Now I will leave you to discover the rest for yourself. But before I do, I'm afraid I must introduce one sour note. Swearing has become commonplace in everyday conversation and Guardian writers have proved more foul-mouthed than most. Much to my dismay, we printed 705 "fucks" last year - 704 of them in the newspaper's digested read. For that my sincere apologies.

John Crace's digested read appears regularly in the Guardian's G2 section

Grammar & punctuation

66It will be proved to thy face that thou hast men about thee that usually talk of a noun and a verb, and such abominable words as no Christian ear can endure to hear99

William Shakespeare, Henry VI Part 2

Ambrose Bierce defined grammar as "a system of pitfalls thoughtfully prepared for the feet of the self-made man". He had a point. Generations of schoolchildren were taught grammar as an arbitrary set of dos and don'ts laid down by people who knew, or thought they knew, best.

Nowadays, grammar might be more helpfully defined as the set of rules followed by speakers of a language. The aim is to communicate effectively, not to feel superior to other people because you know what a conjunction is.

Rather than encourage readers to, say, protest outside cinemas carrying placards drawing attention to Hollywood's perceived syntactical shortcomings, this section is designed to give them a practical guide to some common points of grammar, punctuation, and English usage.

Don't feel too downhearted if you were taught grammar badly, or not at all: as the linguist Steven Pinker says: "A preschooler's tacit knowledge of grammar is more sophisticated than the thickest style manual."

apostrophes are used to indicate a missing letter or letters (can't, we'd) or a possessive (David's book).

Don't let anyone tell you that apostrophes don't matter and we would be better off without them. Consider these four phrases, each of which means something different:

my sister's friend's books (refers to one sister and her friend).

my sister's friends' books (one sister with lots of friends).

my sisters' friend's books (more than one sister, and their friend).

my sisters' friends' books (more than one sister, and their friends).

The possessive in words and names ending in S takes an apostrophe followed by a second S (Jones's, James's).

Plural nouns that do not end in S take an apostrophe and S in the possessive: children's games, old folk's home, people's republic, etc.

Phrases such as butcher's knife, collector's item, cow's milk, goat's cheese, pig's blood, hangman's noose, writer's cramp, etc are treated as singular.

Use apostrophes in phrases such as two days' time, 12 years' imprisonment and six weeks' holiday, where the time period (two days) modifies a noun (time), but not in nine months pregnant or three weeks old, where the time period is adverbial (modifying an adjective such as pregnant or old) - if in doubt, test with a singular such as one day's time, one month pregnant.

Some shops use an apostrophe, wrongly, to indicate a plural ("pea's"), but will generally omit the apostrophe when one is actually required ("new seasons asparagus"), a phenomenon sometimes referred to as the greengrocer's (or grocer's) apostrophe. Try to avoid this.

brackets
If the sentence is logically and grammatically complete without the information contained within the parentheses (round brackets), the punctuation stays outside the brackets. (A complete sentence that stands alone in parentheses starts with a capital letter and ends with a stop.)

"Square brackets," the grammarian said, "are used in direct quotes when an interpolation [a note from the writer or editor, not uttered by the speaker] is added to provide essential information."

bullet points take a full stop after each one, ie:
- This is the first bullet point.
- This is the second.
- And this is the third.

collective nouns

Nouns such as committee, family, government, jury, squad and team take a singular verb or pronoun when thought of as a single unit, but a plural verb or pronoun when thought of as a collection of individuals:

The committee gave its unanimous approval to the plans;
The committee enjoyed biscuits with their tea.
The family can trace its history back to the middle ages;
The family were sitting down, scratching their heads.
The squad is looking stronger than for several seasons;
The squad are all very confident that they will win promotion this season.

colon

Use between two sentences, or parts of sentences, where the first introduces a proposition that is resolved by the second, eg Fowler put it like this: to deliver the goods invoiced in the preceding words. A colon should also be used (rather than a comma) to introduce a quotation: "He was an expert on punctuation," or to precede a list - "He was an expert on the following: the colon, the comma and the full stop."

This 2010 example from the Guardian is an awful (but by no means isolated) example of the tendency to use a semicolon where only a colon will do (all the more unfortunate for distracting the reader from a funny sentence): "Here's a task for the new coalition government; set up a Drumming Taskforce today, and appoint a Snare Tsar."

We are in danger of losing the distinction between colon and semicolon; many writers seem to think they are interchangeable but to make it clear: they are not.

commas

Use a comma to help the reader by inserting breathing space into a sentence: "When the Dutch reflect on their performance in the World Cup final, they will not find it hard to see why their aggressive tactics lost them many friends in 2010."

"The editor, Alan Rusbridger, is a man of great vision" –
commas if there is only one editor.

"The subeditor Amelia Hodsdon is all style and no substance"
– no commas if there is more than one subeditor.

A misplaced comma can sabotage a sentence, as in this
example from the paper: "Neocon economists often claim a
large, black economy turbo-powers growth ... " (the writer was
talking about a big black economy, not a big and black one,
which is not the same at all).

A comma is also crucial to avoid ambiguity in examples such
as this: "Part of the report will heavily criticise a so-called power
culture among the Dublin bishops who have been accused of
not taking the allegations seriously." We should have inserted a
comma after "bishops" to make clear that all the Dublin bishops
have been accused; as published, the sentence implies that only
some of the bishops have. *See Oxford comma*

compare to or with?

The former means liken to, the latter means make a comparison:
so unless you are specifically likening someone or something to
someone or something else, use compare with. A former lord
chancellor compared himself to Cardinal Wolsey because he
believed he was like Wolsey; I might compare him with Wolsey
to assess their relative merits. As so often, we are indebted to
Prince for the grammatically immaculate Nothing Compares 2U.

dangling participles (also known as hanging participles)

Avoid constructions such as "having died, they buried him"; the
pitfalls are nicely highlighted in Mark Lawson's novel Going Out
Live, in which a TV critic writes: "Dreary, repetitive and well past
the sell-by date, I switched off the new series of Fleming Faces."

Another example, from a leading article: "Due out in January
as a white paper, Ms Kelly may be unable to overcome Mr Blair's
apparent determination to stick with A-levels ... "

And this particularly exotic dangling participle somehow
found its way into the paper: "Though long-legged and

possessing a lovely smile, gentleman journalists aren't looking up her skirt and wouldn't even if she weren't gay ... "

dashes

Beware sentences - such as this one - that dash about all over the place - commas (or even, very occasionally, brackets) are often better; semicolons also have their uses. Dashes should be en dashes rather than em dashes or hyphens.

due to or owing to?

If you can substitute "caused by", due to is correct; if you can substitute "because of", owing to is correct:

The train's late arrival was due to leaves on the line; the train was late owing to leaves on the line.

Now, how hard is that?

ellipsis

Use a space before and after ellipses, and three dots (with no spaces between them), in copy and headlines, eg "She didn't want to go there ... "; there is no need for a full point.

gerund

Nothing to be frightened of. Think of it as a verb used as a noun: I like running, smoking is bad for your health, etc. You are supposed to use a possessive: I was worried by his smoking, rather than I was worried by him smoking. In practice, many people - yes, even journalists - don't bother.

hyphens

Our style is to use one word wherever possible. Hyphens tend to clutter up text (particularly when computer programmes break already hyphenated words at the end of lines). This is a widespread trend in the language: "The transition from space to hyphen to close juxtaposition reflects the progressive institutionalisation of the compound," as Rodney Huddleston puts it, in his inimitable pithy style, in his Introduction to the Grammar of English.

Inventions, ideas and new concepts often begin life as two words, then become hyphenated, before finally becoming accepted as one word. Why wait? "Wire-less" and "down-stairs" were once hyphenated, and some old-fashioned souls still hyphenate e-mail.

Words such as chatroom, frontbench, gameplan, housebuyer and standup are all one word in our publications, as are thinktank (not a tank that thinks), longlist (not necessarily a long list) and shortlist (which need not be short).

There is no need to use hyphens with most compound adjectives, where the meaning is clear and unambiguous without: civil rights movement, financial services sector, work inspection powers, etc. Hyphens should, however, be used to form short compound adjectives, eg two-tonne vessel, three-year deal, 19th-century artist. Also use hyphens where not using one would be ambiguous, eg to distinguish "black-cab drivers come under attack" from "black cab-drivers come under attack". A missing hyphen in a review of Chekhov's Three Sisters led us to refer to "the servant abusing Natasha", rather than "the servant-abusing Natasha".

Do not use hyphens after adverbs ending in -ly, eg a hotly disputed penalty, a constantly evolving newspaper, genetically modified food, etc, but hyphens are needed with short and common adverbs, eg ever-forgiving family, much-loved character, well-established principle of style (note, however, that in the construction "the principles of style are well established" there is no need to hyphenate).

When an adverb can also be an adjective (eg hard), the hyphen is required to avoid ambiguity – it's not a hard, pressed person, but a hard-pressed one; an ill-prepared report, rather than an ill, prepared one.

Use a hyphen in verbs where necessary to stop this kind of thing happening in a narrow headline:

Motorists
told: don't
panic buy
petrol

(While not panicking may well have been advisable, they had actually been told not to panic-buy.)

Prefixes such as macro, mega, micro, mini, multi, over, super and under rarely need hyphens: examples are listed separately. Follow Collins dictionary when a word or phrase is not listed in this book.

it's or its?

it's shortened form of it is or has: it's a big dog, it's been ages since I saw her.

its possessive form of it: the dog is eating its bone.

like or as if?

As Ogden Nash pointed out, it is As You Like It, not Like You Like It: like governs nouns and pronouns, not verbs and clauses, so "it looks as if he's finished" not "it looks like he's finished"; "as I say" not "like I say".

like or such as?

"Cities like Manchester are wonderful" suggests the writer has in mind, say, Sheffield or Birmingham; better to say "cities such as Manchester", which is what she actually means.

Do not, however, automatically change "like" to "such as" - the following appeared in the paper: "He is not a celebrity, such as Jesse Ventura, the former wrestler ... "

may or might?

The subtle distinctions between these (and between other so-called modal verbs) are gradually disappearing, but they still matter to many of our readers and can be useful.

may implies that the possibility remains open: "The Mies van der Rohe tower may have changed the face of British architecture for ever" (it has been built); **might** suggests that the possibility remains open no longer: "The Mies tower might have changed the face of architecture for ever" (if only they had built it). Similarly, "they may have played tennis, or they may have gone boating" suggests I don't know what they did; "they might have played tennis if the weather had been dry" means they didn't, because it wasn't.

Our headline "Capello has stayed aloof but personal touch may have kept Bridge onside" says the opposite of what was meant - it suggests that Capello's personal touch could yet keep Bridge in the team; it should have read "Capello has stayed aloof but personal touch might have kept Bridge in the team".

May also has the meaning of "having permission", so be careful: does "Megawatt Corp may bid for TransElectric Inc" mean that it is considering a bid, or that the competition authorities have allowed it to bid?

none

It is a (very persistent) myth that "none" has to take a singular verb: plural is acceptable and often sounds more natural, eg "none of the current squad are good enough to play in the Premier League", "none of the issues have been resolved".

one in six, **one in 10**

Phrases of this sort should be treated as plural. There are good grammatical and logical reasons for this. Compare "more than one in six Japanese is 65 or older ... " with "more than one in six Japanese are 65 or older ... "

Grammatically, we are talking not about the noun "one" but the noun phrase "one in six", signifying a group of people. Logically, the phrase represents a proportion - just like "17%" or "one-sixth", both of which take plural verbs. "Two out of every seven" and "three out of 10" take plurals too, functioning identically.

"One in six is ... " is also unnecessarily (and possibly misleadingly) specific, implying that of any six people from the group you take, exactly one will be as described. "One in six" means one-sixth on average over the whole group, and a plural verb better reflects this. We wouldn't say: "Only 1% of Republican voters is able to point to Iran on a map," just because there's a "one" in there.

Oxford comma

A comma before the final "and" in lists: straightforward ones (he ate ham, eggs and chips) do not need one, but sometimes it can help the reader (he ate cereal, kippers, bacon, eggs, toast and marmalade, and tea), and sometimes it is essential: compare

> I dedicate this book to my parents, Martin Amis, and JK Rowling

with

> I dedicate this book to my parents, Martin Amis and JK Rowling.

prepositions

Say appeal against, protest against/over/at, not "appealed the sentence", "protested the verdict", etc.

Schoolchildren used to be told (by English teachers unduly influenced by Latin) that it was ungrammatical to end sentences with a preposition, a fallacy satirised by Churchill's "This is the sort of English up with which I will not put" and Fowler's "What did you bring me that book to be read to out of for?

Take care after phrases following "to": the subheading "to we Conservatives, Labour looks as if it's heading back to the old horrors of the winter of discontent" drew numerous protests from readers pointing out that it should have been "to us Conservatives ... " (The mistake was ours, not the shadow cabinet minister who wrote the piece.)

quotation marks

Use double quotes at the start and end of a quoted section, with single quotes for quoted words within that section. Place full points and commas inside the quotes for a complete quoted sentence; otherwise the point comes outside – "Anna said: 'Your style guide needs updating,' and I said: 'I agree.'" but: "Anna said updating the guide was 'a difficult and time-consuming task'."

When beginning a quote with a sentence fragment that is followed by a full sentence, punctuate according to the final part of the quote, eg The minister called the allegations "blatant lies. But in a position such as mine it is only to be expected."

Headlines and standfirsts (sparingly), captions and display quotes all take single quote marks. For parentheses in direct quotes, use square brackets.

reported speech

When a comment in the present tense is reported, use past tense: "She said: 'I like chocolate'" (present tense) becomes in reported speech "she said she liked chocolate".

When a comment in the past tense is reported, use "had" (past perfect tense): "She said: 'I ate too much chocolate'" (past tense) becomes in reported speech "she said she had eaten too much chocolate" (not "she said she ate too much chocolate").

Once it has been established who is speaking, there is no need to keep attributing, so long as you stick to the past tense: "Alex said he would vote Labour. There was no alternative. It was the only truly progressive party," etc.

semicolon

Used correctly (which occasionally we do), the semicolon is a very elegant compromise between a full stop (too much) and a comma (not enough). This sentence, from a column by David McKie, illustrates beautifully how it's done: "Some reporters were brilliant; others were less so."

The late Beryl Bainbridge said in the Guardian: "Not many people use it much any more, do they? Should it be used more? I think so, yes. A semicolon is a partial pause, a different way of pausing, without using a full stop. I use it all the time," and George Bernard Shaw told TE Lawrence that not using semicolons was "a symptom of mental defectiveness, probably induced by camp life".

Orwell, on the other hand, thought they were unnecessary and Kurt Vonnegut advised: "Do not use semicolons. They are transvestite hermaphrodites, standing for absolutely nothing. All they do is show you've been to college."

split infinitives

"The English-speaking world may be divided into (1) those who neither know nor care what a split infinitive is; (2) those who do not know, but care very much; (3) those who know and condemn; (4) those who know and distinguish. Those who neither know nor care are the vast majority, and are happy folk, to be envied." (HW Fowler, Modern English Usage, 1926)

It is perfectly acceptable, and often desirable, to sensibly split infinitives – "to boldly go" is an elegant and effective phrase – and stubbornly to resist doing so can sound pompous and awkward ("the economic precipice on which they claim perpetually to be poised") or ambiguous: "he even offered personally to guarantee the loan that the Clintons needed to buy their house" raises the question of whether the offer, or the guarantee, was personal.

Raymond Chandler wrote to his publisher: "Would you convey my compliments to the purist who reads your proofs and tell him or her that I write in a sort of broken-down patois which is something like the way a Swiss waiter talks, and that when I split an infinitive, God damn it, I split it so it will stay split." And after an editor tinkered with his infinitives, Shaw said: "I don't care if he is made to go quickly, or to quickly go – but go he must!"

subjunctive

Fowler noted that the subjunctive was "seldom obligatory" and Somerset Maugham declared half a century ago: "The subjunctive mood is in its death throes, and the best thing to do is put it out of its misery as soon as possible." Would that that were so.

Most commonly, the subjunctive is a third person singular form of the verb expressing hypothesis, typically something demanded, proposed, imagined: he demanded that she resign at once, I propose that she be sacked, she insisted Jane sit down.

It is particularly common in American English and in formal or poetic contexts: If I were a rich man, etc, and you have to admit the song sounds better than "If I was a rich man ... "

We get this wrong at least as often as we get it right. Two examples from the same issue in April 2010 in which "was" should be "were":

"If every election or ballot in which there are cases of bad practice was to be invalidated, democracy would soon become a laughing stock ... " (leading article); "If this was the centred Conservative party that Cameron claims, its strategists wouldn't be half as worried as they are ... " (column).

Nobody died and no great harm was done, but as professional writers we should be aware of the distinction. Used properly, the subjunctive can add elegance to your writing; an object lesson was provided in a Gary Younge column of 5 July 2010: "It was as though Charlie Brown's teacher were standing for leader of the opposition ... " (one of three examples of the subjunctive in the piece).

As with the hyper-correct misuse of whom instead of who, however, using the subjunctive wrongly is worse than not using it at all, and will make you look pompous and silly.

syntax

Beware of ambiguous or incongruous sentence structure - the following appeared in a column in the paper: "This argument, says a middle-aged lady in a business suit called Marion, is just more London stuff ... " (What were her other outfits called?)

tenses

We've Only Just Begun was playing on the radio. He began to drink; in fact he drank so much, he was drunk in no time at all. He sank into depression, knowing that all his hopes had been sunk. Finally, he sneaked away. Or perhaps snuck (according to Steven Pinker, the most recent irregular verb to enter the language).

See burned/burnt, dreamed, drink, hove into view, lay bare, learned, lie, shrank, spelled/spelt, spoiled/spoilt

that

Do not use automatically after the word "said", but it can be useful: you tend to read a sentence such as "he said nothing by way of an explanation would be forthcoming" as "he said nothing by way of an explanation" and then realise that it does not say that at all; "he said that nothing by way of an explanation would be forthcoming" is much clearer.

that or which?

This is quite easy, really – "that" defines, "which" gives extra information (often in a clause enclosed by commas):

> This is the house that Jack built; but this house, which John built, is falling down.
>
> The Guardian, which I read every day, is the paper that I admire above all others.
>
> I am very proud of the sunflowers that I grew from seed (some of the sunflowers);
>
> I am very proud of the sunflowers, which I grew from seed (all the sunflowers).

Note that in such examples the sentence remains grammatical without "that" (the house Jack built, the paper I admire, the sunflowers I grew), but not without "which".

who or whom?

This is how to do it: "When it comes to sci-fi villains, few have endured as well as the Martians, whom HG Wells depicted wielding a weapon called the Heat-Ray in The War of the Worlds, back in 1898."

And this is how not to do it: "A nation's weeping turned to tears of joy with the news that Louie – for who media commentators had to commission new words for camp … – is to star in his own 10-part series."

Only those with a tin ear for language could be unaware that "who" sounds wrong in the second example, but it is not always so obvious.

If in doubt, ask yourself how the clause beginning who/whom

would read in the form of a sentence giving he, him, she, her, they or them instead: if the who/whom person turns into he/she/they, then "who" is right; if it becomes him/her/them, then it should be "whom".

In this example: "Straw was criticised for attacking Clegg, whom he despised" - "whom" is correct because he despised "him".

But in "Straw attacked Clegg, who he thought was wrong" - "who" is correct, because it is "he" not "him" who is considered wrong.

Use of "whom" has all but disappeared from spoken English, and seems to be going the same way in most forms of written English too. If you are not sure, it is much better to use "who" when "whom" would traditionally have been required than to use "whom" incorrectly for "who", something even great writers have been guilty of: "There was a big man whom I think was an hôtelier from Phnom Penh and a French girl I'd never seen before ... " (The Quiet American, Graham Greene - who as a former subeditor should have known better).

Aa

66 We are losing sight of directness. Risk aversion is reaching every corner of the language. Most noticeable is the abuse of the preposition 'around'. The object of the verb to say is rarely 'something' but 'something around'. Rather than disagree with a statement of fact or opinion, we say it 'gives us issues around it'. Around was said to be dying out when Fowler wrote his Modern English Usage, in favour of round, assuming its correct use as a preposition of location. It has come storming back, presumably because around is somehow more elusive than round. It is as if the subject of any discourse were a repelling magnet, to be circled, circumnavigated, treated warily. We should say what we mean and cut the clutter **99**

Simon Jenkins

a or an before H?

Use an before a silent H: an heir, an hour, an honest politician, an honorary consul; use a before an aspirated H: a hero, a hotel, a historian (but don't change a direct quote if the speaker says, for example, "an historic"). With abbreviations, be guided by pronunciation: an LSE student

A* (GCSE or A-level grade) not A-star

A&E accident and emergency

abattoir

abbeys take initial cap, eg Westminster Abbey

abbreviations and acronyms

Do not use full points in abbreviations, or spaces between initials, including those in proper names: US, mph, eg, 4am, lbw, M&S, No 10, AN Wilson, WH Smith, etc.

Use all capitals if an abbreviation is pronounced as the individual letters: BBC, VAT, etc; if it is an acronym (pronounced as a word) spell out with initial capital, eg Nasa, Nato, unless it can be considered to have entered the language as an everyday word, such as awol, laser and, more recently, asbo, pin number and sim card. Note that pdf and plc are lowercase.

If an abbreviation or acronym is to be used more than once in a piece, put it in brackets at first mention: so Association of Chief Police Officers (Acpo), seasonal affective disorder (Sad); alternatively, use the abbreviation with a brief description, eg the conservation charity the RSPB. Remember that our large international readership will not necessarily be aware of even well-known UK abbreviations. If an organisation is mentioned only once, it is not necessary to give its abbreviation or acronym.

Cap up single letters in such expressions as C-list, F-word, "the word assassin contains four Ss", etc

Aborigines, **Aboriginal** uppercase (uc) when referring to native Australians

Aa

aborigines, **aboriginal** lowercase (lc) when referring to indigenous populations

abscess

absorb but **absorption**

abysmal

abyss

a cappella Italian for "in the style of the church", ie unaccompanied singing

Acas the Advisory, Conciliation and Arbitration Service (Acas), at first mention; thereafter just Acas

accents
Use on French, German, Portuguese, Spanish and Irish Gaelic words (but not anglicised French words such as cafe, apart from exposé, lamé, pâté, résumé, roué).

People's names, in whatever language, should also be given appropriate accents where known. Thus: "Arsène Wenger was on holiday in Bogotá with Rafa Benítez"

Accenture formerly Andersen Consulting; the new name was devised by an employee from "accent on the future"

access has been known as contact since the 1989 Children Act

accommodate, **accommodation**

accordion not accordian

achilles heel, **achilles tendon** lowercase

acknowledgment not acknowledgement

acres
Use hectares, with acres in brackets, rounded up or down: eg the field measured 25 hectares (62 acres).

You multiply hectares by 2.47 to convert to acres, or acres by 0.41 to convert to hectares

acronyms *See abbreviations and acronyms*

act initial caps when using full name, eg Criminal Justice Act 1998, Official Secrets Act; but lc on second reference, eg "the act", and when speaking in more general terms, eg "we need a more radical freedom of information act"; bills remain lc until passed into law

actor
Use for both male and female actors; do not use actress except when in name of award, eg Oscar for best actress. The Guardian's view is that actress comes into the same category as authoress, comedienne, manageress, "lady doctor", "male nurse" and similar obsolete terms that date from a time when professions were largely the preserve of one sex (usually men). As Whoopi Goldberg put it in an interview with the paper: "An actress can only play a woman. I'm an actor - I can play anything."

There is normally no need to differentiate between the sexes - and if there is, the words male and female are perfectly adequate: Lady Gaga won a Brit in 2010 for best international female artist, not artiste, chanteuse, or songstress.

As always, use common sense: a piece about the late film director Carlo Ponti was edited to say that in his early career he was "already a man with a good eye for pretty actors ... " As the readers' editor pointed out in the subsequent clarification: "This was one of those occasions when the word 'actresses' might have been used"

AD, BC AD goes before the date (AD64), BC goes after (300BC); both go after the century, eg second century AD, fourth century BC

adaptation not adaption; **adapter** someone who adapts; **adaptor** plug

addendum plural **addendums** not addenda. Latinate -um neuter endings that are a part of the language (eg stadium) take an -s plural. Exceptions: bacteria, which retain the Latin plural and take a plural verb, as do media, but note that spiritualists are mediums

Aa

addresses like this: 90 York Way, London N1 9GU

Adidas initial cap, although adidas is lc in the company logo

administration the Obama administration, etc

admissible not -able

admit

Take care: as a reader put it when we referred in July 2010 to Tory MPs who "admitted" being gay: "Admit in modern English is almost exclusively used when conceding or confessing something negative and/or of which one is or should be ashamed. Please be more careful. Language can offend." Quite. The former Washington Post editor Ben Bradlee urged reporters not to "hide their biases and emotions behind subtly pejorative words" such as admit

adoption

Mention that children are adopted only when relevant to the story: a reader points out that "explicitly calling attention to adoptions in this way suggests that adoption is not as good, and not as real a relationship, as having a child normally". So say biological father, biological family rather than real father, real family, etc

Adrenalin TM, a brand of adrenaline; **adrenaline** hormone that increases heart rate and blood pressure, extracted from animals or synthesised for medical uses

adverbs

Do not use hyphens after adverbs ending in -ly, eg a constantly evolving newspaper, a hotly disputed penalty, genetically modified food, etc; but hyphens are needed with short and common adverbs, eg ever-forgiving family, ill-prepared report, much-loved character, well-founded suspicion

adviser not advisor

advocate member of the Scottish bar (not a barrister)

aeroplane

Aa

affect or effect?
Exhortations in Guardian Style have had little effect on the number of mistakes; the level of mistakes has been little affected by our exhortations; we hope to effect a change in this

affidavit a written declaration made on oath, so "sworn affidavit" is tautologous

affinity with or between, not to or for

Afghans people; **afghanis** currency of Afghanistan

aficionado plural aficionados

African American

African-Caribbean not Afro-Caribbean

Afrikaans language; **Afrikander** cattle breed; **Afrikaner** person

afterlife, aftermath no hyphens

ageing not aging

ages David Cameron, 44 (not "aged 44"); little Lucy, four; the woman was in her 20s (but twentysomething, thirtysomething, etc)

aggravate means to make worse, not to annoy

aggro despite the once-popular terrace chant "A, G, A-G-R, A-G-R-O: agro!"

AGM annual general meeting

ahead of overused; before or in advance of are among the alternatives

aide-de-camp plural aides-de-camp (aide is a noun); **aide-memoire** plural aide-memoires (aide is a verb)

Aids acquired immune deficiency syndrome, but normally no need to spell out.

Do not use such terms as "Aids victims" or someone "suffering from Aids", language that in the words of one reader is "crass, inaccurate and reinforces stigma", implying

Aa

helplessness and inviting pity; "people with Aids" or "living with Aids" are preferable.

Do not use the term "full-blown Aids". Unesco guidelines state: "This term implies that there are varying stages of Aids ... People have Aids only when they present with an Aids-defining illness"

airbase, aircrew, airdrop, airlift, airmail, airspace, airstrip, airtime one word

aircraft designations usually take hyphens after initials, eg B-52, MiG-23

aircraft carrier

air fares, air force, air raid, air show, air strike two words

Air Force One US president's jet

air hostess cabin attendant or flight attendant, please

airports Heathrow, Gatwick, Stansted (normally no need to say airport); Liverpool John Lennon airport, Schiphol airport, etc

air vice-marshal

AKA also known as

al- (note lc and hyphen) before an Arabic name means "the" so try to avoid writing "the al- ... " where possible *See Arabic names*

Alastair or Alistair?
Alastair Campbell (spin doctor), Alastair Cook (cricketer), Alastair Hetherington (late Guardian editor), Alastair Stewart (broadcaster).

Alistair Cooke (late BBC and Guardian journalist), Alistair Darling (politician), Alistair MacLean (late novelist), Alistair McGowan (impressionist).

Aleister Crowley (late satanist)

Alcott, Louisa May (1832-88) American author of Little Women

A-levels

Aa

Al Fayed, Mohamed owner of Fulham FC and former owner of Harrods (Fayed after first mention; Mr Fayed if honorific is needed); the son who died in Paris in 1997 was Dodi Fayed

Alfonsín, Raúl (1927-2009) president of Argentina from 1983-89

alfresco one word

algae plural of alga

Ali, Muhammad was Cassius Clay until 1964

alibi being somewhere else; not synonymous with excuse

alice band as worn by Alice in Lewis Carroll's Through the Looking-Glass (1871) and more recently David Beckham

A-list etc, but to refer to "C-list celebrities" and its variations has become tedious. An edition of G2 referred to "D-list celebrities" and, less than hilariously, in a separate piece about the same reality TV show, "Z-list celebrities"

Allah Arabic for "the God". Both words refer to the same concept: there is no major difference between God in the Old Testament and Allah in Islam. Therefore it makes sense to talk about God in an Islamic context and to use Allah in quotations or for literary effect

Allahu Akbar "God is greatest"

Allende, Isabel Chilean author, niece of Salvador;
Allende, Salvador Chilean president, overthrown and killed in 1973

allies second world war allies, the allied invasion, etc

all mouth and trousers not "all mouth and no trousers"

all right is right; alright is not all right (but note that the Who song, much loved by generations of headline writers, was The Kids are Alright)

All Souls College Oxford, no apostrophe

Almo arm's-length management organisation

Almodóvar, Pedro Spanish film-maker

alpha male

alsatian dog; **Alsatian** person from Alsace

also often redundant

AltaVista

alter ego not "altar ego", as we have been known to spell it

alternative normally a choice between two courses of action; if there are more than two, option or choice may be preferred; beware the trend to use "alternate" instead of alternative: in a piece about French politics we wrote "in this juddering alternate reality ... "

alumnus plural **alumni**; although in the UK graduate is preferable

Alzheimer's disease

AM (assembly member) member of the Welsh assembly

Amazon normally no need for .com or .co.uk

ambassador lc, eg the British ambassador to Washington; "ambassador, you are spoiling us" has become a headline cliche

ambience not ambiance

amendments to the US constitution like this: fifth amendment, 18th amendment, etc

America the country is generally the United States or US, although its citizens are Americans; we should remember that America includes all of North and South America

American English
We follow British English spellings: secretary of defence, Labour Day, World Trade Centre, etc; exceptions are placenames such as Ann Arbor, Pearl Harbor

American Civil Liberties Union not American Civil Rights Union

American universities "University of X" is not the same as "X

University"; most states have two large public universities, eg University of Kentucky and Kentucky State University, University of Illinois and Illinois State University, etc.

Do not call Johns Hopkins University "John Hopkins" or Stanford University "Stamford", as we have done on all too many occasions

America's Cup sailing trophy named after the schooner America, its first winner

Amhrán na bhFiann Irish national anthem

Amicus trade union formed by a merger between the AEEU and MSF, now part of Unite after a further merger with the TGWU

amid not amidst

amok not amuck (the 1980s version of this guide advised: "amok, not amuck" and, a few entries later: "amuck, not amok")

among not amongst

among or between?
Whatever you may have been told, between is not limited to two parties. It is appropriate when the relationship is essentially reciprocal: fighting between the many peoples of Yugoslavia, treaties between European countries, etc; among belongs to distributive relationships: shared among, etc

amount or number? amount refers to a quantity, number to something that can be counted: eg an enormous amount of energy was exerted by a small number of people

ampersand should be used in company names when the company does: Marks & Spencer, P&O, etc

anaesthetic

analysis plural analyses

ancestors precede descendants; we frequently manage to get them the wrong way round

Andalucía

Anderson shelter not Andersen

anglicise, anglophile, anglophone

animals take the pronoun "it" unless gender is established

annex verb, **annexe** noun: I am going to annex the annexe for the afternoon

anorexic is not a superlative of thin. Anorexia is an illness. Like schizophrenia, it should not be used as a cheap and lazy metaphor. Anyone thinking of using a phrase such as "she looked positively anorexic" should think again

Ansaphone TM; use answering machine or answerphone

antenna (insect) plural antennae; (radio) plural antennas

antichrist

anticipate take action in expectation of; not synonymous with expect

anticlimax, antidepressants, antidisestablishmentarianism (not recommended for use in headlines), **antihero** no hyphens

antipodean, antipodes

antisemitic, antisemitism no hyphen: it does not mean "anti-Semitic"

antisocial but **anti-war**

apex plural apexes

any more two words

apostrofly "an insect that lands at random on the printed page, depositing an apostrophe wherever it lands" according to the first Guardian readers' editor

apostrophes *See Grammar & punctuation*

app an application for, typically, a mobile phone

appal but as the Prince of Wales might say, it really is appalling

apparatchik

Aa

appeal
In British English you appeal against a decision, verdict, etc - you do not "appeal the verdict". After we reported on 9 June 2010 that a convicted murderer "successfully appealed the sentence", a despairing reader wrote: "This usage seems to be occurring more and more, sometimes even in headlines. Do Guardian journalists not read the style guide?" Not all of them, evidently

appendix plural **appendices**

Apple no longer Apple Computer

apples lc: cox's orange pippin, golden delicious, granny smith, etc

appraise to evaluate; **apprise** to inform

April Fools' Day also known, less commonly nowadays, as All Fools' Day; an individual prank, or the victim of one, is an April fool, so you might say "one of the greatest April fools was the Guardian's San Serriffe issue of 1977 - it made April fools of all who were taken in"

al-Aqsa Martyrs Brigade

aquarium plural aquariums

Arab
A noun and an adjective, and the preferred adjective when referring to Arab things in general, eg Arab history, Arab traditions. Arabic usually refers to the language and literature: "the Arabic press" means newspapers written in Arabic, while "the Arab press" would include newspapers produced by Arabs in other languages.

There is no simple definition of an Arab. At an international level, the 22 members of the Arab League can safely be described as Arab countries: Algeria, Bahrain, Comoros, Djibouti, Egypt, Iraq, Jordan, Kuwait, Lebanon, Libya, Mauritania, Morocco, Oman, Palestine, Qatar, Saudi Arabia, Somalia, Sudan, Syria, Tunisia, United Arab Emirates, and

Aa

Yemen. At a human level, there are substantial groups within those countries - the Berbers of north Africa and the Kurds, for example - who do not regard themselves as Arabs

Arabic names

Although Arabic has only three vowels - a, i and u - it has several consonants that have no equivalent in the Roman alphabet. For instance, there are two kinds of s, d and t. There are also two glottal sounds. This means there are at least 32 ways of writing the Libyan leader Muammar Gaddafi's name in English, and a reasonable argument can be made for adopting almost any of them. With no standard approach to transliteration agreed by the western media, we must try to balance consistency, comprehensibility and familiarity - which often puts a strain on all three.

Typically, Arabs have at least three names. In some cases the first or second name may be the one that is most used, and this does not imply familiarity (Arabs often address foreigners politely as "Mr John" or "Dr David"). Often Arabs also have familiar names that have no connection with the names on their identity cards: a man might become known after the birth of his first son as "Abu Ahmad", and a woman as "Umm Ahmad", the father or mother of Ahmad (eg the Palestinian leader Ahmed Qureia is commonly known as Abu Ala).

Where a particular spelling has become widely accepted through usage we should retain it. Where an individual with links to the west has clearly adopted a particular spelling of his or her own name, we should respect that. For breaking news and stories using names for which we have no established style, we take the lead given by Reuters wire copy.

Note also that names in some parts of the Arab world have become gallicised, while others have become anglicised, eg the leading Egyptian film director Youssef Chahine uses a French spelling instead of the English transliteration, Shaheen.

Some guidelines (for use particularly where there is no established transliteration):

Aa

al- Means "the". In names it is not capitalised, eg Ahmad al-Saqqaf, and can be dropped after the first mention (Saqqaf). For placenames we drop it altogether. Sometimes it appears as as- or ash- or ad- or ul-: these should be ignored and can be safely rewritten as al-. But some Arabs, including Syrians and Egyptians, prefer to use el- in place of al-. Exceptions: by convention, Allah (al-Lah, literally "the God") is written as one word and capitalised; and in Saudi royal names, Al Saud is correct (in this case, "al" is actually "aal" and does not mean "the").

abdul, abu and bin These are not self-contained names, but are connected to the name that follows: abdul means "slave of ... " and so cannot correctly be used on its own. There are standard combinations, "slave of the merciful one", "slave of the generous one", etc, which all indicate that the person is a servant of God. In transliteration, "abd" (slave) is lowercase, eg Ahmad abd al-Rahman al-Saqqaf, except when used at the start of a name; abu (father of) and bin (son of) are similar. When they appear in the middle of a name they should be lowercase and are used in combination with the following part of the name: Faisal abu Ahmad al-Saqqaf, Faisal bin Ahmad al-Saqqaf. Despite the above, some people are actually known as "Abdul". This is more common among non-Arab Muslims. And some Arabs run "abd" or "abu" into the following word, eg the writer Abdelrahman Munif.

Muhammad Our style for the prophet's name and for most Muhammads living in Arab countries, though where someone's preferred spelling is known we respect it, eg Mohamed Al Fayed, Mohamed ElBaradei. The spelling Mohammed (or variants) is considered archaic by most British Muslims, and disrespectful by many of them.

Muhandis/Mohandes, Qadi Be wary of names where the first word is Muhandis or Qadi: these are honorary titles, meaning engineer and judge respectively

Aran Island is off Co Donegal and the **Aran Islands** off Co Galway in western Ireland; the **Isle of Arran** is the largest island in the Firth of Clyde in Scotland. **Aran sweaters**, whether Irish or Scottish, take an initial cap A

arcane esoteric; **archaic** antiquated (yes, we got them the wrong way round)

archbishops
It is not normally necessary to use their formal title, which for both Anglicans and Catholics is Most Rev: so Rowan Williams, the archbishop of Canterbury, at first mention, thereafter Williams or the archbishop (except in leading articles, where he is Dr Williams); Vincent Nichols, the archbishop of Westminster, on first mention, subsequently Nichols or the archbishop

archdeacon the Ven Paul Olive, archdeacon of Farringdon, at first mention; thereafter Olive or the archdeacon

archery arrows are shot, rather than fired; if they hit the centre of the target, it is a gold rather than a bullseye

archipelago plural archipelagos

arch-rival an arch rival would mean something different

Ardoyne (Belfast), not "the Ardoyne"

Argentina, **Argentinian**

arguably unarguably one of the most overused words in the language

Armageddon

armed forces, **armed services** the army, the British army, the navy, but Royal Navy, Royal Air Force or RAF

arms akimbo hands on hips, elbows out; it is surprising how often the phrase "legs akimbo" turns up, "suggesting that such a posture exists, but lacks a word to define it", as David McKie wrote

around about or approximately are better, eg about £1m or

approximately 2,000 people

around or round? We were driving around aimlessly all weekend; it nearly drove me round the bend

arranged marriages are a traditional and perfectly acceptable form of wedlock across southern Asia and within the Asian community in Britain; they should not be confused with forced marriages, which are arranged without the consent of one or both partners, and have been illegal in the UK since 2007

arse British English; **ass** American English

art movements are generally lowercase, eg art deco, art nouveau, cubism, dadaism, expressionism, gothic, impressionism, pop art, surrealism, etc, but Bauhaus, Modern (in the sense of Modern British, to distinguish it from "modern art"), pre-Raphaelite, Romantic (to differentiate between a romantic painting and a Romantic painting)

artefact

artist not artiste (except, possibly, in a historical context)

Arts and Crafts movement

Arts Council England, **Arts Council of Wales**, **Scottish Arts Council**

as or since? "as" is causal: I cannot check the online style guide as the connection is down; "since" is temporal: Luckily, I have had the latest edition of Guardian Style on my desk since it was published

asbo

ascendancy, **ascendant**

Asean Association of Southeast (sic) Asian Nations

Ash Action on Smoking and Health

Ashura a day of voluntary fasting for Muslims; Shia Muslims also commemorate the martyrdom of Hussein, a grandson of the prophet, so for them it is not a festival but a day of mourning

Asperger's syndrome

aspirin lc

al-Assad, Bashar became president of Syria in 2000 after the death of his father, Hafez al-Assad

assassin, **assassination** the murder of prominent political figures rather than, say, celebrities

assisted dying is preferable to "assisted suicide"

astrologer not astrologist

astronomer royal

Asunción capital of Paraguay

asylum seeker
Someone seeking refugee status or humanitarian protection; there is no such thing as an "illegal asylum seeker", a term the Press Complaints Commission ruled in breach of its code of practice.

Refugees are people who have fled their home countries in fear for their lives, and may have been granted asylum under the 1951 refugee convention or qualify for humanitarian protection or discretionary leave, or have been granted exceptional leave to remain in Britain.

Someone who is refused asylum should be referred to as a refused asylum seeker, not a failed asylum seeker.

An asylum seeker can become an illegal immigrant only if he or she remains in Britain after having failed to respond to a removal notice

athletics 1500m but 5,000m (the former is the "fifteen hundred" not "one thousand five hundred" metres)

Atlantic Ocean or just the Atlantic

attache no accent

attention deficit hyperactivity disorder ADHD after first mention

Attlee, Clement (1883-1967) Labour prime minister 1945-51, often misspelt as Atlee

Aa

attorney general lc, no hyphen; plural **attorney generals** (there will be those who tell you it should be "attorneys general" *See berks and wankers*)

auger used to make holes; **augur** predict or presage

Aum Shinrikyo Supreme Truth sect, but note that "aum" means sect, so to talk about the Aum sect or Aum cult is tautologous

Aung San Suu Kyi
Use her full name (as with other Burmese names), even on second and subsequent mentions, in copy; if absolutely necessary, Suu Kyi is permissible in headlines

Auntie not Aunty if you must refer to the BBC in this way

au pair

Australasia Oceania is preferable *See Oceania*

Australian Labor party not Labour

autism neurological disorder, to be used only when referring to the condition, not as a term of abuse, or in producing such witticisms as "mindless moral autism" and "Star Wars is a form of male autism", both of which have appeared in the Guardian; **autistic** (adjective) someone with autism, not someone with poor social skills

Autocue TM; teleprompter is a generic alternative

autumn

AV the alternative vote electoral system

avant garde no hyphen

average, mean and median
Although we loosely refer to the average in many contexts (eg pay), there are two useful averages worth distinguishing.

What is commonly known as the average is the mean: everyone's wages are added up and divided by the number of wage earners.

The median is described as the value below which 50% of

Aa

employees fall, ie it is the wage earned by the middle person when everyone's wages are lined up from smallest to largest. (For even numbers there are two middle people, but you calculate the mean average of their two wages.)

The median is often a more useful guide than the mean, which can be distorted by figures at one extreme or the other

awards and prizes are generally lc, eg Guardian first book award, Nobel peace prize (but note Academy Awards); lc for categories, eg Sean Penn won the best actor Oscar, Chipmunk was voted best newcomer at the 2008 Mobos, etc

awol stands for "absent without leave" but, having been around since at least the 1920s, has established itself as a word in its own right

awopbopaloobop alopbamboom

axing not axeing, but cutting jobs is less cliched than axing them

axis plural axes

Ayers Rock is now known as Uluru

Azerbaijan noun, **Azerbaijani** adjective; note that there are ethnic Azeris living in, for example, Armenia

Aznar, José María former prime minister of Spain

Bb

 66 Language evolves (well mine does - usually in line with the news editor's demands). He used to say that I wrote like I spoke. So now it annoys me when other people do the same. Top offenders include 'to try and', 'be compared to' and 'get bored of'. Also annoying is the overuse of lazy words - although I'm clearly guilty of that. One recent intro was met by an email from the ed that said: 'The word "issue" is a problem you will have to deal with.' I am, I promise 99

Anushka Asthana

Bb

b bit or binary digit; **B** byte, usually made up of 8 bits *See byte*

BAA formerly the British Airports Authority

Ba'ath party it means renaissance or resurrection

Babybel cheese; **baby Bells** US regional telephone companies formed after the breakup of AT&T in 1984

baby boomer

Babygro TM; a generic alternative is babygrow

Baby P Peter Connelly, who died in Haringey, north London, in 2007, was known as Baby P or Baby Peter

babysitter one word

baccalaureate

bacchanalia originally wild festivals dedicated to the god Bacchus; now drunken revelry as found in most British towns on a Saturday night

Bacharach, Burt US songwriter, born 1928

bachelor now has a slightly old-fashioned ring to it, so probably better to say (if relevant) unmarried man; "confirmed bachelor" should definitely be avoided, as should "bachelor girl" (unless writing about swinging 60s movies)

backbench newspaper or politics; plural backbenches, backbenchers

backstreet, backyard one word

bacteria plural of bacterium, so "the bacteria are"; do not confuse with viruses

BAE Systems formerly British Aerospace, BAE after first mention

Bafta British Academy of Film and Television Arts

bagel not baigel or beigel

Baghdad

Bahá'í faith

Bb

bailout noun; **bail out** a prisoner, a company or person in financial difficulty; **bale out** a boat or from an aircraft

baker's dozen 13

bakewell tart

balk obstruct, pull up, stop short; **baulk** area of a snooker table. As the former world champion Ronnie O'Sullivan generously acknowledged in a previous edition of this book: "At last - a book that tells everyone the difference between balk and baulk"

ballboy, ballgame, ballgirl, ballgown, ballpark one word

ballot, balloted

Band-Aid TM; say plaster or sticking plaster

B&B abbreviation for bed and breakfast

band names
lc the: the Beatles, the Killers, the The; but uc equivalents in other languages, eg Les Négresses Vertes, Los Lobos. Bands that do not take the definite article (although they are often erroneously given it) include Arctic Monkeys, Pet Shop Boys and Ramones; for most bands, this can be easily checked online.

Bands take a plural verb: Snow Patrol are overrated, the Young Radicals' You Get What You Give was the best single of all time, etc. Try to include diacritical marks if bands use them in their name, no matter how absurd: Maxïmo Park, Mötley Crüe, Motörhead, etc; for a comprehensive list see the excellent "metal umlaut" entry on Wikipedia

Bangalore is now known as Bengalooru

bank holiday bank holiday Monday, etc

Ban Ki-moon UN secretary general; Ban on second mention

banknote one word

Bank of England the Bank on subsequent mentions

Bank of Scotland BoS on second mention

Bb

banlieue French for suburbia, not suburb: strictly singular, but a French reader points out that the Petit Robert dictionary listed *les banlieues* among its *nouveaux mots* in 2006; the French for suburb is *faubourg* (literally, "false town")

bar (legal) she was called to the bar; (political) of the House of Commons

barbecue not BBQ or barbeque

Barclays Bank

barcode one word

barmitzvah, batmitzvah not Bar Mitzvah, bat mitzvah, etc

Barnardo's children's charity, formerly Dr Barnardo's; it no longer runs orphanages

barolo wine lc

Baron Cohen, Sacha the man behind Ali G, Borat and Brüno (note umlaut); **Baron-Cohen, Simon** a professor of developmental psychopathology at Cambridge University and cousin of Sacha

barons, baronesses are lords and ladies in our publications, even at first mention: Lord Adonis, Lady Warsi, etc; do not use first names with title ("Lady Patricia Scotland"), even if you claim to be on good terms with the peer in question

Barons Court area of and tube stop in west London

baroque

barracks the army has barracks, the RAF has airfields

Barroso, José Manuel former prime minister of Portugal, subsequently president of the European commission

Barts abbreviation for St Bartholomew's hospital, London

base jumping extreme sport; the acronym stands for four categories of object from which you can jump, if so inclined: building, antenna, span and Earth

basically this word is unnecessary, basically

Bb

Basle not Basel

Basque country

bas-relief

bated breath not baited

Battenberg (not Battenburg) German family name that became Mountbatten; **battenberg cake** lc

Battersea Dogs & Cats Home no apostrophes

battlebus one word

Bauhaus

BBC1, BBC2, BBC3, BBC4 no spaces

BBC News is no longer BBC News 24

BBC Radio 1, 2, 3, 4, 5 Live, 6 Music, Radio 7

BC 1000BC but AD1066 *See AD, BC*

Beaton, Sir Cecil (1904-80) photographer

beau plural beaux

Beaver scouts for boys aged six to eight, when they are eligible to become Cub scouts

bebop, hard bop, post-bop

because can be ambiguous: "I didn't go to the party because Mary was there" may mean that Mary's presence dissuaded me from going or that I went to sample the canapes

Becket, Thomas (1118-70) murdered archbishop of Canterbury, not Thomas à Becket

bed blocking

bedouin

beef wellington

Beeton, Mrs (Isabella Mary Beeton, 1836-65) author of The Book of Household Management

Bb

begs the question

This phrase is almost invariably misused: it means assuming a proposition that, in reality, involves the conclusion. An example would be to say that parallel lines will never meet, because they are parallel. The concept can be traced as far back as Aristotle, but HW Fowler, whose entry on begging the question is listed under the Latin *petitio principii* (assumption of the basis), defines it as "the fallacy of founding a conclusion on a basis that as much needs to be proved as the conclusion itself", giving as an example "foxhunting is not cruel, since the fox enjoys the fun". Now used widely to mean "raise the question", its traditional sense is being lost, which seems a sad fate for a phrase that might be useful or even - in a logical or philosophical context - essential

Beijing

Belarus adjective Belarussian

beleaguered overused, even when we spell it correctly

believable

Belisha beacons flashing orange lamps on black and white poles at zebra crossings, named after Leslie Hore-Belisha, the minister of transport who introduced them in 1934; have given way in many cases to pelican crossings (little red and green men)

bellringers, **bellringing** no hyphens

Bell's whisky

bellwether sheep that leads the herd; customarily misspelt, misused, or both

benefactor, **beneficiary** are sometimes confused: the former gives something; the latter gets it

benefited, **benefiting**

Benetton

Bengalooru formerly Bangalore

Berchtesgaden

berks and wankers
Kingsley Amis identified two principal groups in debates over use of language: "Berks are careless, coarse, crass, gross and of what anybody would agree is a lower social class than one's own; wankers are prissy, fussy, priggish, prim and of what they would probably misrepresent as a higher social class than one's own"

Berlin Wall

Berliner newspaper format, narrower and shorter than a broadsheet, taller and wider than a tabloid; the Guardian switched to Berliner format on 12 September 2005

Bermuda the adjective is Bermudian (not Bermudan) and its citizens are Bermudians

Bernabéu stadium the home of Real Madrid

Berne not Bern

berserk not beserk

Berwick-upon-Tweed is in England, although Berwick Rangers play football in the Scottish League

bestseller, bestselling

Betaferon TM; the generic term for the drug is interferon-beta 1b

bete noire no accents

betting odds
We frequently get this wrong. A brief explanation: long odds (eg 100-1 against, normally expressed as 100-1) mean something unlikely; shorter odds (eg 10-1) still mean it's unlikely, but less unlikely; odds on (eg 2-1 on, sometimes expressed as 1-2) means it is likely, so if you were betting £2 you would win only £1 plus the stake.

Take care using the phrase "odds on": if Labour is quoted by bookmakers at 3-1 to win a byelection, and the odds are cut to 2-1,

it is wrong to say "the odds on Labour to win were cut last night" – in fact, the odds against Labour to win have been cut (the shorter the price, the more likely something is expected to happen).

It gets more complicated when something is genuinely odds-on, ie bookmakers quote a price of "2-1 on": in this case, if the Labour candidate is quoted at 2-1 on and becomes an even hotter favourite, at 3-1 on, the odds have shortened; if Labour loses popularity, and 2-1 on becomes, say, 7-4 on or evens, the odds have lengthened

between 15 and 20 not "between 15 to 20" or "between 15-20"

Bevan, Aneurin (1897-1960) Labour health minister from 1945 to 1951 and architect of the NHS, also known as Nye Bevan

Beverly Hills

Bevin, Ernest (1881-1951) Labour foreign secretary between 1945 and 1951 who helped to create Nato

Beyoncé

beyond the pale not pail; this pale is derived from the Latin palus, a stake as used to support a fence (cf palisade); hence the figurative meaning of beyond the pale as being outside the boundary, unacceptable

biannual twice a year; **biennial** every two years; biannual is almost always misused, so to avoid confusion stick with the alternative twice-yearly; an alternative to biennial is two-yearly

bias, biased

Bible cap up if referring to Old or New Testament, lc in such sentences as "Guardian Style is my bible"; the adjective biblical is always lc

Bible belt

biblical quotations
Use a modern translation, not the Authorised Version. From a reader: "Peradventure the editor hath no copy of Holy Writ in

Bb

the office, save the King James Version only. Howbeit the great multitude of believers knoweth this translation not. And he (or she) who quoteth the words of Jesus in ancient form, sheweth plainly that he (or she) considereth them to be out of date. Wherefore let them be quoted in such manner that the people may understand"

biblical references like this: Genesis 1:1; II Corinthians 2:13; Revelation 3:16 (anyone calling it "Revelations" will burn in hell for eternity)

bicentenary a 200th anniversary; **bicentennial** is its adjective

biceps singular and plural (there is no such thing as a bicep)

bid should be used only in a financial or sporting sense, eg Royal Bank of Scotland's disastrous bid for ABN Amro, Barcelona have put in a bid for Rooney, etc; or when writing about an auction. Say in an attempt to, in an effort to, rather than "in a bid to"; in headlines, move is a useful alternative

big usually preferable to major, massive, giant, mammoth, behemoth, etc

big bang lowercase, whether you are talking about the origin of the universe, about 14bn years ago, or deregulation of the City of London in 1986

bigot, **bigoted**

"big society" described by Simon Hoggart as "surely the vaguest slogan ever coined by a political leader. Nobody knows what it means." Until they do, keep it in quotation marks

bill lowercase; cap up only if it becomes an act

billion one thousand million: in copy use bn for sums of money, quantities or inanimate objects: £10bn, 1bn litres of water; otherwise billion: 6 billion (not six billion) people, etc; use bn in headlines

bin Laden, Osama Bin Laden on second reference. He has been stripped of his Saudi citizenship, so can be described as Saudi-born but not as a Saudi

biodegradable, bioethics, biofuel one word

Birds Eye TM; two words, no apostrophe, named after the frozen food pioneer Clarence Frank Birdseye II (1886-1956)

birdwatchers also known as birders, not "twitchers"; they go birding or birdwatching, not "twitching"

Biro TM; say ballpoint pen

birthdays are for people; institutions, events, etc have anniversaries

birthplace, birthrate, birthright one word

Birtwistle, Sir Harrison British composer, born 1934 (not Birtwhistle)

bishops the Right Rev Clifford Richard, bishop of Wimbledon, at first mention; thereafter just Richard or the bishop

bismillah means "in the name of God" in Arabic

bite-size not bite-sized; very few things are the same size as a bite

bitterest use of this word by the Guardian in 2006 provoked a bitter controversy among readers, many of whom (rightly) pointed out that there is nothing wrong with it

black should be used only as an adjective when referring to race, ie not "blacks" but "black people" or whatever noun is appropriate

blackberry fruit, plural blackberries; **BlackBerry** handheld wireless email device, plural BlackBerrys

black cab-driver a black person who drives a cab; **black-cab driver** a person who drives a black cab

Black Country

Black Death

Bb

black economy hidden or parallel economy are preferable

black-on-black violence is banned, unless in a quote, but even then treat with scepticism (imagine the police saying they were "investigating an incident of white-on-white violence between Millwall and West Ham supporters")

blackout no hyphen

Blackpool Pleasure Beach a giant funfair, not a beach, so do not illustrate with a picture of donkeys on the sand

Blade Runner not Bladerunner

Blair/Booth, Cherie is Cherie Blair when we are referring to her in her capacity as the wife of the former prime minister; if she is appearing in court or at a function related to her work as a lawyer, she is Cherie Booth QC (Booth on second mention)

Blanchett, Cate

blase no accent

blastfurnace

bleeper pager; not to be confused with beeper, a thing that goes "beep" (eg on a microwave)

blitz as in the London blitz of 1940-41, and various other blitzes (eg Liverpool, Sheffield)

blitzkrieg

blog (noun) collection of articles, (verb) action of publishing an article to the blog: "I just blogged about that"; an individual article is a **blogpost**

blokeish rather than blokish

blond adjective and male noun; **blonde** female noun: the woman is a blonde, because she has blond hair; the man has blond hair and is, if you insist, a blond

bloodsports one word

bloody mary vodka and tomato juice

Bb

Bloody Sunday

Take care when writing about the death toll: 13 died in Derry on 30 January 1972, but a 14th victim died from a brain tumour several months later, so we should use a phrase such as "which led to 14 deaths"

Bluffer's Guide TM; beware of using phrases such as "a bluffer's guide to crimewriting", a headline that led to a legal complaint

blunder

One (of many) mentions of this word led to the following comment from a reader: "The term 'blunder' is used most frequently when referring to mistakes made in public services and this only serves to fuel the view commonly propagated by rightwing newspapers that the role of the public sector should be diminished and its functions handed over to private companies. I'm sure the Guardian does not endorse this view, but its use of language may imply that it does"

Blu-ray TM; full name is Blu-ray Disc (not Disk), abbreviation BD

Blu-Tack TM

Boat Race Oxford v Cambridge

Boddingtons popularly known as Boddies, it remains the cream of Manchester, despite the closure of the Strangeways brewery

bodybuilder, bodybuilding one word

boffin tabloid word for scientist

Bogarde, Dirk (1921-99) British actor

Bogart, Humphrey (1899-1957) American actor

bogey golf, nasal mucus, ghost, so bogeyman; **bogie** trolley, truck

Bogotá capital of Colombia

Bolívar, Simón (1783-1830) Venezuelan-born Latin American revolutionary hero; not Simon Bolivar, Simón Bolivar, Simon Bolívar, or Simón Bólivar - all of which appeared in the paper in the space of a year

Bb

Bombay is now known as Mumbai

bombay duck

bona fide, **bona fides**

Bonham Carter, Helena

bon vivant not bon viveur

boo-boo mistake; **Boo Boo** cartoon bear who lives with Yogi in Jellystone Park

bookcase, bookkeeper, bookseller, bookshelf one word

book titles are not italicised, except in the Guardian's Review section and the Observer; lc for a, an, and, at, for, from, in, of, the, to (unless they are the first word of the title): Pride and Prejudice, The Mill on the Floss, etc

bordeaux wine from Bordeaux

bored with, **bored by** not bored of, although usage seems to be changing, particularly among younger people

borstals named after a village in Kent, these institutions were replaced by youth custody centres in 1982, four years after being immortalised by the Sham 69 single Borstal Breakout

borscht

Bosnia-Herzegovina for the former Yugoslav republic, not Hercegovina

Bosphorus not Bosporus

Boston Strangler

both unnecessary in most phrases that contain "and"; "both men and women" says no more than "men and women", takes longer, and can also be ambiguous

Botox TM

Botswana country; **Batswana** plural of people (singular: Motswana); **Setswana** language

Bb

bottleneck

Boudicca not Boadicea

bougainvillea

bouncebackability invaluable word coined by the football manager Iain Dowie and since, thanks to the wonders of Twitter, translated by Guardian Style followers into French (*la rebondissabilité*) and German (*die Rücksprungsfähigkeit*)

Boundary Commission

bourgeois adjective, **bourgeoisie** noun

Boutros Boutros-Ghali former UN secretary general

Boxing Day a public holiday on or soon after 26 December in many countries; in the Irish Republic it is known as St Stephen's Day, and in South Africa as the Day of Goodwill

box office

box set not boxed set

boy male under 18

boyband, boyfriend

Boy's Own

brackets *See Grammar & punctuation*

braggadocio

braille

Bramall Lane famous old football (and former cricket) ground, the home of Sheffield United FC

brand "Wenger brands Ferguson a liar" and similar tabloidese should be avoided

Brands Hatch no apostrophe

Brasilia capital of Brazil

brazil nut

breastfed, breastfeeding one word

Bremner, Ewen actor, not Ewan

briar bush, pipe

bric-a-brac

brickbat is permissible only if you know what a brickbat is

bridges lc, eg Golden Gate bridge, Waterloo bridge

Bridgnorth Shropshire

Bridgwater Somerset

Brighton and Hove a city and unitary council since 2000, and no longer in East Sussex

brilliant "a word applied indiscriminately by the Guardian to anything new, no matter how ordinary" (2010 tweet from a reader)

Brink's-Mat

Britain, UK
These terms are synonymous: Britain is the official short form of United Kingdom of Great Britain and Northern Ireland. Used as adjectives, therefore, British and UK mean the same. Great Britain, however, refers only to England, Wales and Scotland. Take care not to write Britain when you might mean only England and Wales, for example when referring to the education system *See Scotland*

Britart

British and Irish Lions (rugby union); not British Lions

British Council

British empire but **British Empire Medal**

British Film Institute BFI on second mention

British Isles
A geographical term taken to mean Great Britain, Ireland and

Bb

some or all of the adjacent islands such as Orkney, Shetland and the Isle of Man. The phrase is best avoided, given its (understandable) unpopularity in the Irish Republic. Alternatives adopted by some publications are British and Irish Isles or simply Britain and Ireland

British Library

British Medical Association (doctors' trade union), BMA on second mention

British Museum

British Sign Language abbreviate to BSL after first mention

Britpop

Britvic TM

Broadmoor a secure psychiatric hospital, not a prison

Brontë Charlotte, Emily, Anne and their brother, Branwell; they grew up at Haworth (not Howarth) in what is now West Yorkshire

bronze age, ice age, iron age, stone age

brownie points

Brownies for girls aged seven to 10, at which point they may join the Guides

Bruegel family of Flemish painters

Brum, Brummie

brussels sprouts lc

brutalise render brutal, not treat brutally; so soldiers may be brutalised by the experience of war

Brylcreem TM

BSE bovine spongiform encephalopathy; no need to spell out

BST stands for British summer time; **BST** also stands for bovine somatrophin (bovine growth hormone)

Bb

BTec

Buckingham Palace the palace on second mention

buckminsterfullerene a form of carbon, named after the US engineer Buckminster Fuller (1895-1983)

budget, the lc noun and adjective, eg budget talks, budget measures, mini-budget, pre-budget report (PBR), etc

buffaloes for the plural; not buffalo or buffalos

buffet finger food, not to be confused with **Buffett, Warren** investor known as the Sage of Omaha

buildup (noun) no hyphen

Bulger, James not Jamie

bullet points *See Grammar & punctuation*

bullseye

bumblebee

bumf not bumph

Buñuel, Luis (1900-83) Spanish film director

buoyed by not buoyed up by

Burberry TM

bureau plural bureaus (furniture) or bureaux (organisations)

burgeon means to bud or sprout, so you can have someone with burgeoning talent; often misused to describe anything that is growing or expanding, especially population

burgomaster not burgomeister

Burma not Myanmar

burned/burnt burned is the past tense form (he burned the cakes); burnt is the participle, an "adjectival" form of the verb (the cakes are burnt)

Burns Night 25 January

Bb

burqa not burka

Burton upon Trent

buses, bussed, bussing

Bush, George W son of George Bush Sr

businesslike

businessman, businesswoman for individuals, but say business people or the business community rather than "businessmen"

Bussell, Darcey Royal Ballet dancer who retired in 2007

but, however these words are often redundant, and increasingly wrongly used to connect two compatible statements

Butlins but **Pontin's**

butterflies and moths are usually lc: adonis blue, orange-tip, purple emperor, silver-washed fritillary, death's-head hawkmoth, etc; but note the following: Duke of Burgundy, Queen of Spain fritillary, Essex skipper, Lulworth skipper, Scotch argus

buyout but **buy-in**

byelection, bylaw, byline, bypass, bystander no hyphen

byte unit of measurement of computer information storage, eg 320GB hard drive (320 gigabytes)

Byzantine empire; **byzantine** complexity

Cc

 66 Lamentably, 'care in the community' has become a byword for failed – even dangerous – public policy when we should celebrate its success and humanity. Something like 100,000 people who were locked up in Victorian mental hospitals were set free to live ordinary lives. Only a tiny minority ever proved a risk to themselves or others 99

David Brindle

Cc

cabbie plural is cabbies

cabin attendant, crew, staff not air hostesses

cabinet, shadow cabinet but **Cabinet Office**

caddie tee; **caddy** tea

Cádiz

Caernarfon place; **Lord Carnarvon** person (but he lives at Highclere Castle in West Berkshire)

caesar salad; caesarean section; Caesars Palace hotel in Las Vegas

Cafcass Children and Family Court Advisory and Support Service on first mention

cafe no accent

Calcutta is now Kolkata

Californian a person; the adjective is California, which is why Brian Wilson did not write a song called Californian Girls; the same rule applies to other US states, so a "Texan drilling for Texas tea" is an oilman

call girl like vice girl, an old-fashioned term encountered only in the tabloids, where it is always the 1950s

Calor TM

cameraphone one word

Campaign for Better Transport formerly Transport 2000

Campari TM

Canal+ French TV channel, formerly Canal Plus

canal boats
A narrowboat is the popular type of British canal boat, 7ft wide and up to 70ft long - do not call it a barge; a wider version (typically 10-14ft wide) is a broadbeam narrowboat. A barge is a broader (10-14ft wide) cargo-carrying boat - usually towed but sometimes self-powered. The version with accommodation is

Cc

usually a Dutch barge. A cruiser is the white-hulled GRP (glass-reinforced plastic) style of boat, more commonly seen on rivers; smaller versions are cabin cruisers.

The difference between narrowboat and barge is important, particularly if you don't want to get stuck in a narrow lock somewhere outside Birmingham

Canary Wharf the whole development, not the main tower, which is 1 Canada Square

Cancún city in Mexico

cannabis people smoke cannabis rather than "experiment" with it, despite what politicians and young members of the royal family might claim

canon cleric, decree, principle, body of writings, type of music; **cannon** something you fire

Canute (c994-1035) Danish king of England, Denmark and Norway who commanded the tide to turn back, so the legend says - not in a vain attempt to exercise power over nature, but to prove to his toadying courtiers that he was not all-powerful

canvas tent, painting; **canvass** solicit votes

CAP common agricultural policy

capitals
"I am a poet: I distrust anything that starts with a capital letter and ends with a full stop" (Antjie Krog)

Times have changed since the days of medieval manuscripts with elaborate hand-illuminated capital letters, or Victorian documents in which not just proper names, but virtually all nouns, were given initial caps (a Tradition valiantly maintained to this day by Estate Agents). A look through newspaper archives would show greater use of capitals the further back you went. The tendency towards lowercase, which in part reflects a less formal, less deferential society, has been accelerated by the internet: some web companies, and many email users, have

Cc

dispensed with capitals altogether.

Our style reflects these developments. We aim for coherence and consistency, but not at the expense of clarity. As with any aspect of style, it is impossible to be wholly consistent – there are almost always exceptions, so if you are unsure, check for an individual entry in this guide. But here are the main principles:

jobs all lc, eg prime minister, US secretary of state, chief rabbi, editor of the Guardian

titles cap up titles, but not job description, eg President Barack Obama (but the US president, Barack Obama, and Obama on subsequent mention); the Duke of Westminster (the duke at second mention); the Queen

British government departments of state initial caps, eg Home Office, Foreign Office, Ministry of Justice *See departments of state for a full list*

other countries' departments of state lc, eg US state department, Russian foreign ministry

government agencies, public bodies, quangos initial caps, eg Crown Prosecution Service, Equality and Human Rights Commission, Heritage Lottery Fund, Revenue & Customs

acts of parliament initial caps (but bills lc), eg Official Secrets Act, Child Poverty Act 2010, local government bill

parliamentary committees, reports and inquiries all lc, eg trade and industry select committee, royal commission on long-term care for the elderly, Jenkins report

artistic and cultural names of institutions, etc, get initial caps, eg British Museum, National Gallery, Royal Albert Hall, Tate Modern. Books, films, music, works of art, etc have initial caps except a, an, and, at, for, from, in, of, the, to (except in initial positions or after a colon), eg There is a Light That Never Goes Out

churches, hospitals and schools cap up the proper or placename, lc the rest, eg St Peter's church, Pembury; Great Ormond Street children's hospital, Ripon grammar school, Vernon county primary school

Cc

universities and colleges of further and higher education caps for institution, lc for departments, eg Sheffield University department of medieval and modern history, Oregon State University, Free University of Berlin, University of Queensland school of journalism, London College of Communication

airports cap the name but lc the generic part (if necessary at all), eg Heathrow, Gatwick (no need for "airport"), Liverpool John Lennon airport

geographical features lc, eg river Thames, Sydney harbour, Monterey peninsula, Bondi beach, Solsbury hill (but Mount Everest)

words and phrases based on proper names that have lost connection with their origins (alsatian, cardigan, champagne, cheddar cheese, cornish pasty, french windows, wellington boots, yorkshire pudding and numerous others) are usually lc; many are listed individually in this guide, as are exceptions (eg Parma ham, Worcestershire sauce)

cappuccino

car bomb, **car park** but **carmaker**

carcass plural carcasses

cards scratchcard, smartcard, swipecard but credit card, debit card, sim card

careen to sway or keel over to one side; often confused with **career**, to rush along

career girl, **career woman** we don't use these sexist labels

carer an unpaid family member, partner or friend who helps a disabled or frail person with the activities of daily living; not someone who works in a caring job or profession. The term is important because carers are entitled to a range of benefits and services that depend on them recognising themselves as carers

Cc

Caribbean one R, two Bs

cartel
It is dangerous to call a group of companies a cartel unless you want to hear from ...

Carter-Ruck
You might think that, given this law firm's close relationship with newspapers, everyone would know that it's hyphenated. You would, sadly, be wrong

Casanova cap up, whether you are talking about the original (Giacomo Girolamo Casanova de Seingalt, 1725-98), or any latterday womaniser ("he is the Casanova of the Observer")

casbah rather than kasbah

cash for honours noun but cash-for-honours should, like similar phrases, be hyphenated when used adjectivally (the cash-for-honours scandal)

cashmere fabric

caster sugar, wheels on a sofa; **castor** oil; **Caster Semenya** South African runner

castoff one word (noun, adjective); **cast off** two words (verb)

casual (workers) freelance is often preferable

casualties includes dead and injured, so not a synonym for deaths; **casualty** lc, as in she's been taken to casualty (though normally called A&E)

Cat scan or **CT scan**; it stands for computerised (axial) tomography

Catalonia adjective Catalan

catch-22 lc unless specifically referring to Joseph Heller's 1961 novel Catch-22

catchphrase

catchup TV not catch-up or catch up

Cc

cathedrals cap up, eg Béziers Cathedral (its full name is Cathédrale Saint-Nazaire-et-Saint-Celse de Béziers)

catherine wheel

Catholic church but if you mean Roman Catholic, say so

caviar not caviare

CBeebies

CD, **CDs**, **CD-Rom** a CD is a disc, not a disk

CE, **BCE** some people prefer CE (common era, current era or Christian era) and BCE (before common era, etc) to AD and BC, which, however, remain our style

ceasefire

Ceausescu, Nicolae former president of Romania, deposed and executed in 1989, and dug up again in 2010

ceilidh

celibate, **celibacy** strictly refer to being unmarried (especially for religious reasons), but it is now acceptable to use them to mean abstaining from sexual intercourse

cellphone mobile phone in British English

celsius without degree symbol and with fahrenheit equivalent in brackets: 23C (73F), -3C (27F), etc.

To convert celsius to fahrenheit, multiply by 9, divide by 5, then add 32; to convert fahrenheit to celsius, subtract 32, divide the answer by 9, then multiply by 5 (or use one of the many online calculators)

Celtic not Glasgow Celtic

cement or concrete? not interchangeable terms: cement is an ingredient of concrete, which is a mix of aggregates (sand and gravel or crushed stone) and paste (water and portland cement); so a "cement mixer" should always be referred to as a concrete mixer

censor prevent publication; **censure** criticise severely

Cc

census lc, eg the next UK census is due on 27 March 2011

Center Parcs

centimetres abbreviation cm, not cms

Central America comprises Mexico, Belize, Guatemala, Honduras, El Salvador, Nicaragua, Costa Rica, and Panama

central belt the swath across Scotland, containing Glasgow and Edinburgh, where population density is highest. It is in the south, not the centre of the country

centre on or centre in, but revolve around

Centre Court Wimbledon

Centres for Disease Control not singular, and not the American spelling

century sixth century, 21st century, etc; but sixth-century remains, 21st-century boy, etc

Cephalonia eschew the variations

Cern the Geneva-based European laboratory for particle physics

Cézanne, Paul (1839-1906) French artist

CFC chlorofluorocarbon

chablis wines from Chablis

cha-cha-cha the dance, not cha-cha

chair acceptable in place of chairman or chairwoman, being nowadays widely used in the public sector and by organisations such as the Labour party and trade unions (though not the Conservative party, which had a "chairman" in kitten heels); if it seems inappropriate for a particular body, use a different construction ("the meeting was chaired by Ian" or "Kath was in the chair")

Chakrabarti, Shami director of Liberty

champagne

Cc

Champs Elysées

chancellor of the duchy of Lancaster

chancellor of the exchequer

changeable

Channel, the not the English Channel

Channel 4, Channel 5

Channel Islands

Channel tunnel not Chunnel

chaos theory is not a synonym for chaos. It describes the behaviour of dynamic systems that are sensitively dependent on their initial conditions. An example is the weather: under the "butterfly effect", the flap of a butterfly's wing in Brazil can in principle result in a tornado in Texas

chardonnay lc, like other wines, whether named after a grape (as in this case) or a region

chargé, chargée d'affaires

Charity Commission

Chartered Institute of Public Finance and Accountancy Cipfa or the institute after first mention

chassis singular and plural

chateau, chateaux no accent

Chatham House rule often mistakenly called "rules". There is just one, namely: "When a meeting, or part thereof, is held under the Chatham House rule, participants are free to use the information received, but neither the identity nor the affiliation of the speaker(s), nor that of any other participant, may be revealed." Chatham House is more formally known as the Royal Institute of International Affairs, based at Chatham House in London

chatroom, chatshow

Cc

Chávez, Hugo elected president of Venezuela in 1998, and re-elected in 2000 and 2006

chavs a term best avoided

Chechnya inhabited by Chechens

checkout noun, adjective; **check out** verb

cheese normally lc, even if named after a place: brie, camembert, cheddar, cheshire, double gloucester, lancashire, parmesan, stilton, wensleydale, etc

Chekhov

Chek Lap Kok Hong Kong international airport, designed by Sir Norman Foster, opened in 1998

Chennai formerly Madras

chequebook

cherubim plural of cherub

Cheshire cat but **cheshire cheese**

chickenpox one word

chicken tikka masala Britain's favourite dish; note that there is also an Italian dish called chicken marsala

chief ("planning chiefs", etc): try to use proper titles; officers or officials may be preferable

chief constable a job, not a title – John Smith, chief constable of Greater Manchester; Smith at second mention

chief rabbi lc, a style consistent with that followed by Haaretz and the Jerusalem Post

chief secretary to the Treasury, **chief whip**

childcare, **childminder**

ChildLine

child trust funds colloquially known as baby bonds, abolished by the new progressive government in 2010

Cc

chilli with two Ls but note Red Hot Chili Peppers

Chinese names

Mainland China: in two parts, eg Mao Zedong, Zhou Enlai, Jiang Zemin.

Hong Kong, Taiwan: in two parts with hyphen, eg Tung Chee-hwa, Chiang Kai-shek (exception: when a building, park or the like is named after a person it becomes three parts, eg Chiang Kai Shek Cultural Centre); note also that Korean names are written the same way, eg Kim Il-sung.

Singapore, Malaysia: in three parts, eg Lee Kuan Yew.

For people with Chinese names elsewhere in the world, follow their preference – but make sure you know which is the surname

Chloé (fashion) note accent

chock-a-block

chocoholic not chocaholic

Chomsky, Noam US linguist and political activist

choose for some mysterious reason this often appears in the paper as "chose", its past tense

chords musical; **cords** vocal

Christ Church Oxford (not Christ Church College)

christened, christening only when referring to a Christian baptism: don't talk about a boat being christened or a football club christening a new stadium; named is fine

Christian, Christianity but unchristian

Christian name use first name, forename or given name (which in many cultures comes after the family name)

Christian Union an evangelical Christian organisation

Christie's the auction house; Christies the holding company has no apostrophe

Cc

Christmas Day, **Christmas Eve**

chronic means lasting for a long time or constantly recurring, too often misused when acute (short but severe) is meant

Chumbawamba (not Chumbawumba) band whose guitarist, Danbert Nobacon, threw a bucket of iced water over John Prescott, the then deputy prime minister, at the 1998 Brit awards

church lc for the established church, eg "the church is no longer relevant today"; Anglican church, etc, but Church of England

cineaste someone who enjoys films; but note that, in French, a *cinéaste* is someone who makes them

cinemagoer

cinéma vérité

Cites convention on international trade in endangered species of wild fauna and flora

Citizens Advice what the organisation likes to be called, although it still runs bureaux

Citroën

city in Britain a town that has been granted a charter by the crown; it usually has a cathedral; **City** capped when used as shorthand for the City of London financial district

civil partnership rather than gay marriage, but gay wedding is fine and does not need quotation marks

civil servant, **civil service**

CJD Creutzfeldt-Jakob disease, not normally necessary to spell it out; it is acceptable to refer to variant CJD as the human form of BSE, but not "the human form of mad cow disease"

classical music Mozart's 41st Symphony (or Symphony No 41) in C, K551; Rachmaninov's Piano Concerto No 2; Schubert's Sonata in A minor for Piano, D845

Cc

clause IV of the Labour manifesto, rewritten in 1995; also by extension to "clause IV moment" as in "will the Tories experience their own clause IV moment?" (not so far)

clearcut no hyphen

cliches
Overused words and phrases to be avoided, some of which merit their own ignominious entry in this book, include: ahead of, back burner, boost (massive or otherwise), bouquets and brickbats, but hey … , controversial, count 'em, drop-dead gorgeous, elephant in the room, eye-watering, famous, fit for purpose, flagship, landmark, key, major, massive, meanwhile, ongoing, politically correct, raft of measures, special, step change, to die for, upcoming, upsurge; verbs overused or misused in headlines include: bid, boost, downplay, fuel, hike, insist, probe, quiz, set to, signal, spiral, target, unveil.

A survey by the Plain English Campaign found that the most irritating phrase in the language was "at the end of the day", followed by (in order of annoyance): at this moment in time, like (as in, like, this), with all due respect, to be perfectly honest with you, touch base, I hear what you're saying, going forward, absolutely, and blue sky thinking; other words and phrases that upset people included 24/7, ballpark figure, bottom line, diamond geezer, it's not rocket science, ongoing, prioritise, pushing the envelope, singing from the same hymn sheet, and thinking outside the box

cliffhanger one word

Climate Camp its full name is Camp for Climate Action

climate change terminology
A sensitive area. The editor of the Guardian's environment website says: "Climate change deniers has nasty connotations with Holocaust denial and tends to polarise debate. On the other hand there are some who are literally in denial about the evidence." Our guidelines are:

Cc

Rather than opening itself to the charge of denigrating people for their beliefs, a fair newspaper should always try to address what it is that people are sceptical about or deny.

The term sceptics covers those who argue that climate change is exaggerated, or not caused by human activity.

If someone really does claim that climate change is not happening - that the world is not warming - then it seems fair enough to call them a denier

climbdown noun, **climb down** verb

clingfilm

Close, Glenn two Ns (as in bunny boiler)

cloud cuckoo land

CO₂

coalfield, coalmine, coalminer

Coalite TM

coalition government Con-Lib if you are being polite; Lib-Con if you are a sceptic; Con-Dem if you want to be rude

coarse fishing we have been known to spell it course

coastguard

Coca-Cola, Coke TM; the generic term is cola; **coke** for smokeless fuel and cocaine

cockney

coconut

cohabitant not cohabitee

cold war

Coliseum London theatre; **Colosseum** Roman amphitheatre

collectible

collective nouns *See Grammar & punctuation*

collector's item

Cc

College of Arms

colleges take initial caps, eg West Kent College; but not when college forms part of the name of a school, eg Bash Street sixth-form college, Eton college

Colombia South American country that we frequently misspell as "Columbia"

colon *See Grammar & punctuation*

colonel Colonel Napoleon Bogey, subsequently Bogey (Col Bogey in leading articles)

Columbia as in District of Columbia (Washington DC) and Columbia University (New York); Columbus Day (12 October, marking the date Christopher Columbus landed in the West Indies in 1492); Columbus is also the state capital of Ohio

comedian male and female; do not use comedienne

commas *See Grammar & punctuation*

commented "said" is normally adequate

common agricultural policy lc but the abbreviation is CAP

Commons, House of Commons but the house, not the House

Commons committees lc, home affairs select committee, public accounts committee, etc

common sense noun; **commonsense** adjective: "William Hague's 'commonsense revolution' showed little common sense"

Commonwealth, the; Commonwealth War Graves Commission

communique no accent

communism, communist lc, except in name of party, eg Communist party of Great Britain (Marxist-Leninist)

community the subediting community is encouraged to weed out examples of this shockingly overused word

community charge what no one, apart from a handful of

Cc

Conservative ministers, called the poll tax

company names
A difficult area, as so many companies have adopted
unconventional typography and other devices that, in some
cases, turn their names into logos. In general, we use the names
that companies use themselves: c2c, Capgemini, easyJet, eBay,
ebookers, iSoft Group, etc. Some of these look odd, so change if
using as first word in a headline or sentence, eg eBay becomes
Ebay; iSoft becomes Isoft.

Exceptions include Adidas (not adidas), ABN Amro (not ABN
AMRO), BAE Systems (not BAE SYSTEMS), BhS (no italicised H),
Toys R Us (do not attempt to turn the R backwards), Yahoo (no
exclamation mark).

Company names are always singular

compare to or with? *See Grammar & punctuation*

compass points lc for regions: the north, the south of England,
the south-west, north-east Scotland, south Wales; the same
applies to geopolitical areas: the west, western Europe, the far
east, south-east Asia, central America, etc; cap up, however,
when part of the name of a county (West Sussex, East Riding of
Yorkshire) or province (East Java, North Sulawesi, etc); note the
following: East End, West End (London), Middle East, Latin
America, North America, South America

Competition Commission formerly the Monopolies and Mergers
Commission – and yes, there is only one

complement, compliment, complimentary to complement is to
make complete: the two strikers complemented each other; to
compliment is to praise; a complimentary copy is free

complicit you can be complicit in a crime, for example, if you
know about it but fail to report it

comprise to consist of; "comprise of" is wrong

Concord town in Massachusetts; **Concorde** plane

Cc

confidant male, **confidante** female

congestion charge lc

Congo acceptable on second mention for the Democratic Republic of the Congo (or DRC, formerly Zaire); we call its neighbour Congo-Brazzaville; the Congo is the river

Congregational uc when referring to the Congregational Union of England and Wales, formed in 1832, which joined the Presbyterian Church of England in 1972 to form the United Reformed Church (please, not "Reform")

Congress comprises the House of Representatives (the house) and Senate; but lc congressman, congresswoman, congressional

conjoined twins not Siamese twins

connection not connexion

Conservative central office, **Conservative party**

consortium plural consortiums

constitution lc as in the US constitution

Consuelo not Consuela; from a reader: "I really have had enough of show-off ignoramuses messing up my name. Consuelo is a Spanish abstract noun, masculine, invariable. Pilar and Mercedes are also Spanish female names derived, like Consuelo, from titles of the Virgin Mary"

consult not consult with

consumer price index forms the basis for the government's inflation target; CPI after first mention

Consumers' Association now known as Which?, after its magazine

contemporary of the same period, though often wrongly used to mean modern; a performance of Shakespeare in contemporary dress would involve Elizabethan costume, not 21st-century clothes

Cc

continent, the mainland Europe

continual refers to things that happen repeatedly but not constantly; **continuous** indicates an unbroken sequence

contractions
Do not overuse contractions such as aren't, can't, couldn't, hasn't, don't, I'm, it's, there's and what's (even the horrific "there've" has appeared); while they might make a piece more colloquial or easier to read, they can be an irritant and a distraction, and make a serious article sound frivolous. They also look horrible

controversial is overused, typically to show that the writer disapproves of something ("the government's controversial free schools scheme"); like "famous", it can be safely removed from news stories to allow readers to make up their own minds

convener not convenor

conversions
We give metric measures and convert on first mention only to imperial in brackets (exceptions: miles and pints); if a rough figure is given in metric, do not convert it into an exact figure in imperial, and vice versa, eg if someone says the towns are about 50km apart, convert to 30 miles, not "31.07 miles"; the same goes for rough amounts of currencies, though don't round up £3.6bn to £4bn

convertible not -able

convince or persuade? having convinced someone of the facts, you might persuade them to do something

co-operate, co-operation, co-operative

Co-operative Bank, Group, party but you might shop at your local **Co-op**

co-opt, co-ordinate

cop-out

Cc

copy editor what subeditors are known as in the United States and Canada, where they copy-edit

copyright but **copywriter**

Córdoba

cords vocal; **chords** musical

cornflakes in general but Kellogg's Corn Flakes

cornish pasty

coronavirus

corporation of London

corps de ballet

cortege no accent

coruscating means sparkling, or emitting flashes of light; people seem to think, wrongly, that it means the same as excoriating, censuring severely, eg "a coruscating attack on Clegg's advisers"

cosmetic surgery is not the same as plastic surgery, which should be reserved for people treated for deformity or illness

councils lc apart from placename: Lancaster city council, London borough of Southwark, Kent county council; it is normally sufficient to say Lancaster council, Southwark council, etc

Council of Europe

count 'em cliche often seen in parenthesis after a number is mentioned. For example, an article referred to "the seminal Andrex puppy advent calendar with 25 - count 'em - puppy pictures ... "

counteract, counterattack, countermeasures but **counter-terrorism**

County Down, **County Durham** etc at first mention; thereafter Co Down, Co Durham, etc

Cc

coupe no accent

courts all lc, eg court of appeal, court of session, high court, magistrates court (no apostrophe), supreme court, European court of human rights, international criminal court, etc

court martial plural courts martial

court of St James's

couscous

CPRE Campaign to Protect Rural England (formerly the Council for the Protection of Rural England)

CPS Crown Prosecution Service

Cradock, Fanny (1909-94) TV chef, often misspelt as "Craddock"

creche no accent

credibility capable of being believed; **credulity** gullibility; we sometimes mix the two up

creme fraiche no accents

crescendo a gradual increase in loudness or intensity; musically or figuratively, it is the buildup to a climax, not the climax itself (we frequently get this wrong)

cretinism a medical condition, not a term of abuse

cricket leg-side, leg-spinner, off-spin, off-stump, silly mid-on, mid-off, etc, all hyphenated

cripple, crippled offensive and outdated

crisscross

criterion plural criteria

critique a noun meaning review, rather than a verb meaning criticise

Crombie TM

crowdsourcing

crown, the; crown estate, crown jewels

Cc

crucifix not synonymous with cross: a crucifix depicts the body of Christ on the cross

crucifixion, the

Crufts

cruise missile

Crusades, the

Cruz, Penélope

cubism, cubist

Cub scouts boys (and now girls) aged from eight to 10, organised in packs but no longer known as "Wolf Cubs"; avoid dated "Dyb Dyb Dyb, Dob Dob Dob" jokes but if relevant, it is spelt thus (it stands for "do your best" and we will "do our best"), and not "Dib"

cull means pick or choose as in "culled from the best authors". It doesn't mean killed, axed or massacred (though you cull sheep in order to kill them). So a jobs cull does not mean the same as mass sackings

CULV consumer ultra-low voltage

cumberland sausage

Cummings, EE US poet (1894-1962) who, despite what many people think, used capitals in his signature - so don't call him "ee cummings"

Cup, FA after first mention it is the Cup; but other cups are lc on second mention

curate's egg
Used nowadays to mean good in parts ("this was a curate's egg of a match"), the expression originally, and more subtly, meant to deliberately gloss over the truth - the curate was trying to spare his bishop's feelings, or perhaps his own embarrassment, when served a bad egg, by saying: "Oh no, My Lord, I assure you! Parts of it are excellent!" (cartoon in Punch, 9 November 1895)

Cc

curb restrain; **kerb** pavement

currencies

When the whole word is used it is lc: euro, pound sterling, dong, etc. Abbreviate dollars like this: $50 (US dollars); A$50 (Australian dollars); HK$50 (Hong Kong dollars).

Convert all foreign amounts to sterling in brackets at first mention, but use common sense - there is no need to put £625,000 in brackets after the phrase "I feel like a million dollars."

Take care when converting old money to new: some of our attempts have been meaningless, in that they have ignored the relative value of sums involved. We said in an obituary, for example, that Ronnie Barker was paid £1 9s (£1.45) a week for his first job in 1947 - a comparison of average earnings would convert that to around £113 today.

Similarly, in converting the price of a "four shilling dish of rice and vegetables" in 1967 to 20p in today's money we forgot to allow for its relative value; taking into account changes in the retail price index it would now be worth £2.23.

There are some excellent websites to assist with such conversions

currently "now" is usually preferable, if needed at all

cusp

A place where two points meet (eg "on the cusp of Manchester and Salford", "on the cusp of Taurus and Gemini"), which may be extended metaphorically to a place or time where two things or groups of things come into contact, as in this elegant example from the Review: "It was a world caught on the cusp between postwar recession, stasis and a dying moral code, and the colour, mobility and licence of the 60s."

Writers who use cusp under the impression that it is a clever way to say on the brink of or about to ("on the cusp of adolescence", "on the cusp of the final", "the garlic was on the cusp of bursting into a constellation of white stars") are, sadly, mistaken

Cc

custody since the 1989 Children Act the correct term for what used to be known as custody in cases involving care of children is residence

Customs, **Revenue & Customs** (singular) but customs officers

cutbacks avoid; cuts will suffice

cybercrime but **cyber attacks**, **cyber criminals**

cyberspace

Cyprus Cyprus, properly known as the Republic of Cyprus, joined the EU in 2004, 30 years after Turkey invaded the northern part of the island, which should be referred to as "Turkish-occupied northern Cyprus" (the self-styled "Turkish Republic of Northern Cyprus" is recognised only by Turkey)

Czech Republic

Dd

❝ May I suggest that the phrase 'heart of darkness' be retired altogether? Conrad recycled colonial stereotypes of the 'dark continent' in order to parody them, but now ... oh, the horror, the horror. It isn't just that it's a cliche, though that's sin enough - but that it is invariably the first thing reached for in stories about dark-skinned people, and carries such a freight of 'us' (pale, civilised, good) v 'them' (benighted, ignorant, savage). Stop it, please **❞**

Aida Edemariam

Dd

Dad or dad? I'll have to ask Dad, then you can check with your dad

dadaism, dadaist

Dáil Éireann lower house of parliament in the Irish Republic, normally just the Dáil

DaimlerChrysler

Dalek takes initial cap, whether used literally (as in referring to Doctor Who), or figuratively (as in describing, say, your boss)

Dalí, Salvador (1904-89) Spanish surrealist

dancefloor one word (thanks to Arctic Monkeys for this one)

dangling participles *See Grammar & punctuation*

DA notices issued by the Defence, Press and Broadcasting Advisory Committee, "advising" that the media do not publish sensitive information; formerly D notices

dark ages

dashes *See Grammar & punctuation*

data though strictly a plural, takes a singular verb (like agenda): the data is clear, etc; no one ever uses agendum or datum

dates Guardian, Observer and guardian.co.uk style is 14 June 2010 (day month year; no commas). In the 21st century but 21st-century boy; fourth century BC; AD2007, 2500BC, 10,000BC; for decades use figures: the swinging 60s or 1960s

daughter, son
Think twice before referring to people in these terms. Often only the person's father is described and such descriptions can smack of snobbery as well as sexism. Simplistic labels may also be misleading: we had to publish a clarification after calling Captain James Cook the son of a Scottish farm labourer. True enough, but Cook's mother was a Yorkshirewoman and Cook is a famous son of Yorkshire

Dd

Davison, Emily suffragette who died four days after stepping in front of George V's horse at the 1913 Derby

daybreak, **daydream**

Day-Glo TM

Day Kundi province in Afghanistan

daylong but **month-long**, **year-long**; **daytime** but **night-time**

day trip two words, as in Day Trip to Bangor by (trivia question) ... Fiddler's Dram

D-day 6 June 1944, or used figuratively ("Monday is D-day for the Blades' promotion hopes")

deaf ears avoid or say "closed ears": the phrase is not just a rather lazy cliche but offensive to many deaf people; for the same reason, do not use "dialogue of the deaf": most deaf people are perfectly capable of conducting a dialogue using BSL and other sign languages

deathbed but **death row**

debacle no accents; like farce and fiasco, to be used sparingly in news reporting

debatable

decades 1950s, etc; use figures if you abbreviate: roaring 20s, swinging 60s, a woman in her 70s, the first reader's email of the 00s (pronounced, unfortunately, "noughties")

decimate nowadays used to mean to partly destroy (yes, we know it originally meant to kill one in 10) *See Latin*

declarations lc, eg Lacken declaration on the future of Europe

decorations do not give OBE, KCMG, or anything similar, after names

deep south of the US

defensible

defriend or **unfriend** Facebook

defuse render harmless; **diffuse** spread about

Degas, Edgar (1834-1917) French artist

de Gaulle, Charles (1890-1970) French military leader and statesman; De Gaulle on second mention

degrees like this: my sons all got firsts, but I only got a second - although it was a 2:1 - and I did go on to a master's

deja vu no accents

Delhi unless specifically referring to the small area of the city that is New Delhi

Deloitte not Deloittes, Deloitte Consulting, or Deloitte & Touche

delphic

delusion or illusion? "That the sun moves round the Earth was once a delusion, and is still an illusion" (Fowler)

DeMille, Cecil B (1881-1959) Hollywood producer and director; the B stood for Blount

Democratic party not "Democrat party", despite attempts by some Republicans to call it this

Dench, Dame Judi not Judy

Deng Xiaoping

denier one who denies, as in "Holocaust denier"; there is no such word as "denialist" *See climate change terminology*; denier is also a unit of weight for fibre, eg 10-denier tights

De Niro, Robert

denouement no accent

departments of state
British government ministries (but not ministers) take initial caps, as follows:
　　Cabinet Office (but the cabinet)

Dd

Home Office

Foreign Office (abbreviate to FCO - for Foreign and
Commonwealth Office - after first mention)

Treasury

Department for Business, Innovation and Skills (BIS)

Communities and Local Government

Department for Culture, Media and Sport (DCMS)

Department for Education (DfE)

Department of Energy and Climate Change (Decc)

Department for Environment, Food and Rural Affairs (Defra)

Department for International Development (DfID)

Department for Transport (DfT)

Department for Work and Pensions (DWP)

Department of Health (DH)

Ministry of Defence (MoD)

Ministry of Justice (MoJ)

Office of the leader of the House of Commons

Northern Ireland Office

Scotland Office (not Scottish Office)

Wales Office (not Welsh Office)

Use the abbreviations in brackets sparingly, especially the
clumsy ones: business department, culture and sport department,
and so on are fine, or just the department, the ministry, etc. The
rebranded Communities and Local Government is tricky, having
decided to drop "Department" from its name: if we say, for
example, "Communities and Local Government yesterday
announced a shakeup in council tax" it makes us sound equally
silly, so best to call it the communities and local government
department (lc) or just communities department or local
government department, depending on the story.

Departments and ministries of other countries are lc, eg
French ministry of the interior, Iraqi foreign ministry

dependant noun, **dependent** adjective, **dependence**

depositary person; **depository** place

Dd

deprecate express disapproval; **depreciate** reduce in value

de rigueur the two Us are de rigueur

derring-do not daring-do

Derry, Co Derry (County Derry at first mention) not Londonderry, Co Londonderry

descendants come after ancestors; you wouldn't think we would get this simple thing wrong as often as we do

deselect

desiccated not dessicated

despoil but **despoliation**

dessert pudding, but **just deserts**

Dettol TM

developing countries rather than third world

devil, the

de Villepin, Dominique Villepin on second mention

DeVito, Danny

Diabetes UK formerly known as the British Diabetic Association

Diaghilev, Sergei (1872-1929) Russian impresario; founder of the Ballets Russes

dialects cockney, estuary English, geordie, scouse

diaspora

DiCaprio, Leonardo

Dictaphone TM

diehard although the film series is Die Hard

dietitian must be trained and qualified in dietetics, and registered with the Health Professionals Council; not the same as a nutritionist, a less precise term (although some nutritionists are also registered dietitians)

Dd

different from is traditionally the correct form, although different to is widely accepted nowadays (but note that you would always say differs from, not differs to); different than is wrong, at least in British English

digital rights management can be abbreviated to DRM after first mention

dignitary, **dignitaries**

dilapidated not delapidated

dilemma means a choice between two difficult options, not any general problem

dilettante

dim sum

Dinky Toys TM

diphtheria

diplomatic service

director general

direct speech
People we write about are allowed to speak in their own, not necessarily our, style, but be sensitive: do not, for example, expose someone to ridicule for dialect or grammatical errors. Do not attempt facetious phonetic renditions such as "oop north", "fooking" and "booger" when interviewing someone from the north, or "dahn sarf" when writing about south London

disabled people not "the disabled"
We aim to use positive language about disability, avoiding outdated terms that stereotype or stigmatise. Terms to avoid, with acceptable alternatives in brackets, include victim of, suffering from, afflicted by, crippled by (prefer person who has, person with); wheelchair-bound, in a wheelchair (uses a wheelchair); invalid (disabled person); mentally handicapped, backward, retarded, slow (person with learning difficulties or

Dd

disabilities); the disabled, the handicapped, the blind, the deaf (disabled people, blind people, deaf people); deaf and dumb, deaf-mute (deaf and speech-impaired, hearing and speech-impaired)

disc rotating optical disc: CD, CD-Rom, DVD, etc; **disk** rotating magnetic disc: disk drive, floppy disk

discernible not discernable

discharged a patient is discharged, not released, from hospital; a prisoner is released from jail

discolour but **discoloration**

discomfit thwart, readily confused with **discomfort**, make uncomfortable

discreet circumspect; **discrete** separate

disfranchise not disenfranchise

disinterested means free from bias, objective (the negative form of interested as in interested party); often used incorrectly instead of **uninterested**, not taking an interest (the negative form of interested as in interested in football)

Disneyland (California), **Disneyland Paris** (formerly Euro Disney), **Disney World** (Florida)

dispatch, **dispatch box** (Commons), **dispatched**; not despatch, despatched

Disprin TM; call it aspirin

dissociate, **dissociation** not disassociate, disassociation

distributor not distributer

ditching not a synonym for crashing: if you ditch a helicopter, you make a controlled landing on the water after an emergency - we have got this wrong several times

divorcee a divorced person, male or female

Doctor Who the title of the series - do not abbreviate to Dr Who; the character's name is **the Doctor**; also Daleks, Time Lords

Dd

docudrama, docusoap

dogs normally lc, eg alsatian, doberman, jack russell, rottweiler, yorkshire terrier; but note Irish setter, old English sheepdog

D'oh! as Homer Simpson would say (note the apostrophe)

Dolby TM

doll's house

dome, the Millennium Dome at first mention, thereafter the dome; now the O2

Domesday Book but **doomsday scenario**

Dominica former British colony in the Windward Islands, south-east of the Dominican Republic

Dominican Republic independent Spanish-speaking country that shares the island of Hispaniola with Haiti

doner kebab *See kebabs*; **donor** gives money

doppelganger no accent

dos and don'ts

Dostoevsky, Fyodor Mikhailovich (1821-81) Russian novelist, author of Crime and Punishment and The Idiot

dotcom

Double, the as in Chelsea won the Double in 2010 (FA Cup and Premier League)

dove is a bird, not the past tense of dive, which is dived

dover sole lc

Dow Jones industrial average

downmarket

downplay play down is preferable

Down's syndrome a baby with Down's syndrome (if relevant), not "a Down's syndrome baby" - we wouldn't say "a cerebral palsy

Dd

baby". The diagnosis is not the person

down under should not be used to refer to Australia or New Zealand

dozen precisely, not approximately, 12

Dr at first mention for medical and scientific doctors and doctors of divinity (not, for example, a politician who happens to have a PhD in history); thereafter, just use surname except in leading articles

draconian

draftsman of document; **draughtsman** of drawing

dreamed not dreamt

dressing room two words

drier, **dryer** this shirt will only get drier after an hour in the tumble dryer (while I use the hairdryer)

drily not dryly

drink past tense **drank**, past participle **drunk**: he drinks too much - last night he drank 10 pints, the least he has drunk on any night this week

drink-driver, **drink-driving**, **drunk-driving**

driving licence not driver's licence in British English

drone honeybee whose function is to mate with the queen, and by extension therefore someone who lives off the work of others (the worker bees); however, it seems to be used increasingly to mean something like an obedient, unimaginative worker ("office drone")

drug companies, **drug dealer**, **drug raid**, **drug squad**, **drug tsar** not drugs raid, etc

drug use a more accurate and less judgmental term than "drug abuse" or "misuse" (often all three terms have been scattered randomly through the same reports)

Dd

druid

drum'n'bass

drunkenness

DSG International the former Dixons; owns Currys and PC World. DSG stands for Dixons Store Group, but in June 2010 the company, belatedly realising that no one in the world was aware of this, decided to change back to Dixons

dub avoid such tabloidese as "they have been dubbed the nation's leading experts on style" (even if true)

duct tape not duck tape

due to or owing to? *See Grammar & punctuation*

dugout

Duke of Westminster or wherever, first mention; thereafter the duke; **Duke of York** first mention; thereafter Prince Andrew or the prince

dumb do not use when you mean speech-impaired

du Pré, Jacqueline (1945-87) English cellist, Du Pré at second mention; **Dupré, Marcel** (1886-1971) French organist and composer

Dürer, Albrecht (1471-1528) German painter

dutch courage not Dutch

DVD stands for digital versatile disc

dwarves plural of dwarf (not dwarfs); but the verb is to dwarf, eg Kings Place dwarfs the surrounding buildings

dyke not dike

dynamo plural dynamos; **Dynamo** football teams from the former Soviet Union are Dynamo; teams from Romania are **Dinamo**

Dd

dyslexia write "Paul has dyslexia" rather than labelling him "a dyslexic" or saying he "suffers from" dyslexia

Ee

 I'm not really a stickler for language, but the abuse of 'enormity' and 'disinterested' drive me mad. It's always the same kind of people misusing them in the same kind of way - politicians who want to sound super smart. But if you are talking about the size of something stick with enormous or enormousness (however crap it sounds), don't use a word that means something totally different, ie a monstrous offence or evil. As for disinterested, aaaagh - fine if you mean impartial but not fine if you mean uninterested 99

Simon Hattenstone

Ee

each other of two only (Iniesta and Xavi hugged each other); otherwise one another (all 11 Spanish players hugged one another)

EADS European Aeronautic Defence and Space Company; the group includes the aircraft manufacturer Airbus and is the major partner in the Eurofighter consortium

earlier often redundant: "they met this week" is preferable to "they met earlier this week" and will save space

Earl's Court station and district; **Earls Court** exhibition centre

earn rather than learn that a banker or footballer earns, say, £15m a year, readers have indicated that they would prefer us to say "is paid £15m a year" or "receives £15m a year"

earned not earnt

earring, **earshot** no hyphen

Earth but moon, sun

east Africa; **East Anglia**; **east Asia** or **south-east Asia** rather than far east

east coast mainline but the train operating company set up by the government in 2009 is East Coast

East End inner east London north of the river; the equivalent district south of the Thames is south-east London; **EastEnders** TV soap; in real life, people from the East End are East Enders

Easter Day not Easter Sunday

eastern Europe

East Jerusalem

east Midlands but **East Midlands airport**

East Riding of Yorkshire council

easyCouncil approach to local government favoured by some Conservative authorities, modelled on the no-frills approach of budget airlines such as easyJet

Ee

eBay but Ebay if you cannot avoid starting a sentence or headline with it

Ebola a virus and a disease, Ebola haemorrhagic fever (EHF)

ebook, **email** but **e-commerce**, **e-reader**

ebookers online travel company

eccles cake

ecclesiastical titles Most Rev (archbishop), Right Rev (bishop), Very Rev (dean or provost), the Ven (archdeacon), the Rev John (or Joan) Smith - not "Rev John Smith", "Rev Smith", "the Revs Smith and Jones". Surname only on subsequent mentions, except in leading articles

E coli as with other taxonomic names, italicise in copy but roman in headlines and standfirsts; no full point

eco-friendly but **ecohome**, **ecosystem**, **ecotown**, **ecowarrior**

ecstasy state and drug

ecu European currency unit, superseded by the euro

Edinburgh festival comprises the following: **Edinburgh international festival**, **Edinburgh festival fringe** (not fringe festival, but **the fringe** is OK), **Edinburgh international book festival**

editor lc: editor of the Observer, editor of the Redditch Indicator series, etc

editors
An editor is to newspaper or website as captain is to ship.
  "Editors are craftsmen, ghosts, psychiatrists, bullies, sparring partners, experts, enablers, ignoramuses, translators, writers, goalies, friends, foremen, wimps, ditch diggers, mind readers, coaches, bomb throwers, muses and spittoons - sometimes all while working on the same piece" (Gary Kamiya, salon.com).
  "Trust your editor, and you'll sleep on straw" (John Cheever)

educationist not educationalist

Ee

-ee endings -ee means something happens to you; -er means you do something: so employee, invitee (if you must), refugee but attender, escaper, etc, rather than attendee, escapee, etc

eerie weird; **Erie** North American lake; **eyrie** of eagles

effect or affect? *See affect*

effectively is not a synonym for in effect: "the Balls campaign was launched effectively after Brown resigned" means the launch was official and its intended effect was achieved; "the Balls campaign had in effect been launched before Brown resigned" means this was not the official launch, but events at the time described did have the effect of launching it, whether intended or not.

Effectively is almost invariably misused, and can often be omitted

effete does not mean effeminate or foppish, but "weak, ineffectual or decadent as a result of over-refinement ... exhausted, worn out, spent" (Collins)

efit (electronic facial identification technique) program used to create police drawings

eg no full points

EGM extraordinary general meeting

Eid al-Adha (Festival of Sacrifice) Muslim festival laid down in Islamic law, celebrates the end of the hajj. Note that eid means festival, so it is tautologous to describe it as the Eid festival; **Eid al-Fitr** Muslim festival of thanksgiving laid down in Islamic law, celebrates the end of Ramadan (al-fitr means the breaking of the fast)

eid mubarak not a festival but a greeting (mubarak means "may it be blessed")

Eire no: say Republic of Ireland or Irish Republic

elan no accent

Ee

ElBaradei, Mohamed former director general of the International Atomic Energy Agency, ElBaradei after first mention

elderly people or older people, not "the elderly"; do not use to describe anyone under 75

El Dorado fabled city of gold; **Eldorado** fabled flop of a TV soap

electra complex the female equivalent of oedipal complex

electrocution death by electric shock, so don't say survivors of torture were electrocuted during their ordeal – rather that they were given electric shocks

elegiac

elephant in the room
Like governments and reality TV series, metaphors that we once welcomed into our lives as refreshing can become all too familiar, to the point of tedium – and this cliche is a fine example. At its height, elephants were not only in the room, but had taken over the whole house: "elephants in the room" included trade figures, policy, lack of policy, climate change, Iraq, the US, Europe, anti-Americanism, men, women, single women, a new French football league, race, religion, Islam, Catholicism, Tessa Jowell, Andrew Neil, Jimmy Greaves, fatness, thinness, Stalinism, Hitler and Tony Blair's departure from office.

The phrase seemed destined for the elephants' graveyard but there is evidence that, used imaginatively, it may still be effective: "There's only so long they can ignore this elephant in the room [the Iraq war] before it takes a dump on the carpet" (Gary Younge, 5 July 2010)

11-plus

elide, **elision** means omission, not the conflation of one or more things

elite

ellipsis *See Grammar & punctuation*

Ee

email

emanate is intransitive; use **exude** if you need a transitive verb

Embankment, the in London; the tube station is just Embankment

embargo plural embargos

embarrass, embarrassment

embassy lc, eg British embassy; not necessarily an excuse to use the Ferrero Rocher joke yet again

emigrate leave a country; **immigrate** arrive in one

émigré

Emin, Tracey not Tracy

empathic not empathetic

Empire State Building

empires lc British empire (but British Empire Medal), Roman empire, etc

employment tribunal not industrial tribunal

EMS European monetary system; **Emu** economic and monetary union

enamoured of not by or with

enclose not inclose

encyclopedia not encyclopaedia

enervate to deprive of strength or vitality

enforce, enforceable

England, English should not be used when you mean Britain or British, unless you are seeking to offend readers from other parts of the UK (we published a map of England's best beaches, with the headline "Britain's best beaches") *See Scotland*

Enlightenment, the

Ee

en masse

enormity means monstrous or wicked, not big

enquiry use inquiry

enrol, **enrolling**, **enrolment**

en route not on route

en suite two words, whatever estate agents might claim

ensure make certain; **insure** against risk; **assure** life

enthral, **enthralling**

entr'acte

E.ON

epicentre point on the Earth's surface directly above the focus of an earthquake or underground explosion; frequently misused to mean the centre or focus itself and is also not a synonym for "dead centre". After our latest misuse in July 2010 a reader (of more than 60 years) wrote: "How is it that so many highly educated people, whose business is words and communication, do not understand that a prefix such as epi is there for a purpose: it changes the meaning of the root word"

epilepsy seizures are epileptic, people are not - we do not define people by their medical condition; so say (if relevant) "Joe Bloggs, who has epilepsy" not "Joe Bloggs, an epileptic"

EPO erythropoietin, a performance-enhancing drug

Equality and Human Rights Commission abbreviation EHRC; set up in 2007 to replace the Commission for Racial Equality, Disability Rights Commission and Equal Opportunities Commission; may be called simply the commission, after first mention

equator, the

Equatorial Guinea formerly Spanish Guinea, a country in central Africa that became independent in 1974; do not confuse with

Guinea or Guinea-Bissau, other African former colonies

equable unvarying; **equitable** fair

Erdogan, Recep Tayyip Turkish politician, elected prime minister in 2003

ere long not e'er long

Eriksson, Sven-Göran

ERM exchange rate mechanism

Ernie electronic random number indicator equipment: the machine that picks winning premium bond numbers

escapers not escapees, despite the apparently unstoppable advance of the -ee suffix (can it be long before readers become "readees"?)

Eskimo is a language spoken in Greenland, Canada, Alaska and Siberia. Note that it has no more words for snow than English does for rain. The people are Inuit (singular Inuk), not Eskimos

espresso not expresso

establishment, the

estuary English

Eta Basque separatists; **ETA** estimated time of arrival

ethnic never say ethnic when you mean ethnic minority, which leads to such nonsense as "the constituency has a small ethnic population"

ethnic cleansing should not be used as a euphemism for genocide unless quoting someone

EU European Union (no need to spell out at first mention); formerly EC (European Community); before that EEC (European Economic Community)

EU presidents
There are three, so don't say "EU president" or "president of the union" without making clear which you mean: president of the

Ee

European commission, president of the European parliament, or holder of the rotating presidency (technically "president in office of the council of the European Union"), which rotates among the member states every six months

euro currency; plural euros and cents; **Euro** should not be used as a prefix to everything European, but Euro-MP is an acceptable alternative to MEP

Euro Disney runs what is now called Disneyland Paris

euroland, **eurozone**

Europe includes Britain, so don't say, for example, something is common "in Europe" unless it is common in Britain as well; to distinguish between Britain and the rest of Europe the phrases "continental Europe" or "elsewhere in Europe" may be useful

central Europe, **eastern Europe**, **western Europe**

European commission the commission after first mention; do not abbreviate to EC

European convention on human rights

European council EU institution, not to be confused with the Council of Europe

European court of human rights nothing to do with the EU: it is a Council of Europe body; sits in Strasbourg; **European court of justice** the highest court in the European Union in matters of EU law; sits in Luxembourg

Eurovision song contest

evangelical fundamentalist wing of Christianity; **evangelist** someone who spreads the gospel

eventually often unnecessary, as in "the FTSE 100 drifted back, eventually closing 33.9 points lower at 5244.2"; the stock market always closes eventually

every day adverb meaning often: it happens every day; **everyday** adjective meaning ordinary: an everyday mistake

Ee

every parent's nightmare avoid this cliche

exchequer, the

exclamation marks Do not use! (As F Scott Fitzgerald said, it is like laughing at your own jokes)

exclusive term used by tabloid newspapers to denote a story that is in all of them

execution the carrying out of a death sentence by lawful authority, so a terrorist, for example, does not execute someone

ex officio by right of position or office; **ex parte** on behalf of one party only

exorcised having had evil spirits removed; often used erroneously for **exercised** having one's passions inflamed by something

expat, expatriate not ex-pat or expatriot; this is "ex" meaning out of (as in export, extract), not ex- meaning former (as in ex-husband)

explained "said" is normally sufficient

exploitative rather than exploitive

Export Credits Guarantee Department ECGD at second mention

exposé

extracurricular, extramarital, extraterrestrial, extraterritorial all one word

extrovert not extravert

eye level no hyphen

eyes is being used increasingly for "considers", but it doesn't mean that. You might get away with "BoS eyes up Abbey" meaning considers it as a takeover target, but not "BoS eyes online insurance" meaning BoS is considering setting up an online sales operation

eyewitness one word, but witness is preferable, except in the Guardian's Eyewitness picture spread

Ee

eye-watering

The pace at which a fresh metaphor becomes a tired cliche seems to have increased in recent years; this one saw a huge increase in 2009 - although curiously, while "eye-watering" is only ever applied to money ("eye-watering sums"), its adverbial near relative is more versatile ("an eye-wateringly beautiful woman", "an eye-wateringly sharp sauvignon" and so on). The danger, as ever, is that the expression loses its force from overuse *See elephant in the room*

Eyjafjallajökull Icelandic volcano that brought peace to the skies for a short time in 2010

Ff

 **66** Is there anything more dull than 'going forward'? It is not about bravery - seeing the danger ahead but still pressing on. It only suggests a robotic and mandatory optimism. There you are, faced with global meltdown and double-dip recession, and you just 'go forward', in a bland and positive way, like the Light Brigade pretending it's off for a picnic **99**

Michele Hanson

Ff

Fabergé

Fàbregas, **Cesc** note the Catalan accent

facade no cedilla

Facebook no need to call it "the social networking site" every time - we know what it is *See Pov*

facelift

factchecker, **factchecking**

factoid not a trivial fact, but a mistaken assumption repeated so often that it is believed to be true (a word coined by Norman Mailer, who defined it as "something that everyone knows is true, except it ain't!")

FA Cup the Cup (the cap C is hallowed by convention); all other cups lc at second mention

fahrenheit
Use in brackets, without degree symbol, after celsius figure, eg 37C (98.6F); to convert, multiply the celsius temperature by 1.8, then add 32; alternatively, double the celsius figure, subtract one-10th of the result, and add 32; or you could save yourself the bother by using a conversion website

Fáilte Ireland Ireland's tourism authority

Fairtrade a certification system run by the Fairtrade Foundation; products are given a Fairtrade mark and entitled to be called Fairtrade (cap F) if they meet the following criteria: a price that covers producers' costs, a premium for producers to invest in their communities, and long-term and more direct trading relations; **fair trade** refers to the movement as a whole, eg Only fair trade will enable farmers in developing countries to become self-sufficient

fairytale noun and adjective

faith schools may be called religious schools without fear of divine retribution

falafel

Ff

fallopian tubes

fallout

Falluja

families word favoured by politicians to make them sound caring and concerned ("hard-working families"), which doesn't mean we have to do so, as in this 2010 Guardian splash headline: "Families face nuclear tax on power bills". As a reader pointed out: "So don't older people, single people, etc, face the same tax? ... the implicit attitude [is] that those not part of families are of secondary significance." Quite

family-size, fun-size not family-sized, fun-sized

famous, famously but if it actually is famous, there is no need to say so

fanbelt, fanclub, fanmail all one word

far, farther, farthest of distances; otherwise **further, furthest**

far away adverb; **faraway** adjective: she moved to a faraway place, and now lives far away

far east lc but east Asia or south-east Asia are preferable

farm worker not farm labourer

Faroe Isles or just Faroes

farrago a hotchpotch or jumbled mixture; not synonymous with fiasco, a humiliating failure

Farsi language spoken by the majority of Iranians (not Persian)

fascism, fascist not facism, facist, a careless but common error

fashion weeks lc, eg London fashion week

fatality a fatality is worse than death, and like most euphemisms best avoided

fat cats should be used sparingly, even if writing about overweight moggies

Ff

father of two, **mother of two** etc (no hyphens); only describe people in this way if relevant

Father's Day

fatwa an edict, not necessarily a death sentence

fayre belongs to the world of Ye Olde Gift Shoppe and Merrie England, not our publications; use fair

fazed overwhelmed; **phased** staged

FBI Federal Bureau of Investigation, but normally no need to spell out

FDA what the former First Division Association now calls itself; you will need to say it is the senior civil servants' union or no one will know who you are talking about; note that FDA also stands for the US food and drug administration

fedayeen Arab fighters (the word means those who risk their lives for a cause); can be capped up when referring to a specific force, eg the Saddam Fedayeen militia, which fought coalition forces in the 2003 Iraq war

Federal Reserve at first reference, the Fed thereafter

fed up with not fed up of

feelgood factor

fellow lc, eg a fellow of All Souls, fellow artist, fellow members, etc (and do not hyphenate)

female not "woman" or "women" in such phrases as female home secretary, female voters

female genital mutilation not "female circumcision"

ferris wheel no need for a cap F, although the first was built by George Washington Gale Ferris Jr for the World's Fair in Chicago in 1893

festivals lc, whether artistic or sporting: Cannes film festival, Cheltenham festival, Edinburgh festival fringe, Reading festival, etc

Ff

fete no accent

fetid not foetid

fewer or less? fewer means smaller in number, eg fewer coins; less means smaller in quantity, eg less money

Ffestiniog

fiance male, **fiancee** female; note that divorcee is both male and female

Fianna Fáil Irish political party

fiasco like debacle and farce, overused in news reports: who says it's a fiasco?

field marshal

50-50 not 50/50

figures spell out from one to nine; numerals from 10 to 999,999; thereafter 1m, 3.2bn (except for people and animals, eg 2 million viewers, 8 billion cattle); spell out ordinals from first to ninth, thereafter 10th, 31st, etc

filesharing one word

fillip not filip

film-maker but **film star**

Filofax TM; use personal organiser unless you are sure

finalise as long as complete and finish survive, and human beings with breath in their bodies to utter them, there will be no need for this word

Financial Services Authority FSA on second mention

financial years 2010-11, etc

Fine Gael Irish political party

fine-tooth comb not fine toothcomb (even if you are in the habit of combing your teeth)

Finnegans Wake book by James Joyce that many have started, though fewer have finished; note the absence of apostrophe

firebomb

fire brigade, **fire service** lc, eg Cheshire fire and rescue service

firefight involves fighting fire, not a military skirmish or gun battle

firefighter not fireman

firewall

firing line the people who do the firing; if they are aiming at you, you are in the line of fire

firm strictly a partnership without limited liability, such as solicitors or accountants, but may be used in place of company in headlines

first, **second**, **third** rather than firstly, secondly, thirdly, etc; spell out up to ninth, then 10th, 21st, millionth

first aid; **first lady**; **first minister** (Scottish parliament, Welsh assembly, Northern Ireland assembly)

first-hand

first name; **forename**; **given name** not Christian name. Use them first time, but not subsequently (except for peers, who never use their first names). Avoid just initials, unless that is how a person is known - TS Eliot, AA Gill, etc. In stories about more than one member of a family, first names can be used to distinguish between them. Occasionally, we will use first names in interviews if this strikes an appropriate tone

First Nations indigenous peoples of Canada, excluding the Inuit and Métis

first things first not thing's (there's more than one thing)

first world war

fit for purpose a recent cliche that quickly proved itself unfit for the purpose of good writing

Ff

fit the bill not fill the bill

flagship cliche alert: a flagship is a ship; a flagship store would be a store where one bought flagships

flak not flack

flammable rather than inflammable (although, curiously, they mean the same thing); the negative is non-flammable

flash memory computer memory that can be erased and reused, used for example in mobile phones, digital cameras and MP3 players

Flat racing

flatmate one word

flaunt or flout? to flaunt is to make a display of something, as in flaunting wealth; to flout is to show disregard for something, as in flouting the seatbelt law

fledgling not fledgeling

Fleet Street nickname for Britain's national newspapers (their former home)

flexitime

floor If, say, a policeman knocks you over, you fall on to the ground, not the floor (unless you are indoors)

flotation whether in a tank or on the stock market

flounder or founder? to flounder is to perform a task badly, like someone stuck in mud; to founder is to fail: a business might be foundering because its bosses are floundering

flu

fluky not flukey

flyer not flier

flying squad

flypast noun

Ff

fo'c'sle abbreviation of forecastle (and the longest surviving entry in this book)

focus, focused, focusing

foetus not fetus

fogey not fogy

folklore, folksong

following prefer after, eg Wednesday went to pieces after their latest relegation

font (typeface) not fount

foolproof

foot-and-mouth disease

footie abbreviation for football, but note that in Australia (particularly Victoria), footy is what they call Australian rules football

for all its worth but **for what it's worth**

forbear abstain; **forebear** ancestor

foreign accents
Use accents on French, German, Portuguese, Spanish and Irish Gaelic words – and, if at all possible, on people's names in any language, eg Sven-Göran Eriksson (Swedish), José Manuel Durão Barroso (Portuguese). This may be tricky in the case of some languages but we have had complaints from readers that it is disrespectful to foreign readers to, in effect, misspell their names *See Spanish names and accents*

foreign names
The French (or French origin) de or le and the Dutch van are normally lowercase when the name is full out: eg Charles de Gaulle, Graeme le Saux, Giovanni van Bronckhorst; but De Gaulle, Le Saux, Van Bronckhorst when written without forenames. Note, however, that the Dutch president of the European council is Herman Van Rompuy on first mention. The

Ff

Italian De or Di is normally uppercase, eg Antonio Di Natale

Foreign Office abbreviated to FCO, not FO, as its official name is Foreign and Commonwealth Office

foreign placenames

Style for foreign placenames evolves with common usage. Leghorn has become Livorno, and maybe one day München will supplant Munich, but not yet. Remember that many names have become part of the English language: Geneva is the English name for the city that Switzerland's French speakers refer to as Genève and its German speakers call Genf.

Accordingly, we opt for locally used names, with these main exceptions (the list is not exhaustive, apply common sense): Archangel, Basle, Berne, Brittany, Cologne, Dunkirk, Florence, Fribourg, Genoa, Gothenburg, Hanover, Kiev, Lombardy, Milan, Munich, Naples, Normandy, Nuremberg, Padua, Piedmont, Rome, Sardinia, Seville, Sicily, Syracuse, Turin, Tuscany, Venice, Zurich.

And the next time someone says we should call Burma "Myanmar" because that's what it calls itself, tell them Colonel Gaddafi renamed Libya "The Great Socialist People's Libyan Arab Jamahiriyya"

foreign secretary (we have heard the jokes about French shorthand typists, thank you)

foreign words and phrases

Italicise, with roman translation in brackets, if it really is a foreign word or phrase and not an anglicised one, in which case it is roman with no accents (exceptions: exposé, lamé, pâté, résumé, roué). Remember Orwell: do not use a foreign word where a suitable English equivalent exists

forensic is not a synonym for scientific: it derives from forum (Latin for court) and that is what it means - all evidence in court is forensic; forensic scientist means a scientist whose work is done for legal purposes (so a page 1 headline in which we

Ff

referred to "new forensic evidence" should have said "new scientific evidence", which is what was meant)

foresee, **foreseeable**

forever continually: he is forever changing his mind; **for ever** for always: I will love you for ever

for free avoid: we said police recruits might be forced to work "for free"; it would have been more elegant to say "for nothing"

forgo go without; **forego** go before

for goodness sake

forklift truck

former Soviet republics These are:
   Armenia adjective Armenian
   Azerbaijan adjective Azerbaijani (though there are ethnic
      Azeris in, eg, Armenia)
   Belarus adjective Belarussian
   Estonia adjective Estonian (Estonia did not join the
      Commonwealth of Independent States)
   Georgia adjective Georgian
   Kazakhstan adjective Kazakh
   Kyrgyzstan adjective Kyrgyz
   Latvia adjective Latvian (not in the commonwealth)
   Lithuania adjective Lithuanian (not in the commonwealth)
   Moldova adjective Moldovan
   Russia adjective Russian
   Tajikistan adjective Tajik
   Turkmenistan adjective Turkmen (its citizens are Turkmen,
      singular Turkman)
   Ukraine (not "the Ukraine") adjective Ukrainian
   Uzbekistan adjective Uzbek

Formica TM

formula plural formulas, but formulae in a scientific context

Formula One in copy; F1 is fine in headlines and standfirsts

Ff

fortuitous by chance, not (as most people seem to think) by good fortune; if we manage to use the word correctly, it is entirely fortuitous

fosbury flop

Fourth of July

foxhunting one word

FPA Family Planning Association at first mention, thereafter the FPA, although the organisation has decided to style itself "fpa" (lc, no definite article) in its literature and on its website

FRS fellow of the Royal Society

fractions two-thirds, three-quarters, etc, but two and a half, although use ⅓, ¾ in tables, recipes, etc. Avoid mixing fractions and percentages in the same story

Frankenstein the monster's creator, not the monster; **Frankenstein food** has become a cliche to describe GM food: do not use

fraud squad

freefall

french fries, horn, kiss, letter, polish, window all lowercase

French Guiana an overseas *département* of France on the Caribbean coast of South America; do not confuse with Equatorial Guinea, Guinea, or Guinea-Bissau, which are all in Africa, or Guyana, which is also in South America

fresco plural frescoes

Freud, Lucian British artist, not Lucien

Freudian slip

friendlily curious adverb defined by the OED as "in a friendly manner, like a friend"

friendly fire no quotation marks necessary

Friends of the Earth abbreviated to FoE after first mention

Friends Provident no apostrophe

Frisbee TM; if in doubt, call it a flying disc

frontbench, frontline, frontman, frontrunner

frostbite, frostbitten

FTSE 100

fuck not "a good, honest old-fashioned Anglo-Saxon word" (as it is often described) because there is no such thing as an Anglo-Saxon word (they spoke Old English) and, more important, its first recorded use dates from 1278 *See swearwords*

fuel overused as a verb, although handy in headlines

Fulbright scholarship not Fullbright

fulfil, fulfilling, fulfilment

full-time unless saying X works full time

fulsome another example of a word that is almost never used correctly, it means "cloying, excessive, disgusting by excess" (and is not, as some appear to believe, a clever word for full); so "fulsome praise" should not be used in a complimentary sense

fundraiser, fundraising

fungus plural fungi

furniture (also known as page furniture) explanatory text accompanying a story (headline, standfirst, caption, etc)

Gg

66 The whole pronouns-must-agree-with-subjects thing causes me utter agony. Do you know how many paragraphs I've had to tear down and rebuild because you can't say 'Somebody left their cheese in the fridge', so you say 'Somebody left his/her cheese in the fridge' but then you need to refer to his/her cheese several times thereafter and your writing ends up looking like a explosion in a pedants' factory? Billions, that's how many 99

Lucy Mangan

Gg

G8 Canada, France, Germany, Italy, Japan, the United Kingdom, the United States and the newest member, Russia

Gaddafi, Muammar Libyan leader rather than president (he holds no government office and is generally known in Libya as "leader of the revolution"); Gaddafi on second mention

gaff hook or spar, also slang for house; **blow the gaff** give away a secret; **gaffe** blunder

Galápagos

Gallagher Oasis brothers (Noel and Liam); **Gallaher** cigarette company

Gambia, the not Gambia

gambit an opening strategy that involves some sacrifice or concession; so to talk of an opening gambit is tautologous – an opening ploy might be better

Game Boy

gameplan, **gameshow**

Gandhi not Ghandi

García Lorca, Federico (1898-1936) Spanish writer; García Lorca (not "Lorca") after first mention

García Márquez, Gabriel Colombian novelist, born 1927; García Márquez after first mention

Garda Síochána Irish police force; **garda** (plural gardaí) police officer

garotte not garrotte or garrote

garryowen up-and-under kick in rugby union; **Garryowen** Irish rugby club that gave the garryowen its name

gases plural of gas, but the verb is **gasses**

Gategate
The hapless quintet who broke into Democratic headquarters at the Watergate building in Washington DC in 1972 can have had

Gg

no idea of the forces they were unleashing - forces that in due course led to the resignation of President Richard Nixon, and began a proud tradition of inane journalism that shows no sign of diminishing 40 years later. Examples range from the mildly droll - Gatecrashergate, Henry Gatesgate (also known as Stupidgate) - to the utterly feeble (Sexy Photo Gate). Among numerous other instances are Bertiegate, Betsygate, Billygate, Camillagate (not to be confused with Dianagate, also known as Squidgygate), Cheriegate, Closetgate, Contragate, Fajitagate, Flakegate, at least two Grannygates, Hobnobgate, Irangate, Iraqgate, Irisgate (it is compulsory for stories about this to be headlined "And here's to you, Mrs Robinson ... "), Katrinagate, Koreagate, Monicagate, at least two cases of Nannygate, Nipplegate, Smeargate, various Strippergates, Toiletgate, three different outbreaks of Troopergate, and Whitewatergate.

Sporting gates include Beachballgate, Bloodgate, Buttongate, Chicanegate, Crashgate, Handgate/Henrygate/Thierrygate, Liargate, Pizzagate, Tevezgate and, of course, Tigergate.

Occasionally, as with Climategate, such an epithet may be useful as a way to pull together a lot of material on the same subject, but most gates are lazy and more likely to put readers off than engage them

gatecrash

Gatt general agreement on tariffs and trade

Gaudí, Antoni (1852-1926) Catalan architect

Gauguin, Paul (1848-1903) French painter

gay should be used an adjective rather than a noun: a gay man, gay people, gay men and lesbians, not "gays and lesbians"

Gaza Strip

Gb gigabits; **GB** gigabytes

gender issues
Our use of language reflects our values, as well as changes in

Gg

society. Phrases such as career girl or career woman, for example, are outdated (more women have careers than men) and patronising (there is no male equivalent).

So we use actor or comedian for women as well as men, not actress or comedienne (but waiter and waitress are acceptable – at least for the moment); firefighter, not fireman; PC, not WPC (the distinction was abolished by the Sex Discrimination Act), postal workers, not postmen, etc.

Avoid terms such as businessmen, housewives, male nurse, woman driver, woman (lady!) doctor, etc, which reinforce outdated stereotypes. If you need to use an adjective, it is female and not "woman" in such phrases as female MPs, female president.

Do not gratuitously describe a woman as a "mother of three": family details and marital status are only relevant in stories about families or marriage.

Use humankind or humanity rather than mankind, a word that, as one of our readers points out, "alienates half the population from their own history".

Never say "his" to cover men and women: use his or her, or a different construction; in sentences such as "a teacher who beats his/her pupils is not fit to do the job", there is usually a way round the problem – in this case, "teachers who beat their pupils ... "

Men (rarely women – funny, that) who occasionally question our policy and accuse us of "political correctness" may care to reflect on the fact that Fowler's used to list such "established feminine titles" as adventuress, authoress, editress, executrix, giantess, huntress, inspectress, Jewess, poetess, procuress, quakeress, songstress, tailoress, wardress; it also proposed new ones such as danceress and doctress ("everyone knows the inconvenience of being uncertain whether a doctor is a man or a woman")

general General David Petraeus at first mention, then Petraeus, except in leading articles, where he would be Gen Petraeus

Gg

general election

General Medical Council (GMC) doctors' disciplinary body

General Strike of 1926

General Synod but synod after first mention

Geneva conventions (not convention); four treaties, last revised and ratified in 1949, which with three more recently adopted protocols set out international standards for the humanitarian treatment of prisoners of war and civilians caught up in war

geography distinct areas are capped up: Black Country, East Anglia, Lake District, Midlands, Peak District, Potteries, West Country, etc; but areas defined by compass points are lc: the north, the south-east, the south-west, etc

geordie noun and adjective; refers to people from Tyneside, and their accent

geriatrics branch of medicine dealing with elderly people, not an amusing way to describe them in an attempt to make yourself sound cool

german measles but rubella is a preferable term

gerund *See Grammar & punctuation*

ghetto plural ghettoes

ghoti alternative spelling of the word "fish" (gh as in trough, o as in women, ti as in nation) sometimes attributed to George Bernard Shaw, although there is no evidence that he ever said or wrote it

giant We know that BP and Vodafone are big companies, so don't need to be told that they are "the telecoms giant" or "the oil giant"

giantkiller, giantkilling no hyphen

Gibraltar overseas territory, not a British colony; its inhabitants are Gibraltarians

Gg

gift not a verb (unless, perhaps, directly quoting a football manager or player: "We gifted Barnsley their fifth goal")

girl female under 18

girlfriend

girlie noun (only when quoting someone); **girly** adjective (eg girly clothes); **girlish** behaviour

giro banking; **gyro** stabilisation aid

Giscard d'Estaing, Valéry former French president, Giscard on second mention

Giuliani, Rudolph or **Rudy** (not Rudi) former New York mayor

Giuseppe regularly misspelt as Guiseppe; this is sloppy

GLA does not stand for "Greater London assembly": there is no such thing. The Greater London authority comprises the mayor, who runs it, and the London assembly, which holds the mayor to account

glamorous not glamourous

Glasgow kiss a head-butt

glasnost

GlaxoSmithKline GSK on second mention and in headlines

globish a form of simple English used by non-native English speakers

GM crops, **GM food** normally no need to write genetically modified in full

GMT Greenwich mean time: the ship ran aground at 8am local time (0700 GMT)

goalline, **goalpost**

goat's cheese

gobbledegook not gobbledygook

gobsmacked is best used only if directly quoting someone

Gg

God but he, him etc rather than He, Him

godchild, **godfather**, **godmother**, **godparents**, **godson**, **goddaughter** no hyphens

going forward unappealing jargon when employed as an alternative to "in the future"

Goldsmiths College no apostrophe

golf holes are given as figures: 1st, 2nd, 18th, etc

Good Friday agreement

goodnight one word

Google cap up, even when used as a verb ("I Googled myself"); named after googol, the number 10^{100} (1 followed by 100 zeros)

Gorbachev, Mikhail

Gormley, Antony

go-slow noun; **go slow** verb

Goths (uc) Germanic tribe that invaded the Roman empire; **goths** (lc) Sisters of Mercy fans who invaded the Shepherd's Bush Empire

government lc in all contexts and all countries; resist the awful trend to say such things as "Lord Browne fended off accusations of being too close to government" - it should be the government

government departments *See departments of state*

graffiti are plural; the singular is **graffito**

grammar the set of rules followed by speakers of a language, rather than a set of arbitrary dos and don'ts people half remember from their schooldays *See Grammar & punctuation*

Grammer, Kelsey actor best known as Dr Frasier Crane

grandad but **granddaughter**

grandparent
Mention this status only when relevant: leave "battling

Gg

grannies" and similar examples of ageism and sexism to the tabloids; in particular we should avoid such patronising drivel as "How this 55-year-old granny came to earn $25m a year" (page 1 blurb) - just in case anyone still didn't get the message, the front of G2 said: "She's five foot two, she's a grandmother and she earns $25m a year".

Our policy on this matter prompted the Spectator columnist Rod Liddle to ask: "Why has the word 'grandmother' been banned by the Guardian?" It hasn't

grand prix plural grands prix; lc for British grand prix, etc

grand slam (lc) a term originating in contract bridge, now used in various sports, notably golf and tennis - in both of which it refers to winning all four major tournaments in the same year - and rugby union, where it involves beating all five opponents in the Six Nations championship

grassroots one word

great-aunt, **great-grandfather**, **great-great-grandmother** etc

Great Britain England, Wales and Scotland; if you want to include Northern Ireland, use Britain or the UK

Great Leap Forward Mao Zedong's ill-fated attempt to modernise Chinese agriculture and industry from 1958 to 1961

Great Train Robbers, **Great Train Robbery** of 1963

Greek placenames
We normally use generally accepted anglicised names: Andros, Cephalonia, Corfu (not Kerkira), Ithaca, Kos, Paxos, Rhodes, Santorini (not Thira), Symi (with a Y); but note Lefkada (not Lefkas), Peloponnese (not Peloponnesus), Thessaloniki (not Salonika)

green a green activist, the green movement, but uc when referring to so-named political parties, eg the Green party

green belt designated areas around cities subject to strict planning controls, not open countryside in general

greenfield site one that has not been built on before, in contrast to a brownfield site

greengrocer's apostrophe *See Grammar & punctuation: apostrophes*

greenhouse effect
Energy from the Earth's surface is trapped in the lower atmosphere by gases that prevent it leaking into space, a natural phenomenon that makes life possible, whose enhancement by natural or artificial means may make life impossible. Not the result of the hole in the ozone layer, whose thinning in the upper atmosphere is due to CFCs; the connection is that CFCs are also greenhouse gases

green paper

grisly gruesome; **grizzly** bear

Grossman, Loyd TV presenter and chef with his own brand of pasta sauces, singer with Jet Bronx and the Forbidden (relaunched in 2009 as the New Forbidden)

Ground Zero initial caps for the former site of the World Trade Centre in New York; lc when referring to the point on the ground nearest to an explosion, eg ground zero at Hiroshima in 1945

grow is an intransitive verb, so flowers may grow but companies don't grow profits and governments don't grow economies; horrors such as "grow the business" should only be used when quoting someone

grownup, grown up you become a grownup when you have grown up

Guantánamo Bay

guerrilla two Rs, two Ls

Guevara, Che (1928-67) Argentinian-born revolutionary

Guggenheim Museum cap M if you use the word, although it is not normally necessary. Frank Lloyd Wright designed the

Gg

Guggenheim in New York, Frank Gehry the one in Bilbao (and another proposed for Abu Dhabi). We have sometimes confused the two

Guides not Girl Guides; the organisation is Girlguiding UK

Guildhall (City of London), not "the Guildhall"

Guinea formerly French Guinea, a republic in north-west Africa that became independent in 1958; do not confuse with Equatorial Guinea, French Guiana, Guinea-Bissau, or Guyana

Guinea-Bissau formerly Portuguese Guinea, independent since 1974, lying on the coast to the north-west of Guinea

guinea pig

guineas
Younger readers may not be aware that a guinea was worth £1 1s (£1.05) unless they buy or sell racehorses (the buyer still pays the auction house in guineas, and the auction house then gives the vendor the same number of pounds, thus netting the auctioneer their 5% commission)

Guinness World Records formerly the Guinness Book of Records

Gulf, the not the Persian or Arabian Gulf

Gulf war the first Gulf war is now known as the Iran-Iraq war (1980-88); 1991 was the Gulf war: 2003 was the Iraq war

gun battle not gunbattle or firefight

Guns N' Roses may be abbreviated to GNR after first mention

Gurkha

GUS the former Great Universal Stores split into the credit rating agency Experian and Home Retail Group in 2006

guttural not gutteral

Guyana formerly British Guiana, a nation in South America that gained its independence in 1812; not to be confused with French Guiana or the three African states of Equatorial Guinea, Guinea,

Gg

and Guinea-Bissau; its inhabitants are Guyanese (noun and adjective), not Guyanan

gymnasium plural gymnasiums not gymnasia (although this has found its way into the paper)

Gypsies are recognised as an ethnic group under the Race Relations Act, as are Irish Travellers, hence capped up

Hh

66 Pity poor irony, a word corrupted and debased by sports commentators. It is not ironic, for example, that footballers often score against their old clubs. Nor is it ironic when a team loses a crucial game at a ground where they had previously recorded a famous victory. Week after week I hear this error repeated on televised coverage of football, and allow myself a coincidental smile 99

Michael Hann

Hh

Häagen-Dazs American ice-cream; despite appearances, the name was made up to give a European cachet to a product emanating from the Bronx in New York City

Haaretz Israeli newspaper; no longer has an apostrophe

Haarlem the Netherlands; **Harlem** New York City

habeas corpus

Haberdashers' Aske's school

Habsburg not Hapsburg

haemorrhaging is best avoided, even if you manage to spell it correctly, as it has become a cliche - in expressions such as "haemorrhaging cash" - and completely wrong as an adjective meaning big, eg "in the face of haemorrhaging financial losses"

haemorrhoids

Hague, The always cap up the The

hairbrush, haircut, hairdresser, hairdryer, hairstyle all one word

Haiti is not an island: Haiti and the Dominican Republic make up the Caribbean island of Hispaniola

hajj pilgrimage to Mecca; **haji** Muslim who has made such a pilgrimage

haka Maori war dance, as performed by the New Zealand All Blacks rugby team

Hale-Bopp comet its appearance in 1997 prompted mass suicide in the Heaven's Gate cult

half no hyphen when used adverbially: you look half dead; half wine, half water; his trousers were at half mast; the scores were level at half time; hyphen when used adjectivally: a half-eaten sandwich; a half-cut subeditor; half-time oranges.

The boy is six and a half, but a six-and-a-half-year-old boy

half a dozen, half past six

half-life (radioactivity)

Hh

half-term known in Scotland as **mid-term**

halfway, **halfwit**

Hallé orchestra founded in Manchester by Karl Hallé in 1857

Halley's comet

Halloween no apostrophe

halo plural haloes

Hambros former British bank, now SG Hambros Bank, the private banking division of Société Générale

Hamed, Prince Naseem former boxer; Hamed at second mention

Hamilton Academical not Academicals; nickname the Accies

Hamleys toyshop

handbill, handbook, handbuilt, handheld, handmade, handout no hyphens

handicapped should not be used to refer to people with disabilities or learning difficulties

hangar aircraft; **hanger** clothes

hanged, hung the woman was found hanged; the sheet was hung out to dry

hanging participles See *Grammar & punctuation*

Hanover

Hanukah

happy-clappy avoid

hara-kiri known less vulgarly in Japan as *seppuku*

harass, harassment

hardcore one word, whether noun or adjective and whether you are talking about music, rubble, a hardcore of rebels or hardcore pornography

hardline adjective, **hard line**, **hardliner** nouns

Hh

harebrained not hairbrained

hare lip never use: say cleft lip or cleft palate

Haringey north London borough, one ward of which is **Harringay**

Hariri, Rafik former prime minister of Lebanon, assassinated in Beirut in 2005

Harley-Davidson

HarperCollins

Harper's Bazaar US fashion magazine marketed as Harper's Bazaar UK in Britain, where it was known as Harpers & Queen from 1970 to 2006; **Harpers Bizarre** 60s US harmony group and exponents of "cotton candy rock", named after the magazine

Harris tweed

Harrods

Hassidic

hat-trick

haver widely used to mean hesitate, but in some places (notably Scotland) means to talk nonsense

Haverfordwest in south-west Wales, not "Haverford West" as we managed to call it

Havisham, Miss (not Haversham) in Dickens's Great Expectations

Hawaiian

Hawk-Eye (not Hawkeye) tracks the ball in cricket and tennis

Hay the **Guardian Hay festival** takes place at **Hay-on-Wye** in Wales

hay fever

hazard or risk? Scientists use hazard to mean a potential for harm and risk to mean the actual probability of harm occurring; though headline writers may feel more at home with risk than hazard, the distinction is worth bearing in mind

Hh

HBOS (not HBoS) created in 2001 by the merger of Halifax and Bank of Scotland

HDTV, HD DVD

head-butt

headdress, headhunter, headroom but **head-on**

headlines *See end of this section*

headquarters can be used as a singular (a large headquarters) or plural (our headquarters are in London); HQ, however, takes the singular

headteacher one word, not headmaster, headmistress; but Association of Head Teachers

Health and Safety Executive HSE on second mention

healthcare

hear, hear exclamation of approval that we have misspelt as "here, here" on more than one occasion

heartbroken, heartfelt, heartsearching, heartwarming but **heart-rending, heart-throb**

Heart of Midlothian Edinburgh football club commonly known as Hearts; said to be named after a dancehall that in turn took its name from Sir Walter Scott's 1818 novel The Heart of Midlothian

Heathrow airport or simply Heathrow; not "London's Heathrow"

heatwave

heaven

hectares should be converted to acres in brackets at first mention by multiplying by 2.47, so 10 hectares is 24.7 acres; to convert acres to hectares, multiply by 0.41, so 10 acres is about 4 hectares (we get this the wrong way round embarrassingly often)

height in metres with imperial conversion, eg 1.68 metres (5ft 7in)

Hh

heir apparent someone certain to inherit from a deceased person unless he or she dies first or is taken out of the will; don't use to mean likely successor

hell, hades

hello not hallo (and certainly not "hullo", unless quoting the former Private Eye columnist the Rev ARP Blair)

Hells Angels no apostrophe

help help to decide or help decide, not "help and decide"

helpline

hemisphere lc: northern hemisphere, southern hemisphere

herculean

here generally avoid if what you mean is in Britain (your readers might not be)

Hergé pen name of Georges Remi (1907-83), Belgian creator of Tintin

Heritage Lottery Fund

Hermès scarves and shawls; **Hermes Group** stocks and shares

Hewlett-Packard or HP

Hezbollah means "party of God"

Hibernian Edinburgh football club commonly known as Hibs, nickname the Hibees

hiccup not hiccough

hi-fi short for high fidelity; how we listened to music in the days before iPods

highchair

high commissioner sent from one Commonwealth country to another (rather than an ambassador)

high court

Hh

highfalutin

high flyer noun, **high-flying** adjective

highland fling

Highlands, the (Scotland)

high street lc in retail spending stories: "the recession is making an impact in the high street"; capped only in proper name: "I went shopping in Godalming High Street"

hijab covering for the head worn by some Muslim women

hijack of movable objects only, not of schools, embassies, etc

hike a walk, not an increase in interest rates; "Motorists face new petrol hike" (not one of our better headlines) suggested a long walk to a garage

Hindi language; **Hindu** religion

Hips home information packs, scrapped by the new government in 2010

hip-hop

hippopotamus plural hippopotamuses not hippopotami

hippy plural hippies

Hirst, Damien

His Master's Voice TM (picture of Nipper the dog with gramophone)

historian, historic use a not an, unless in a direct quote

HIT Entertainment

hitchhiker, hitchhiking no hyphens

hi-tech

HIV a virus, not a disease, but do not call HIV "the Aids virus" or an HIV test an "Aids test"; an HIV-positive man (hyphen) is HIV positive (no hyphen)

Hh

HM or **Her Majesty** for the Queen, not HRH

HMS Her Majesty's Ship: does not need the definite article, so it is HMS Pinafore rather than the HMS Pinafore

hoard or horde? a hoard of treasure; a horde (or hordes) of tourists

Hobson's choice a "choice" between taking what is offered and nothing at all

Ho Chi Minh City formerly Saigon

hockey mom We "translated" this to describe Sarah Palin as a "hockey mum", which sounds daft

hoi polloi common people, the masses; "the hoi polloi" is acceptable, even for speakers of ancient Greek

holidaymaker

Holland should not be used to mean the Netherlands (of which it is a region), with the exception of the Dutch football team, who are conventionally known as Holland

Holocaust
Do not trivialise by comparing piles of cattle during a foot-and-mouth outbreak to the Holocaust, or through phrases such as "Belsen-skinny" which, incredibly, found its way into one of our stories about Kate Winslet

holy communion, holy grail but **Holy Land**

Holyrood home of Scotland's parliament, in Edinburgh; **Holyroodhouse** the Queen's official residence in Scotland

homebuyers, homeowners

home counties

home in on not hone in on, which suggests you need to hone your writing skills

homeland but **home town**

homemade

Hh

Home Office but **home secretary** (although the official title is "Secretary of State for the Home Department")

homeopathy

homepage

homogeneous uniform, of the same kind; **homogenous** (biology) having a common descent; the latter is often misused for the former

homosexual rape is rape (or male rape if necessary)

honeybee

Hong Kong names as with Taiwanese and Korean names, Hong Kong names are written in two parts with a hyphen, eg Tung Chee-hwa (Tung after first mention)

hon members of parliament

honorarium plural honorariums

honorary knights are not given titles, so it is still plain Geldof rather than Sir Bob

honorifics
Use just surname after first mention, except in leading articles.

So: David Cameron at first mention, thereafter Cameron; Harriet Harman at first mention, subsequently Harman; Sir Richard Branson at first mention, thereafter Branson; Lady Warsi at first mention, subsequently Warsi; Prof John Wells at first mention, thereafter Wells; Dr Bill Bailey (and all other medical and scientific doctors and doctors of divinity) at first mention, subsequently Bailey; the Rev George Herbert at first mention, thereafter Herbert, etc.

As always, use common sense: in a story where two people have the same name (eg a court case about a husband and wife or brothers), it may be necessary to use Mr and Mrs or Ms, or forenames. In news stories particularly we should use an honorific if it sounds jarring or insensitive not to do so - for example, a woman whose son has been killed on active duty in

Iraq should be "Mrs Smith" and not "Smith". We need to use our judgment and be guided by the tone of the piece.

Follow traditional Guardian style in leading articles (but not other comment pieces and columns on leader pages): use honorifics after first mention, unless writing about an artist, author, journalist, musician, criminal or dead person; use Ms for women on second mention unless they have expressed a preference for Miss or Mrs.

So: at first mention David Cameron, Harriet Harman, Sir Richard Branson, Lady Warsi, Prof John Wells, Dr Bill Bailey, the Rev George Herbert; thereafter Mr Cameron, Ms Harman, Sir Richard, Lady Warsi, Prof Wells, Dr Bailey, Mr Herbert, etc.

Under-18s should normally be referred to by their first names

"honour" killings always in quotes; as a reader says: "There is no honour involved in these murders and calling them honour killings belittles the victims and plays down the crime"

hoodie a hooded top, as well as someone who wears one

Hoover TM; say vacuum cleaner unless you are sure it is a Hoover (uc); but lc for figurative hoovering up (eg "the Guardian website hoovered up all the awards")

hopefully like many other adverbs, such as frankly, happily, honestly and sadly, hopefully can be used as a sentence adverb indicating the writer's view of events – "hopefully, we will reach the summit" – or as a manner adverb modifying a verb: "we set off hopefully for the summit". Why some people are upset by "hopefully we will win" and not "sadly we lost" is a mystery

horrendous sounds like a rather ugly combination of horrific and tremendous, but is in fact from the Latin for fearful; horrific is generally preferable

horticulturist not horticulturalist

hospitalised do not use; say someone was taken (never "rushed") to hospital

Hh

hospitals lc for the generic part, eg Derby city general hospital, Great Ormond Street children's hospital, Royal London hospital

hotdog

hotels a hotel not "an"; do not cap up "hotel": the Dorchester, the Ritz, the Grand hotel, Brighton, etc (but don't be silly and lowercase Hotel California)

hotline, hotspot

hot-water bottle

houseboat, housebreaker, housebuyer, householder, housekeeper

househusband, housewife should be used with care; avoid sexist stereotyping such as lower food prices being "good news for housewives" (it's good news for shoppers)

House Un-American Activities Committee (Huac) anti-communist investigating body of the House of Representatives, often associated with "McCarthyism", although Joseph McCarthy was in fact head of the Senate permanent subcommittee on investigations

hove into view not heaved or hoved, as we sometimes write

hovercraft

Howards End by EM Forster: no apostrophe; **Howards' Way** (vintage BBC TV series) had one

Hubble space telescope

Hudson Bay but Hudson's Bay Company

Human Genome Project

humanity, humankind not man, mankind *See gender issues*

hummus you eat it; **humus** belongs in the ground

humour but **humorist, humorous**

hundred years war

hunky dory

Huntington's disease formerly known as Huntington's chorea

huntsman a paid servant of the hunt, rather than a hunter or hunt follower

hurricane lc, eg hurricane Katrina

Hutchison Telecommunications International (not Hutchinson) part of Hutchison Whampoa; Hutchison Essar in India, known as Hutch

hydroelectric

hyperbole what used to be known in newspapers as "flamming up" a story - which, on the whole, we aim to avoid *See sexing up*

hyperthermia hot; **hypothermia** cold

hyphens *See Grammar & punctuation*

Headlines

What makes a great, or at least memorable, headline? They can be historic ("Man walks on moon"), campaigning ("He lied and lied and lied"), classical ("Between Cilla and Charybdis"), subtle ("Flo quiets the Dons"), funny ("Super Caley go ballistic - Celtic are atrocious"), notorious ("Gotcha!"), salacious ("Zip me up before you go-go"), or downright absurd ("Freddie Starr ate my hamster"). Some of the most fondly remembered headlines are, in fact, apocryphal: the archives of the Manchester Guardian reveal it is a myth that our reports of the exploits of the explorer Vivian Fuchs ever carried the headline "Fuchs Off To Antarctic". The following did, however, appear: "Sir Vivian Fuchs At Palace" (16 May 1958) and "Sir Vivian Fuchs For Antarctic" (6 December 1963).

The explosion in online publishing has led to a change in the nature of headline writing because of the need to attract readers via SEO (search engine optimisation): relatively few people are likely to type Charybdis, say, into Google. Web headlines are expected to contain key terms that are not vital in print. For example, in a story about an earthquake, a headline such as "After 10 days in the rubble, a small voice called out ... " might work very well in the newspaper with an appropriate photograph; on the web, it would probably be something like "China earthquake kills thousands". If a lot of people in the US are Googling the name of an American politician who is not particularly well known in the UK, using his name in a headline on guardian.co.uk will bring more readers to the site, although we might not use the name in the paper. Not everyone welcomes this - according to a Washington Post columnist: "When the stories arrive on the web, even the best headlines will be changed to something dull but utilitarian." On the other hand, surely telling a news story simply and clearly, with the most arresting words, is something that all headline writers - in whatever medium - should strive for. The web is still young, the "rules" of SEO still evolving, and good headlines will be around for a while yet.

Writing them, whether for print or web, is harder than it looks. Here are a few guidelines.

Use active verbs where possible, particularly in news headlines: "Editor updates style guidelines" is much better than "Style guidelines updated" (although the latter is more SEO friendly).

Avoid tabloid cliches such as bid, brand, dub and slam, and their broadsheet counterparts such as insist, signal and target. Imagining that you are describing an event, in words, to real people, is a good antidote to journalese: no one in a pub says: "Did you see that Clegg slammed Cameron in a dramatic power bid?"

Just as we would in copy, we need to take care with words such as debacle, farce and fiasco, especially when combined, which we contrived to do in the headline "Hips fiasco descends into farce" - the fact that "Hips farce descends into fiasco" would work just as well tells you something is probably wrong here.

Strive to be fresh: tired plays on the phrase "Mind the gap", familiar to passengers on the London underground, have become tedious, as well as either baffling or infuriating to readers who do not happen to live in the capital. This reached its nadir, surely, in the feeble (not in our papers) "Millions mind the Watford Gap" (on a story about the so-called north-south divide). Similar headline cliches include variations on "Back to the future", "New kids on the block", "A bridge too far" or any headlines about tax that include the word "taxing".

Take care over ambiguity: "Landmine claims dog UK arms firm", which appeared in the paper, contains so many successive nouns, some of which may or may not be verbs, that you have to read it several times to work out what it means. And it's not even funny, unlike a more exotic example that suffered from a similar confusion between verbs and nouns: "French push bottles up German rear".

Exclamation marks are generally an attempt to say "Look, I've written something funny!" and should not be used.

Question marks should be employed very sparingly, although "But is it weather?" (when Tate Modern exhibited a giant sun and created its own indoor climate) is as perfect a headline as you will find. Quotation marks, unless essential to signify a quote or for legal reasons, are also best avoided. And we should resist the temptation to save space by replacing "and" with a comma: "Cameron and Clegg agree coalition deal" not "Cameron, Clegg agree coalition deal".

Puns are fine – "Where there's muck there's bras", about a farmer's wife who started a lingerie business from a barn, was voted headline of the year by our staff – but do not overuse, or resort to tired puns such as "flushed with success" (this story has got a plumber in it). It is possible to try just a little too hard ("To baldly grow where no mane's grown before"). In the 1970s and 80s the Guardian suffered from a reputation for excruciating puns; today, we want to be known for clever, original and witty headlines.

Unexpected twists, or subtle plays on words and phrases, show the subeditor's craft at its best: a power failure in a theatre became, in the Guardian, "Bad lights stop play". A light touch can work beautifully: "Drop dead, gorgeous", on a story about office jealousy, added one comma to create the perfect headline.

Be careful when making references to popular culture: "I fed the newts today, oh boy" (on a story revealing that the young John Lennon was a nature lover) works, because most people are familiar with the lyric, but allusions to your favourite obscure prog-rock LP are likely to pass over most readers' heads. Long after people had forgotten the 1960s movie Charlie Bubbles, tabloid sports subeditors continued to mystify their readers by using the headline "Charlie bubbles" whenever anyone called Charlie scored a goal. "Book lack in Ongar", about a shortage of resources in Essex libraries, remains one of the all-time great headlines, but it only works if you get the reference to John Osborne's 1956 play Look Back in Anger (or at least it did until Oasis helpfully recorded a song called Don't Look Back in Anger).

It's time for some formulaic headlines to be given a decent burial, or at least a long rest. "The kids are alright" (based on a song by the Who, and subsequently a film) crops up, with minor variations, on a weekly and sometimes daily basis in British newspapers: "The kids are alright online", "The kids are all right (and left)", "The kids are all right, left and centre", and so on.

Even more ubiquitous are "Size isn't everything" and its close relative "Size doesn't matter", used to refer to a car (in two different newspapers), school uniforms, Simon Callow's height, a hotel in Turkey, new houses, national economies, motorbikes, a footballer, the gallery following a golf tournament, and - once - penis size.

The ever-popular "Brighton rocks" and its variations are an allusion, still common, to the Graham Greene novel and subsequent film, both more than 50 years old. How many people still understand the reference? "So lucky, lucky, lucky", a headline we used above a photograph of Kylie Minogue, quoted lyrics from a hit she had two decades ago. How many of our readers would be aware of this? You have to use your judgment.

If you are quoting, be sure to get it right. "Talkin' about their generation", from a classic 1960s song by the Who, fails as a headline because it literally lacks rhythm (it should be "Talkin' 'bout"). We claimed that Millwall fans sing "No one likes us and we don't care"; they don't sing that, and the mistake made it look as if we don't care.

The most important thing is to think of the readers and remember that we are writing headlines for their benefit, not for our own amusement or to show how clever we are.

Ii

66 I hate the way even problems are euphemised. They are now 'issues'. (Insurmountable problems have become 'challenges'.) 'Issues' now has far too many meanings. Imagine a parenting magazine that had a special edition on problem children - which ran into difficulties at the printers. Would these become the 'issue issues issue issues'? Probably 99

Simon Hoggart

Ii

ice age

ice-cream

iconic is in danger of losing all meaning after an average three appearances a day in the Guardian and Observer, employed to describe anything vaguely memorable or well-known – from hairdressers, storm drains in Los Angeles and the Ferrero Rocher TV ads to Weetabix, the red kite and the cut above the eye David Beckham sustained after being hit by a flying boot kicked by Sir Alex Ferguson. Our advice, even if our own writers rarely follow it, is to show a little more thought, and restraint, in using this term

icons

A selection of the things described in the Guardian as "iconic" in a heady fortnight in 2010:

Archaeopteryx, bluefin tuna, Castro's cigar, David Beckham wearing an anti-Glazer scarf, Grace Kelly in casual wear, Imperial War Museum North, Liberty prints, limestone stacks in Thailand, Nigel Slater, Mad Men, Variety, the John Hughes films Breakfast Club, Ferris Bueller's Day Off and Weird Science, postboxes, prints of the Che Guevara image, Stephen Fairey's Obama Hope design, the parliamentary constituency of Hove, Brandenburg Gate, Bach's St Matthew Passion, a community-owned wind turbine, Kraft cheese slices, salmon farming, the blue and white stripes of Cornishware pottery, Penarth Pavilion, Cardiff, the Norwegian church and Pierhead Building in Cardiff Bay, a multimillion-pound arena in Leeds, a "rock-built engine house at Bottalack near St Just", the Royal Albert Hall, wind turbines ("iconic renewable energy technology"), Wembley Arena, and the video for Kylie Minogue's Can't Get You Out of My Head

ID cards now "consigned to history" in the UK

Identity and Passport Service subsumed the Passport Agency; also responsible for the registration of births, marriages and deaths in England and Wales

Ii

ie no full points or commas, ie like this

if not can be ambiguous: does "it is the most beautiful castle in France, if not the whole of Europe" mean "and maybe in the whole of Europe" or "but not in the whole of Europe"?

IJ if a Dutch word starts with IJ then both letters are always capped (there is a waterway called the IJ so a lot of places have IJ in their name, eg IJsselmeer, IJmuiden, etc)

illegitimate should not be used to refer to children born outside marriage (unless in a historical context, eg "the illegitimate son of Charles the Good")

iMac, **iPad**, **iPhone**, **iPod**, **iTunes**
The trend for sticking an "i" in front of new products to make them seem whizzy began in 1997, when Ken Segall, a creative director at Apple, came up with the iMac name while the computer was in development. "The i meant internet," Segall says. "But it also meant individual, imaginative and all the other things it came to stand for." Apple's founder, Steve Jobs, initially pooh-poohed the name

Imax cinemas so named in 1968

immaculate conception has nothing to do with the birth of Jesus: it is the doctrine that Mary herself was conceived by her mother (St Anne) without the stain of original sin. The virgin birth is the doctrine of Christ's birth without a human father. This is one of our most frequent errors

immigrate to arrive in a country; **emigrate** to leave one

Immigration and Nationality Directorate may be called "the immigration service"

immune to not immune from

impact a noun, not a verb

Imperial College London (no commas) is no longer part of the University of London

Ii

impinge, **impinging**

impostor not imposter

impracticable impossible, it cannot be done; **impractical** possible in theory but not workable at the moment

impressionism, **impressionist** painting

in can lead to ambiguous headline constructions as "Marconi chief in board clearout" - is the chief clearing out the board or being cleared out with them?

in or on? in the team not the US version "on the team"

inadmissible not -able

inchoate means just beginning or undeveloped, not chaotic or disorderly

incidence amount, eg a high incidence of mistakes

incident has political connotations, so attack or clash is often preferable; within a couple of years of the massacre in Tiananmen Square the Chinese government was referring to it as an "incident" or even "alleged incident"

income support, **income tax** lowercase

Independent Police Complaints Commission replaced the Police Complaints Authority

index plural indexes, except for scientific and economic indices

Indian placenames the former Bombay is now known as Mumbai, Madras is now Chennai, Calcutta is now Kolkata and Bangalore is now Bengalooru

indie music, films, etc; **Indy** short for the Independent, a newspaper (and Sindy for the Independent on Sunday)

indispensable not -ible

Industrial Revolution

industrial tribunals have not existed since 1998, when they

Ii

became employment tribunals; they still appear in the pages of the paper with embarrassing frequency despite regular corrections from the readers' editor

infer or imply? to infer is to deduce something from evidence; to imply is to hint at something (and wait for someone to infer it)

infinite means without limit, not very big

inflammable means the same as flammable, which we prefer; the negative is non-flammable

information commissioner but Information Commissioner's Office

initials no spaces or points, whether businesses or individuals, eg WH Smith, AJ Strauss

injunction the verb is **enjoin**, not injunct

Inland Revenue *See Revenue & Customs*

inner city noun two words, adjective hyphenated: inner-city blues made Marvin Gaye wanna holler

innocent civilians the adjective is superfluous

innocuous

innuendo plural innuendoes

inoculate not innoculate

inpatient

inquiry not enquiry

inshallah means "God willing" in Arabic

insignia are plural

insisted overused, especially in political reporting, perhaps to imply that you don't believe the speaker; "said" should normally suffice

install, instalment

instil, instilled, instilling

Ii

Institute for Fiscal Studies

Institute for Government not Institute of Government

Institute for Public Policy Research

insure against risk; **assure** life; **ensure** make certain

insurgency, **insurgents** *See terrorism, terrorists*

Intellectual Property Office formerly the Patent Office

Intergovernmental Panel on Climate Change

International Atomic Energy Agency not Authority; abbreviate to IAEA after first mention

international date line

International Institute for Strategic Studies

International Union for Conservation of Nature IUCN after first mention; formerly the World Conservation Union

interned imprisoned; **interred** buried (yes, we have got them confused)

internet net, web, world wide web

Interpol International Criminal Police Organisation (and a New York band)

InterRail

intifada

into or in to? one word if you go into a room or look into something, but two words in such sentences as I called in to complain, I listened in to their conversation and I went in to see my friend; on to two words *See on to*

in-tray

introducing people
Never use the following construction to introduce a speaker or a subject: "Foreign secretary William Hague said ... " Use the definite article and commas to separate the job from the name,

like this: "William Hague, the foreign secretary … " (there is only one person with this specific post).

Commas are not used if the description is more general and could apply to more than one person, like this: "The health minister Paul Burstow said … " (there are several health ministers); or like this: "The Liberal Democrat MP Paul Burstow said … " (after the 2010 election, there were 57).

Another example: "Jonathan Glancey, the Guardian's architecture critic, gave his verdict … " is correct; "The architecture critic Jonathan Glancey gave his verdict … " is fine as well

introductory words at the start of a sentence such as "However", "Nonetheless", "Instead", should be followed by a comma

Inuit not Eskimos; an individual is an Inuk

invalid means not valid or of no worth; do not use to refer to disabled or ill people

invariable, **invariably** unchanging; often used wrongly to mean hardly ever changing

invitation noun, **invite** verb; so you do not send someone an invite

IPCC may refer to the Independent Police Complaints Commission or the Intergovernmental Panel on Climate Change

iPod only when you are sure it is an Apple iPod; the generic term is MP3 player or digital audio player

Iraqi placenames
Use these spellings for Iraq's biggest cities and towns: Amara, Baiji, Baghdad, Baquba, Basra, Diwaniya, Dohuk, Falluja, Haditha, Hilla, Irbil, Kerbala, Kirkuk, Kut, Mosul, Najaf, Nassiriya, Ramadi, Rutba, Samarra, Samawa, Sulaimaniya, Tikrit (note that these transliterations do away with al- prefixes and the final H)

Ireland, **Irish Republic** not Eire or Southern Ireland

iridescent one R

Ii

Irish Travellers initial caps, as they are recognised as a distinct ethnic group under race relations legislation

iron age, **iron curtain** but **ironmonger**, **ironworks**

ironic, **ironically**
Do not use when what you mean is strange, coincidental, paradoxical or amusing (if you mean them say so, or leave it up to the reader to decide). There are times when ironic is right but too often it is misused, as in this typical example from the paper: "Santini's Tottenham won 2-0 at Nottingham Forest, ironic really with the north London club having a big interest in Forest's Republic of Ireland midfielder Andy Reid ... " (not that sport are the only, or biggest, offenders).

As Kingsley Amis put it: "The slightest and most banal coincidence or point of resemblance, or even just-perceptible absence of one, unworthy of a single grunt of interest, gets called 'ironical'." The idiotic "post-ironic", which Amis would be glad he did not live to see, is banned

Isa individual savings account, but no need to spell it out

-ise not -ize at end of word, eg maximise, synthesise (exception: capsize)

Islam means "submission to the will of God".
Muslims should never be referred to as "Mohammedans", as 19th-century writers did. It causes serious offence because they worship God, not the prophet Muhammad.

"Allah" is Arabic for "God". Both words refer to the same concept: there is no major difference between God in the Old Testament and Allah in Islam. Therefore it makes sense to talk about "God" in an Islamic context and to use "Allah" in quotations or for literary effect.

The holy book of Islam is the Qur'an (not Koran)

Islamist an advocate or supporter of Islamic fundamentalism; the likes of Osama bin Laden and his followers should be described as Islamist, not Islamic or Muslim, terrorists

Islamophobia

issue not a synonym for problem ("she has stylebook issues")

italics

Use roman for titles of books, films, etc; the only exceptions are the Review and the Observer, which by special dispensation are allowed to ignore the generally sound advice of George Bernard Shaw:

"1 I was reading The Merchant of Venice.

2 I was reading 'The Merchant of Venice'.

3 I was reading *The Merchant of Venice*.

The man who cannot see that No 1 is the best-looking, as well as the sufficient and sensible form, should print or write nothing but advertisements for lost dogs or ironmongers' catalogues: literature is not for him to meddle with."

Use italics for foreign words and phrases (with roman translation in brackets), poetry and scientific names.

Never use italics in headlines or standfirsts

it's or its? *See Grammar & punctuation*

ITV1, ITV2, ITV3, ITV4

Ivory Coast not "the Ivory Coast" or Côte d'Ivoire; its nationals are Ivorians

Ivy League universities Brown, Columbia, Cornell, Dartmouth College, Harvard, Princeton, University of Pennsylvania, Yale

Jj

66 The trickiest word in British political journalism is Tory. It's a strange word, since it is not the official name of the Conservative party, yet most of the party's members and leaders are comfortable with it. And yet, in some contexts, mostly Labour ones, Tory is also a pejorative and even insulting usage. What to do to avoid appearing to be a reflexive Tory-basher? My rule is always to use Conservative for the first reference to the party in any story and then mostly to use Tory - not least because it is shorter - thereafter. In a longer piece, though, I would always try to use Conservative again, at least once, an an effort to stress and maintain objectivity - even in a very critical piece 99

Martin Kettle

Jj

J joules; **kJ** kilojoules

Jack Daniel's note apostrophe; technically it is a Tennessee whiskey, not a bourbon

jack-in-the-box but **jack of all trades**

jack russell terrier first bred by the Rev John Russell in the early 19th century

Jacuzzi TM; named after its US inventors, Roy and Candido Jacuzzi; call it a whirlpool bath unless you're sure it really is a Jacuzzi

jail not gaol (the Guardian persisted with this style well into the 1980s, long after everyone else had changed)

Jalalabad city in Afghanistan; **Jalal-Abad** is in Kyrgyzstan

al-Jazeera

JCDecaux sells outdoor advertising space, but has no spaces in its name

Jeep TM

Jehovah's Witness

jejune naive, unsophisticated (not necessarily anything to do with being young)

jellaba loose cloak with a hood, worn especially in north Africa and the Middle East

Jerez

jerry-built

Jerusalem is not the capital of Israel; Tel Aviv is (a mistake we have made more than once)

jerusalem artichoke not an artichoke and nothing to do with Jerusalem - this jerusalem comes from *girasole*, the Italian for sunflower

jetski

Jj

jewellery in British English, not jewelry

jib triangular sail or arm of a crane; "I don't like the cut of his jib" means you don't like the look or manner of someone

jibe (not gibe) taunt

jihad is used by Muslims to describe three different kinds of struggle: an individual's internal struggle to live out the Muslim faith as well as possible; the struggle to build a good Muslim society; and the struggle to defend Islam, with force if necessary (holy war)

jobcentres are run by Jobcentre Plus

jobseeker's allowance

job titles are all lc: editor of guardian.co.uk, governor of the Bank of England, prime minister, etc

jodhpurs

Joe Public, **John Doe**

john dory fish

Johns Hopkins University not John Hopkins

jokey not joky

Joneses as in keeping up with the Joneses; also note the Joneses' house (not the Jones' house)

Jonsson, Ulrika

judgment not judgement

judgment call works much better without the word "call"

7 July 2005 the London suicide bombings may be referred to as 7/7 in headlines; the bombers, who killed 52 people, were Hasib Hussain, Mohammad Sidique Khan, Germaine Lindsay and Shehzad Tanweer

jumbo jet but **jump-jet**

junior abbreviate to Jr not Jun or Jnr, eg Sammy Davis Jr

Jj

just deserts not just desserts, unless you are saying you only want pudding

juvenile the Criminal Justice Act 1991 replaced this term with youth, and raised the age at which you cease to be one from 17 to 18

Kk

66 Even in this hymn book to linguistic probity, might I make a case for occasional rule-breaking?

Certainly, any would-be sinner must give the impression of being proficient with the rules before they can break them - the reason many people dislike a conceptual artist such as Damien Hirst is because they suspect he couldn't draw a convincing horse if his life depended upon it. But there are times when flouting the laws adds a certain something. For instance, despite being an obvious howler, describing Keith Chegwin as 'off of the telly' lends something that 'TV presenter' simply doesn't provide.

Second, without wishing to invoke the Sarah Palin defence for word-mangling - 'Shakespeare liked to coin new words too!' - the refudiating Republican has a partial point. The fact that in 30 years, more people than not will probably say 'pacific' when they mean 'specific' may infuriate many in the short term, but rest assured that the etymologists of the future will regard it as a charming and entertaining quirk in our mother tongue's evolution. And so with phrases such as 'beg the question' - if they eventually come to be so widely misused as to effectively change in meaning, we mustn't get our knickers in too much of a twist about it. Within reason, the fact that language is vital and metamorphic is something we should celebrate as opposed to lament 99

Marina Hyde

Kk

Ka'bah cube-shaped shrine in the centre of the great mosque in Mecca towards which all Muslims face in prayer; the shrine is not worshipped but used as the focal point of the worship of God

Kabbalah

Kaiser Chiefs band from Leeds (no "the"); **Kaizer Chiefs** football club from Soweto; **Kaiser Wilhelm II** last German emperor and king of Prussia

Kajagoogoo 80s band best known for their silly haircuts and No 1 hit Too Shy

Kaká Brazilian footballer

kapok

Kara Suu (not Korasuv) town in Uzbekistan

Kashmir adjective Kashmiri; but **cashmere** fabric

Kasparov, Garry former world chess champion, born in Azerbaijan in 1963

Kathmandu capital of Nepal

Kazakhstan adjective **Kazakh**

kebabs a doner kebab is made using meat from a rotating spit; shish kebabs are made from skewered cubes of meat

Keir Hardie, James (1856-1915) first leader of the Labour party

Kellogg's Corn Flakes but cornflakes in general

key a useful headline word, but overused

keyring

keywords the most important terms in a story, often used when searching for a specific item on the web: for example, putting the keywords "guardian" and "style guide" into Google will help a user find the Guardian style guide online

key stage 1, 2 etc (education)

Kk

KFC not Kentucky Fried Chicken

K-For stands for Kosovo Force, the Nato peacekeepers who entered Kosovo in June 1999 (and were still there 11 years later)

Khachaturian, Aram (1903-78) Armenian composer

Khartoum

khaki

Khrushchev, Nikita (1894-1971) Soviet leader

Khyber Pakhtunkhwa one of the four provinces of Pakistan formerly known as North-West Frontier province

kibbutz plural kibbutzim

kibosh

kick-off noun, **kick off** verb

kickstart noun or verb

Kilimanjaro not Mount Kilimanjaro

kilograms, kilojoules, kilometres, kilowatts abbreviate as kg, kJ, km, kW

King Edward potatoes

King's College, Cambridge comma; **King's College London** no comma

King's Cross London

King's Lynn Norfolk

Kings Place home of the Guardian, Observer and guardian.co.uk; a building in King's Cross, north London (it wasn't our idea to leave out the apostrophe)

Kings Road a road in Chelsea, west London; try not to call it "the Kings Road"; no apostrophe, although until 1830 it was a private royal road

Kingston upon Hull normally just Hull

Kk

Kingston upon Thames

Kirkcaldy not Kirkaldy, a town in **Fife**, not Fyfe

kir royal

kiss'n'tell

kissogram

Kitemark TM on items approved by the British Standards Institution

KitKat chocolate; there is a **KitKatClub** in Berlin, named after the fictional **Kit Kat Klub** in the musical Cabaret

km/h kilometres an hour (not kph)

kneejerk reaction

Knightley, Keira

knockout noun, **knock out** verb

knots measure of nautical miles an hour; do not say knots an hour

knowhow

knowledgable

koala not koala bear

Koh-i-noor diamond

koi not koi carp

Kolkata formerly Calcutta

Korean names as with Hong Kong and Taiwanese names, Korean names are written in two parts with a hyphen, eg Kim Jong-il, Kim Dae-jung; on second mention they become Kim, etc (except in leading articles: Mr Kim, etc)

Kosovo, Kosovans the adjective is Kosovan, not Kosovar

kowtow

Krajina not the Krajina

Kk

krona plural kronor (Sweden); **krona** plural kronur (Iceland); **krone** plural kroner (Denmark); **krone** plural kroner (Norway)

krugerrands

Ku Klux Klan

kukri Gurkha knife

kung fu

KwaZulu-Natal

Kyrgyzstan adjective Kyrgyz

Kyrie Eleison

L1

66 Look at this: 'Blank died literally in harness.' He didn't ...
This man says that we shall have to pay literally through the
nose. He knows we shan't 99

CP Scott

L1

laager South African encampment; **lager** beer

La Coruña Spanish port

Lady Gaga not GaGa

Lady Macbeth of Mtsensk Shostakovich opera, usually misspelt in the Guardian as Mtensk, with occasional variations such as Mtsenk

Lady Thatcher (and other ladies) not Baroness

lag pipes are lagged; other things lag behind

LaGuardia New York airport

Lailat al-Miraj Islamic holy day; **Lailat al-Qadr** Islamic holy day, time for study and prayer

laissez-faire not laisser-faire

Lake District or the Lakes or Lakeland: note that, with the exception of Bassenthwaite Lake, bodies of water in the Lake District do not have "lake" in their names (eg Buttermere, Derwent Water, Ullswater, Windermere)

lambast

lamb's lettuce, lamb's wool

lamp-post

lance corporal

Land state of Federal German Republic: use state, eg Hesse, the German state

landmark overused as an adjective, randomly strewn through stories as an alternative to flagship

landmine

Land Registry government department that registers title to land in England and Wales; the Scottish equivalent is Register of Scotland

Land Rover

Ll

Land's End but the clothing firm is Lands' End

lang, kd Canadian singer

Laos officially the Lao People's Democratic Republic; the language is Lao; adjective Laotian

laptop

largesse

larva (plural larvae), insects; **lava**, volcanic magma; we sometimes say the former when we mean the latter

La's, the defunct Liverpool rock band; keep apostrophe (abbreviation for Lads)

laser word dating from 1960 formed from the phrase "light amplification by stimulated emission of radiation", and an example of why not all acronyms need to be capped up

lasso noun (plural lassos) and verb: you lasso a horse with a lasso

Last Night of the Proms

last post

later often redundant as context will inform the reader: "They will meet this month" rather than "later this month"

Latin
"Away with him! Away with him! He speaks Latin" (Shakespeare, Henry VI Part 2)

Some people object to, say, the use of decimate to mean destroy on the grounds that in ancient Rome it meant to kill every 10th man; some of them are also likely to complain about so-called split infinitives, a prejudice that goes back to 19th-century Latin teachers who argued that as you can't split infinitives in Latin (they are one word) you shouldn't separate "to" from the verb in English. Others might even get upset about our alleged misuse of grammatical case (including cases such as dative and genitive that no longer exist in English).

Ll

As our publications are written in English, rather than Latin, do not worry about any of this even slightly

latitude like this: 21 deg 14 min S

latter is to last as greater is to greatest: an increasingly common error is to list, say, three things, then refer to the last named as "the latter"

launderette but Stephen Frears' 1985 film was My Beautiful Laundrette

law lords are now known as justices of the supreme court

lawsuit

lay bare (revealed) past tense laid, not lay: so "almost a decade after the human genome project lay bare ... " should have read "laid bare"

layby plural laybys

lay off does not mean to sack or make redundant, but to send workers home on part pay because of a temporary lack of demand for their product

lay waste a hurricane can lay waste an island, or lay an island waste, but it does not lay it to waste or lay waste to it (the word comes from the same root as devastate)

lbw

lc abbreviation for lowercase

Lea or Lee? the river Lea flows to the Thames; the Lee Navigation canal incorporates part of it; the Lee Valley park is the site for much of the 2012 Olympic development

Lead Belly (1888-1949) US musician, real name Huddie Ledbetter

leader article expressing a newspaper's opinion, also known as leader comment, leading article or editorial

leap year

Learjet

L l

learned not learnt (he learned his tables, a message well learned, etc)

Lebanon no definite article

le Carré, John

Le Corbusier Swiss-French architect (1887-1955), real name Charles-Édouard Jeanneret-Gris

led past tense of the verb lead; it is surprising how often such sentences as "he lead them to the scene of the crime" find their way into the paper

left, the left wing, leftwinger nouns; leftwing adjective; hard left, old left

lefty plural lefties

Legal Services Commission responsible for legal aid in England and Wales; in Scotland it is the Scottish Legal Aid Board

legal terms
In England and Wales, in camera is now known as in secret and in chambers in private; a writ is a claim form and a plaintiff a claimant; leave to appeal is permission to appeal. Since the Children Act 1989, access has been known as contact and custody is known as residence; do not use the older terms

legionnaires' disease named after an outbreak at a conference of American Legionnaires

Leibovitz, Annie US photographer

lent past tense of lend; we sometimes misspell it as leant as in "a gritty drama, leant added authenticity by Jean Tournier's monochrome photography ... "

Leonardo da Vinci Leonardo on second mention

Le Pen, Jean-Marie Le Pen on second mention

lepers a term that is now regarded as inappropriate and stigmatising; prefer people with leprosy or, if they are being

L1

treated, leprosy patients

lese-majesty no accents

less or fewer? less means smaller in quantity, eg less money; fewer means smaller in number, eg fewer coins. Note the difference between "do you have less able children in your class?" (children who are less able) and "do you have fewer able children in your class?" (not so many able ones)

letdown, **letup** nouns; **let down**, **let up** verbs

leukaemia

level crossing

Levi's jeans; the company is Levi Strauss

Lévi-Strauss, Claude structural anthropologist (1908-2009)

liaise, **liaison**

Lib Dems for Liberal Democrats after first mention and in headlines

libretto plural librettos

licence noun, **license** verb; you might enjoy your drinks in a licensed premises or take them home from an off-licence

Liechtenstein

lie (tell an untruth), past tense lied; **lie** (down), past tense lay: he lay there for an hour; **lay** (a table, an egg, put something down), past tense laid

lied German musical setting for a poem, plural lieder

Liège but the adjective is Liégeois

lieutenant colonel, **lieutenant general** eg Lieutenant Colonel Christopher Mackay at first mention, subsequently Mackay (except in leading articles where it would be Col Mackay)

lifelong

lifesize one word, not sized

L1

lightbulb

lighthearted

light year a measure of distance, not time

likable not likeable

like or as if? *See Grammar & punctuation*

like or such as? *See Grammar & punctuation*

likely takes the infinitive (he is likely to win) or a qualifier (he will very likely win), not "he will likely win" - if you want to use that form, say "he will probably win"

lilliputian lc

lilo something you take to the beach to lie on;
LiLo Lindsay Lohan

limpid means clear or transparent, not limp

linchpin not lynchpin

lineup, lineout (nouns)

link (noun) takes the reader to a related reference on guardian.co.uk or the web; (verb) to insert such a reference into an article or blog

LinkedIn social networking site aimed at business people

liquefy not liquify

liquorice not licorice

listed buildings
In England and Wales, Grade I-listed (note cap G, roman numeral I) buildings are of exceptional interest; Grade II* are particularly important buildings of more than special interest; Grade II are of special interest, warranting every effort to preserve them. In Scotland and Northern Ireland these categories are replaced by the more logical Grade A, Grade B and Grade C

L1

literally a term used, particularly by sports commentators, to denote an event that is not literally true, as in "Manchester City literally came back from the dead." *See ironic, ironically*

live blog rolling online commentary on a live event

Live 8 not Live8

Liverpool John Lennon airport

Lloret de Mar not del Mar

Lloyd's of London Lloyd's names are lc; **Lloyds TSB** bank

Lloyd-Webber, Lord but **Andrew Lloyd Webber**

loan noun; the verb is **lend**

loathe detest; **loth** unwilling, not loath

lobby requires great care: unless you are writing about, say, the parliamentary lobby or US lobby system, it will at best sound vague and patronising, and at worst pejorative or offensive ("the Jewish lobby"). If you are talking about specific pressure groups, say who they are

local a pub, not a person: talk about local people rather than locals

loch Scottish; **lough** Irish

Lockerbie bombing in September 1988 killed 270 people; the two Libyans eventually put on trial for murder were Abdelbaset al-Megrahi and Al-Amin Khalifah Fhimah. Megrahi was convicted in 2001 and jailed for 27 years, then released in 2009 on compassionate grounds; his co-accused was acquitted

lock-in, **lockout** noun; **lock in**, **lock out** verbs

logbook, logjam

London
Surprising as it may be to some London-based journalists, most of our readers do not work or live in the capital (or, indeed, the UK). So give location, not just name: ie King's Cross, north

London, not just King's Cross; there is a Victoria station in Manchester as well as in London, so make clear which one you mean

London assembly elected body of 25 members whose role is to hold the mayor of London to account. Together, assembly and mayor constitute the Greater London authority (GLA); note that there is no such organisation as the Greater London assembly

London boroughs and counties

Parts of the traditional counties of Essex, Middlesex, Kent and Surrey that are close to London retain the county link in their postal address (eg Bromley, Kent), even when they are administratively part of a London borough (eg the London borough of Bromley), and represented in the London assembly. This leads to inconsistencies, as when we refer to "Chingford, Essex" in one story and "Chingford, east London" in another. It is hard to be totally consistent - the preferences even of people who live in such places may vary (according to how long they have lived there, for example). In general, use London rather than the traditional counties - Ilford, east London; Bexley, south-east London, etc - unless a group or organisation specifically includes a county designation in its title

Londonderry use Derry and County Derry (first mention, thereafter Co Derry)

London Eye official name of the millennium wheel

London's do not say "London's Covent Garden" (or London's anything else); it is Covent Garden, London, etc

London School of Economics abbreviated to LSE after first mention; **London Stock Exchange** is also abbreviated to LSE, and there is no real way round this (especially for headlines); the context should make clear which we are talking about

London Transport Users Committee now refers to itself as London TravelWatch

Ll

Long Island iced tea

longitude like this: 149 deg 18 min E

longlist

longtime adjective, as in longtime companion

look to is used too often in place of hope to or expect to

looking-glass

lord chancellor post abolished in 2003, then reprieved; but the Lord Chancellor's Department was replaced by the Department for Constitutional Affairs, which in 2007 was absorbed into the new Ministry of Justice, at which point the lord chancellor also became secretary of state for justice

lord chief justice

lord lieutenant no hyphen, plural lords lieutenant

Lords, **House of Lords** but **the house**, not the House; **their lordships**

Lord's cricket ground

lottery, **national lottery** lc but Lotto and National Lottery Commission

lovable not loveable

Love's Labour's Lost

lowlife plural **lowlifes**, not lowlives (for an eloquent explanation, see Steven Pinker's Words and Rules)

loyalists (Northern Ireland)

luddite

Luiz Inácio Lula da Silva elected president of Brazil in 2002, he is normally known simply as Lula

lumpenproletariat

Lundy not Lundy Island

Ll

luvvies a silly cliche, best avoided

Luxembourgers live in Luxembourg

LVMH the luxury goods firm is, in full, Moët Hennessy Louis Vuitton

Lycra TM; the briefly fashionable term "lycra louts" led to complaints from the Lycra lawyers

lying in state no hyphens

Lynyrd Skynyrd late US rock band (named after a man called Leonard Skinner)

Lyon not Lyons

Mm

66 Why must all legal rulings be described as 'landmark'? A genuinely 'landmark ruling' is one which significantly changes the course of the common law, by departing from previous court decisions on an issue with obvious consequences. Few cases fall into this category, but that doesn't stop the words 'landmark' and 'ruling' from appearing almost inseparable in copy 99

Afua Hirsch

Mm

Mac or Mc?

Andie MacDowell (actor), Sue MacGregor (broadcaster), Kelvin MacKenzie (ex-editor), Shirley MacLaine (actor), Murdo MacLeod (photographer).

Sir Cameron Mackintosh (impresario), Elle Macpherson (model).

Sir Paul McCartney (composed song about frogs), Steve McClaren (football manager), Sir Trevor McDonald (ex-newsreader), Ian McEwan (novelist), Ewan McGregor, Sir Ian McKellen (actors), Malcolm McLaren (late impresario).

MacDonald, James Ramsay (1866-1937) first Labour prime minister, known as Ramsay MacDonald

mace, the (parliament); **Mace** riot control spray

machiavellian after Niccolò Machiavelli (1469-1527)

machine gun noun, **machine-gun** verb

Machu Picchu Peruvian "lost city of the Incas"

mackem refers both to a person from Sunderland and their accent

Macmillan, Harold (1894-1986) Tory prime minister

MacMillan, Kenneth (1929-92) choreographer

MacNeice, Louis (1907-63) Belfast-born poet

Madagascar geographical; Malagasy Republic political; Malagasy inhabitant or inhabitants of Madagascar and the name of their language; the adjective for the country is Madagascan

Madama Butterfly is the correct title of Puccini's 1904 opera; Madame Butterfly and Madam Butterfly are the French and English versions

Madame Tussauds no apostrophe, even though there was a Mme (Marie) Tussaud

madeira wine and cake

Madejski stadium home of Reading FC

Madison Square Garden (not Gardens) in New York City

Madras is now known as Chennai

madrasa normally used to mean Islamic school, although in both Arabic and Urdu the word is used to refer to any kind of school

mafia

Mafikeng now spelt thus, although it was Mafeking when it was relieved

Magdalen College, Oxford; Magdalene College, Cambridge

magistrates court no apostrophe

maglev high-speed trains (it is short for magnetic levitation)

Magnum a .44 Magnum is a cartridge, not a gun (although Dirty Harry used a .44 Magnum revolver)

maharajah

Mahathir Mohamad prime minister of Malaysia from 1981 to 2003; Mahathir on second mention (except in leading articles, where he is Mr, not Dr, Mahathir)

mailbag, **mailvan** but **mail train**

mainland should not be used to refer to Great Britain in reports about Northern Ireland

mainmast, mainsail

major a major case of overuse; avoid except in military context: big, main and leading are among the alternatives

major general in leading articles, abbreviate on second mention to Gen: Major General Ben Summers, subsequently Gen Summers; otherwise just Summers

makeover, makeup (nouns) one word; **make over, make up** (verbs) two words: making up is hard to do

Málaga

Malaysian names the given name generally comes first, and Muslim Malays tend not to use surnames, so Mahathir Mohamad (Mahathir the son of Mohamad) becomes Mahathir on second reference. Chinese Malaysian names, like Singaporean names, are in three parts: eg Ling Liong Sik (Ling after first mention)

al-Maliki, Nouri (not Nuri) became prime minister of Iraq in 2006

Mall, the in London

Malloch-Brown, Lord a former deputy secretary general of the UN, Mark Malloch Brown acquired a peerage and a hyphen when he became a Labour minister

Mallorca not Majorca

Mamma Mia! musical show and film featuring Abba songs

mammon

Man Booker prize at first mention; thereafter the Booker prize or just Booker

mañana

mangetout

manifesto plural manifestos

mankind humankind or humanity are preferable

manoeuvre, manoeuvring

mantis plural mantids

Maori singular and plural

Mao Zedong Mao on second mention

margarita cocktail; **margherita** pizza

marines Royal Marines, but US marines

Marks & Spencer at first mention, then M&S

Mm

marquis not marquess, except where it is the correct formal title, eg Marquess of Blandford

Marrakech

Mars bar

Marseille not Marseilles

marshal (military rank) not marshall, a very frequent error; a reader sent in this guide: "Air Chief Marshal Marshall presided at the court martial of the martial arts instructor"

Marshall plan US aid to help rebuild Europe after the second world war

Martí, José (1853-95) writer and leader of Cuba's war of independence against Spain

martial arts, law

Marxism, Marxist

Mary Celeste not Marie Celeste

Mariinsky theatre St Petersburg home of the Mariinsky Ballet, known as the Kirov Ballet when touring outside Russia

mass lc; mass is celebrated or said, not read

massacre the savage killing of large numbers of people, not Stockport County beating Macclesfield Town 6-0 in the big Cheshire derby

massive massively overused

masterful imperious; **masterly** skilful

master's as in "I did my master's at UCL"

matchplay (golf) lc, one word but World Match Play Championship

Mathews, Meg former model and ex-wife of Noel Gallagher; they have a daughter, Anais

matinee no accent

matins

matt finish

maxidress

may or might? *See Grammar & punctuation*

mayday distress signal (from the French "m'aidez!");
May Day 1 May

mayor of London or anywhere else: lowercase

MB megabytes (storage capacity)

Mbps megabits per second (communication speed); take care to get such terms right: we referred to a "2mbps internet connection" which, at two millibits a second, is about the speed of smoke signals

McAlpine note the "Sir" in the building and civil engineering company Sir Robert McAlpine (named after the baronet who founded it); not to be confused with Alfred McAlpine construction and support services

MCC, the founded in 1787 as Marylebone Cricket Club

McCarthy & Stone retirement homes

McDonald's hamburgers; the possessive is the same word, eg "McDonald's new vegan-friendly image"

McJob defined by the OED as "an unstimulating, low-paid job with few prospects, esp one created by the expansion of the service sector"

McLuhan, Marshall (1911-80) Canadian author who coined the phrase "the medium is the message"

meanwhile usually means "here's a slight change of subject"

Meat Loaf sings; **meatloaf** doesn't sing - to quote "the Loaf" himself: "When I see my name spelt with one word, I want to slap and choke people. If you do that, you got to be a moron. It's on every poster, every album and every ticket as two words. If you spell it as one, you're an idiot. Bottom line"

Mm

Mecca holy city in Saudi Arabia; **mecca** as in "Ashton-under-Lyne is a mecca for tripe-eaters"

medals military medals uc: British Empire Medal, George Cross, Victoria Cross, etc; non-military medals like this: Fields medal, etc

Médecins sans Frontières international medical aid charity (don't describe it as French)

Medellín Colombia

media plural of medium: the media are sex-obsessed, etc, but a convention of spiritualists would be attended by mediums

Medicaid, Medicare are both US federal health insurance programmes, but Medicare primarily covers people over 65 and has no financial requirements for eligibility; Medicaid is targeted at those on low incomes

medieval not mediaeval

Medvedev, Dmitry (not Dmitri) became president of Russia in 2008

meet, met not meet with, met with someone

mega fine for megabits, megabytes and megawatts, not as an adjective meaning big

memento plural mementoes

memorandum plural memorandums

menage no accent

Menorca not Minorca

menswear

mental handicap, mentally handicapped, mentally retarded do not use: say person with learning difficulties or disabilities

mental health
Take care using language about mental health issues. In addition to such clearly offensive and unacceptable expressions as loony, maniac, nutter, psycho and schizo, terms to avoid –

because they stereotype and stigmatise - include victim of, suffering from, and afflicted by; "a person with" is clear, accurate and preferable to "a person suffering from".

Terms such as schizophrenic and psychotic should be used only in a medical context: for example never use schizophrenic to mean "in two minds".

Avoid writing "the mentally ill" - say mentally ill people, mental health patients or people with mental health problems

merchant navy

Meridian ITV region; **Meridien** hotels

Messiaen, Olivier (1908-92) French composer

metaphor the application to one thing of a name belonging to another, eg all the world's a stage, bowling blitz, economic meltdown, "every language is a temple in which the soul of those who speak it is enshrined" (Oliver Wendell Holmes)

method acting (lc) techniques associated with the Russian Constantin Stanislavski (1865-1938) and the American Lee Strasberg (1901-82)

Met Office

metres should be written out in full, to avoid confusion with million (an obvious exception would be athletics, eg she won the 400m)

metric system
We use the metric system for weights and measures; exceptions are the mile and the pint. As understanding of the two systems is a matter of generations, conversions (in brackets) to imperial units should be provided wherever this seems useful, though usually one conversion - the first - will suffice. Imperial units in quoted matter should be retained, and converted to metric [in square brackets] if doing so doesn't ruin the flow of the quote.

It is not necessary to convert moderate distances between metres and yards, which are close enough for rough and ready

purposes (though it is preferable to use metres), or small domestic quantities: two litres of wine, a kilogram of sugar, a couple of pounds of apples, a few inches of string. Small units should be converted when precision is required: 44mm (1.7in) of rain fell in two hours. But be sensible: don't convert a metric estimate into a precise imperial figure (round the conversion up or down). Tons and tonnes are close enough for most purposes to do without conversion; use tonnes (except in shipping tonnage).

Body weights and heights should always be converted in brackets: metres to feet and inches, kilograms to stones/pounds. Geographical heights and depths, of buildings, monuments, etc, should be converted, metres to feet. In square measurement, land is given in sq metres, hectares and sq km, with sq yards, acres or sq miles in brackets where there is space to provide a conversion. The floor areas of buildings are conventionally expressed in sq metres (or sq ft). Take great care over conversions of square and cubic measures: 2 metres is about 6.5 feet, but 2 sq metres is about 21.5 sq feet

Metropolitan police the Met at second mention; commissioner of the Metropolitan police, Met commissioner is acceptable; but note Metropolitan Police Authority (MPA)

mexican wave

meze not mezze

Miami Beach US city

mic abbreviation for microphone

microblogging is what people do on Twitter

mid-60s, **mid-90s** etc

mid-Atlantic but **transatlantic**

midday

middle ages

middle America, **middle England**

Middle-earth (Tolkien) not Middle Earth

Middle East never Mid, even in headlines

Middlesbrough, Teesside not Middlesborough, Teeside

midget considered by some to be offensive, certainly more so than dwarf; best to ask the people you are writing about how they prefer to describe themselves

Midlands, east Midlands but **West Midlands**

Midsummer Day 24 June

midterm elections, etc but **mid-term** in Scottish education

midweek, midwest no hyphens

MiG-21 Soviet Union-built fighter plane, still in use in some countries

Milad al-Nabi Islamic festival celebrating the birth of the prophet; many Muslims disapprove of celebrating this event

mileage

Militant tendency

militate or mitigate? to militate against something is to influence it (his record militated against his early release); to mitigate means to lessen an offence (in mitigation, her counsel argued that she came from a broken home) or make something less severe

millenary but **millennium** plural millennia

Millennium Dome (now historical) at first mention, then just the dome; reopened in 2007 as the O2

millennium wheel its official name is London Eye

million in copy use m for sums of money, units or inanimate objects: £10m, 45m tonnes of coal, 30m doses of vaccine; but million for people or animals: 1 million people, 23 million rabbits, etc; use m in headlines

mimic, mimicked, mimicking

Mm

min contraction of minute/minutes

mineworker

minibus, minicab, miniskirt, minivan

MiniDisc TM

minimum plural minima

ministers are all lc: prime minister, etc

Minnelli, Liza "Liza with a Zee, not Lisa with an Ess", and Minnelli with two Ns; her father was the film director Vincente Minnelli (1903-86)

minority ethnic (adjective) rather than ethnic minority eg black and minority ethnic support services

minuscule not miniscule

mis-hit, **mis-sell** but **misspell**, **misspent**

mistress best reserved for historical contexts; girlfriend or lover is less judgmental and sexist

misuse, misused

MLA member of the Northern Ireland assembly (it stands for member of the legislative assembly)

MLitt master of letters, not master of literature

Mobo awards it stands for Music of Black Origin

Moby-Dick Herman Melville's classic is, believe it or not, hyphenated

Modern in the sense of Modern British, to distinguish it from modern art

Moët & Chandon champagne

moment magnitude scale measures earthquakes

Mönchengladbach

moneyed eg moneyed classes; moneys not monies

Mm

Mongol one of the peoples of Mongolia

mongooses (not mongeese) plural of mongoose

moniker not monicker

Monk, Thelonious (1917-82) American jazz pianist and composer, generally but erroneously referred to in the Guardian and elsewhere as "Thelonius"; a pleasing mnemonic is that he made a melodious thunk

Montenegro inhabited by Montenegrins

moon lc for the Earth's moon

moon walk what Neil Armstrong did; **moonwalk** what Michael Jackson did

Moors murders committed in the 1960s by Ian Brady and Myra Hindley

morbidity can mean the state of being morbid (taking an unusual interest in death or unpleasant events); but morbidity, also known as the morbidity rate, also means the relative incidence of a disease in a specific locality

more than generally preferable to over: there were more than 20,000 people at the game, it will cost more than £100 to get it fixed; but she is over 18

More Than not MORE TH>N, which is how the insurance arm of Royal & Sun Alliance styles itself

Morissette, Alanis

morning-after pill

morris dancing often seen with a capital M, for no apparent reason

Morrisons for the stores (not Morrison or Morrison's), Morrisons Supermarket plc is the name of the company (formerly Wm Morrison); just to make it more confusing, Morrison is a support services company owned by AWG plc (Anglian Water)

Mm

morse code

mortgages the person borrowing the money is the mortgagor, the lender is both the mortgagee and the mortgage holder; to avoid confusion, call the mortgagor the mortgage borrower and the mortgagee the mortgage lender

mortise lock not mortice

mosquito plural **mosquitoes**

Mosquito "youth dispersal device" that emits a piercing noise inaudible to over-25s

mother of parliaments the great 19th-century Liberal politician and Manchester Guardian reader John Bright described England, the country (not Westminster, the institution), as the mother of parliaments

Mossad, the Israeli secret service; note definite article

mother of three etc, not mother-of-three; but do not use unless relevant to the story

Mother's Day

Mötley Crüe, Motörhead include "metal umlauts"

motorbike, motorcar, motorcycle

motor neurone disease

motorways just M4, etc, not M4 motorway

mottoes

movable

mph

MP, **MPs** if spelling out, lowercase: member of parliament

MP3, **MP3 player** not mp3

Mr, Ms, Mrs, Miss
In leading articles: use the appropriate honorific after first mention (unless you are writing about an artist, author,

journalist, musician, sportsman or woman, criminal or dead person, who take surname only); use Ms for women subsequently unless they have expressed a preference for Miss or Mrs.

Everywhere apart from leading articles: generally use first name and surname on first mention, and thereafter just surname. Use an honorific, however, if this strikes the wrong tone, or to identify different members of the same family *See honorifics*

MSP member of the Scottish parliament

Muhammad
Muslims consider Muhammad to be the last of God's prophets, who delivered God's final message. They recognise Moses and Jesus as prophets also.

The above transliteration is our style for the prophet's name and for most Muhammads living in Arab countries, though where someone's preferred spelling is known we respect it, eg Mohamed Al Fayed, Mohamed ElBaradei. The spelling Mohammed (or variants) is considered archaic by most British Muslims today

Muhammad Ali (formerly known as Cassius Clay)

mujahideen collective noun for people fighting a jihad; the singular is mujahid

mukhabarat secret police in the Arab world (it means "informers")

multicultural, **multimedia**, **multimillion** but **multi-ethnic**

mum or Mum? How is your mum? I don't know, I've not spoken to Mum for two years

Mumbai formerly Bombay, but no need to say so

Murphy's law
"If there are two or more ways to do something, and one of those ways can result in a catastrophe, then someone will do it"; also

Mm

known as sod's law. Not to be confused with **Muphry's law** – "the editorial application of the better-known Murphy's law" – which states: "If you write anything criticising editing or proofreading, there will be a fault of some kind in what you have written"

museums initial caps, eg British Museum, Natural History Museum, Victoria and Albert Museum (V&A on second reference), Metropolitan Museum of Art, etc

Muslim not Moslem

Muzak TM; better to call it easy listening, loungecore, or a similar variant

MW megawatts; **mW** milliwatts

myriad a large, unspecified number; use as an adjective (there are myriad people outside) or a noun (there is a myriad of people outside), but not "myriads of"

MySpace

myxomatosis

Nn

66 There are many irritating things in life, but the less of them the better. After all - no, I can't even finish the sentence. The mere sight of that construction - less, when it should be fewer - can bring me out in hives. I felt an unfamiliar twinge of sympathy for the education secretary, Michael Gove, when he dispensed with his usually perfect manners to upbraid Labour's Tristram Hunt in the House of Commons for referring to 'less' when the English language demanded 'fewer'. It's like seeing a picture hanging askew: the urge to fix it is overwhelming **99**

Jonathan Freedland

Nn

Nabokov, Vladimir (1899-1977) Russian-born author of Lolita; not Nabakov

nailbomb

naive, **naively**, **naivety** no accent

Nakba the Palestinian "catastrophe"

names
Prominent figures can just be named in stories, with their function at second mention: "George Osborne said last night ... " (first mention); "the chancellor added ... " (subsequent mentions).

Where it is thought necessary to explain who someone is, write "Arsène Wenger, the Arsenal manager, said" or "the Arsenal manager, Arsène Wenger, said".

In such cases the commas around the name indicate that there is only one person in the position, so write "the Tory leader, David Cameron, said" (only one person in the job), but "the former Tory leader Michael Howard said" (there have been many).

Do not leave out the definite article in such constructions as "style guru David Marsh said ... " It should be "the style guru David Marsh said" (if there are other style gurus) or "David Marsh, the style guru, said" (if you feel only one person merits such a description)

Nanjing not Nanking

narrowboat the popular type of British canal boat, 7ft wide and up to 70ft long – do not call it a barge. A wider version (typically 10-14ft wide) is a broadbeam narrowboat

Nasa National Aeronautics and Space Administration, but no need to spell out

nation should not be used to mean country or state, but reserved to describe people united by language, culture and history so as to form a distinct group within a larger territory. Beware of attributing the actions of a government or a military

Nn

force to a national population ("the Israelis have killed 400 children during the intifada"). Official actions always have opponents within a population; if we don't acknowledge this, we oversimplify the situation and shortchange the opponents

national anthem

National Archives the former Public Record Office, now merged with the Historical Manuscripts Commission

National Association of Schoolmasters Union of Women Teachers (NASUWT) call it "the union" after first mention if you want to avoid using these unlovely initials; note that an "and" seems to have gone missing somewhere

National Audit Office NAO or audit office after first mention

national curriculum

National Endowment for Science, Technology and the Arts Nesta after first mention

National Grid distributes gas as well as electricity

National Health Service but NHS or health service are normally sufficient

National Hunt horseracing over fences and hurdles

National Institute for Health and Clinical Excellence Nice after first mention

national insurance lc; abbreviate national insurance contributions to NICs after first mention

nationalists (Northern Ireland)

national lottery

National Offender Management Service formed in 2004 from a merger between the prison and probation services, it moved from the Home Office to the Ministry of Justice in 2007; Noms after first mention (but note that in the US, Noms stands for national outcomes measurement system)

Nn

national parks lc, eg Peak District national park, Yellowstone national park

National Savings & Investments may be abbreviated to NS&I

national service peacetime conscription in the UK lasted from 1949 until 1960

Native Americans Geronimo was a Native American (not an American Indian or Red Indian); George W Bush is a native American

Nato North Atlantic Treaty Organisation, but no need to spell out

Natural England formerly English Nature

naught nothing; **nought** the figure 0

navy but **Royal Navy**

Nazi but **nazism**

'Ndrangheta Calabrian version of the mafia

Neanderthal man scientific name and style is *Homo neanderthalensis*. While it may be tempting to describe certain attitudes or, say, politicians as neanderthal, we should bear in mind that archaeologists have known for many years that Neanderthal man was not stupid. British Archaeology magazine has complained about the media's use of neanderthal as a term of abuse

nearby one word, whether adjective or adverb: the pub nearby; the nearby pub

nearsighted

nemesis an agent of retribution and vengeance, not a synonym for enemy

neocon, neoconservative, neoliberal

neophilia
Even if you have always wanted to appear in Private Eye, resist

the temptation to write such nonsense as "grey is the new black", "billiards is the new snooker", "Barnsley is the new Tuscany", etc

Nepalese not Nepali

nerve-racking

Nestlé

Netanyahu, Binyamin not Benjamin

Netherlands, the not Holland, which is only part of the country; use Dutch as the adjective. Exception: the Dutch football team is generally known as Holland

Never Never Land or simply Neverland (JM Barrie used both in his Peter Pan works)

nevertheless

new often redundant, as in "a new report said yesterday"

new age travellers

newbie

Newcastle-under-Lyme hyphens; **Newcastle upon Tyne** no hyphens

New Deal capped up, whether you are talking about Franklin D Roosevelt's job creation policies in the 1930s or Gordon Brown's 1990s version

newfound

New Labour but **old Labour**

news agency but **newsagent, newsprint, newsreel**

newspaper titles the Guardian, the Observer, the New York Times, etc, do not write "the Sun newspaper", etc: people know what you mean

New Testament

Newtownards Northern Irish town pronounced, and frequently misspelt, as Newtonards

Nn

New Wave initial caps for the film movement known in French as the Nouvelle Vague; **new wave** lowercase for music of the late 70s and early 80s (the likes of Talking Heads); also for any other new wave (eg the Moroccan new wave in cinema)

new year lc; but New Year's Day, New Year's Eve

New Year honours list

New York City but **New York state**

next of kin

Nietzsche, Friedrich (1844-1900) German philosopher; occasionally misspelt, even in the Guardian

Nigerian names surnames do not exist in the north of Nigeria: a typical name would be Isa Sani Sokoto (Isa the son of Sani who comes from the town of Sokoto); so best to write in full

nightcap, nightdress, nightfall, nightgown, nightshirt but **night-time**

nimby, nimbys, nimbyism it stands for "not in my back yard"

Nineteen Eighty-Four not 1984 for Orwell's novel

Niño, El

niqab veil that covers the face apart from the eyes

Nissan cars; **Nissen** hut

No 1 in the charts, the world tennis No 1, etc

No 10 (Downing Street)

no plural noes

Nobel prize Nobel peace prize, Nobel prize for literature, etc

no-brainer means something along the lines of "this is so obvious, you don't need a brain to know it" not "only someone with no brain would think this"

no campaign, yes campaign not No campaign, "no" campaign or any other variant

Nn

no doubt that, **no question that** are opposites: "There was no doubt that he was lying" means he was lying; "There was no question that he was lying" means he wasn't; the two are routinely confused

Noel no accent on Noel as in Christmas (The First Noel, not Nowell); use an accent if that's how the person spells his or her name: Noël Coward had one, Noele Gordon didn't

no-fly zone

no man's land no hyphens

noncommissioned officer

nonconformist

none *See Grammar & punctuation*

nonetheless

no one not no-one

Nordic countries Denmark, Norway, Sweden, Finland and Iceland

north north London, north Wales, north-west England, the north-west, etc

north-east England Tyneside (Newcastle), Wearside (Sunderland), Teesside (Middlesbrough); we often confuse these or get them wrong in some way that makes it look as if the farthest north-east Guardian journalists have ventured is Stoke Newington

northern hemisphere

northern lights also known as aurora borealis; the southern hemisphere counterpart is aurora australis

north of the border avoid this expression: we work on national newspapers

north pole

Northumbria an ancient Anglo-Saxon kingdom, a university and

a police authority; the county, however, is Northumberland

North York Moors national park but **North Yorkshire Moors railway** 18-mile heritage line between Pickering and Grosmont

nosy not nosey

notebook, **notepaper**

noticeboard

Nottingham Forest, **Notts County** the former should never be abbreviated to "Notts Forest"

Notting Hill carnival

now occasionally useful for emphasis, but is now used far too often

npower retail arm of RWE npower; nothing to do with nuclear power

numbers
Spell out from one to nine; numerals from 10 to 999,999; thereafter use m or bn for sums of money, quantities or inanimate objects in copy, eg £10m, 5bn tonnes of coal, 30m doses of vaccine; but million or billion for people or animals, eg 1 million people, 3 billion rabbits, etc; spell trillion in full at first mention, then tn; in headlines use m, bn or tn

numeracy
Numbers have always contained power, and many a journalist will tremble at the very sight of them. But most often the only maths we need to make sense of them is simple arithmetic. Far more important are our critical faculties, all too often switched off at the first sniff of a figure.

It's easy to be hoodwinked by big numbers in particular. But are they really so big? Compared with what? And what is being assumed? A government announcement of an extra £Xm a year will look far less impressive if divided by 60 million (the British population) and/or 52 (weeks in the year). That's quite apart from the fact that it was probably trumpeted last week already,

Nn

as part of another, bigger number.

Never invent a big figure when a small one will do. Totting jail sentences together ("the six men were jailed for a total of 87 years") is meaningless as well as irritating. Similarly, saying that something has an area the size of 150 football pitches, or is "eight times the size of Wales", is cliched and may not be helpful.

Here is an easy three-point guide to sidestepping common "mythematics" traps:

1 Be careful in conversions, don't muddle metric and imperial, or linear, square and cubic measures. Square miles and miles square are constantly confused: an area 10 miles square is 10 miles by 10 miles, which equals 100 square miles.

2 Be extremely wary of (or don't bother) converting changes in temperature; you run the risk of confusing absolute and relative temperatures, eg while a temperature of 2C is about the same as 36F, a temperature change of 2C corresponds to a change of about 4F.

3 When calculating percentages, beware the "rose by/fell by X%" construction: an increase from 3% to 5% is a 2 percentage point increase or a 2-point increase, not a 2% increase

Nuremberg

Oo

66 Do I get annoyed when people ask themselves their own questions and answer them (rendering the interviewer irrelevant)? Yes I do. Should we allow this virus in the paper? No we shouldn't. Cricket in recent years has been a science lab for cliches, from 'stepping up' to 'hitting the right areas' and 'backing yourself'. Now calling teams 'the group' (from the Australian captain Ricky Ponting) is spreading. And will someone kill the next person who lets 'back in the day' loose - especially if combined with 'old school'? No they won't 99

Kevin Mitchell

Oo

OAPs, **old age pensioners**
Do not use: they are pensioners or elderly people; do not use elderly to describe someone under 75 (the editors reserve the right to increase this upper limit, as appropriate)

obbligato not obligato

obtuse means "mentally slow or emotionally insensitive" (Collins); often confused with **abstruse** (hard to understand) or **obscure**

Occam's razor philosophical principle, attributed to the 14th-century English friar William of Ockham, that broadly means prefer the simplest explanation, adopting the one that makes the fewest assumptions and "shaving away" the rest

occupied territories Gaza and the West Bank

occurred two Rs

Oceania a preferable term to Australasia, it is sometimes divided into Near Oceania and Remote Oceania, and comprises, according to the UN:
> **Australia/New Zealand**
> **Melanesia** (Fiji, New Caledonia, Papua New Guinea, Solomon Islands, Vanuatu)
> **Micronesia** (Guam, Kiribati, Marshall Islands, Federated States of Micronesia, Nauru, Northern Mariana Islands, Palau)
> **Polynesia** (American Samoa, Cook Islands, French Polynesia, Niue, Pitcairn, Samoa, Tokelau, Tonga, Tuvalu, Wallis and Futuna Islands)

OECD Organisation for Economic Co-operation and Development at first mention

oedipal complex the female equivalent is electra complex

Ofcom Office of Communications - the broadcasting and telecommunications regulator or the media regulator

Offa eighth-century king of Mercia, best known for Offa's Dyke, a giant earthwork that separated the kingdom from Powys; **Offa** Office for Fair Access (to higher education)

Oo

offbeat, offhand, offside

Office for National Statistics ONS on second mention

Office of Fair Trading OFT on second mention

off-licence

Ofgem regulates the gas and electricity markets in Britain

Ofsted Office for Standards in Education, but normally no need to spell out

Ofwat regulates the water and sewerage industry in England and Wales

Oh not O except in phrases of invocation or hymn titles, eg O God, Our Help in Ages Past

oilfield, oilwell; oil production platform for production of oil; **oil rig** for exploration and drilling

oilseed rape

OK is OK; okay is not

Old Etonian

old Labour but **New Labour**

old master lc for paintings as well as ageing schoolteachers

Old Testament

O-levels GCE O-levels and CSEs were combined to become GCSEs

Olympic Games or just Olympics, or the Games

omelette not omelet

one one should generally find an alternative, preferably "you" (unless one is making fun of one's royal family)

one nation Tory

Onetel UK telecom company, not One.Tel, which is Australian

ongoing annoys a lot of people; prefer continuous or continual

online

Oo

only can be ambiguous if not placed next to the word or phrase modified: "I have only one ambition" is clearer than "I only have one ambition"; however, be sensible: do not change the song title to I Have Eyes Only for You.

Say "the only" or "one of the few" rather than "one of the only", which has found its way into the paper

on to not onto; Kingsley Amis, perhaps slightly overstating his case, argued: "I have found by experience that no one persistently using onto writes anything much worth reading" *See into*

Op 58, No 2 for classical music

Opec Organisation of the Petroleum Exporting Countries, but not necessary to spell out

opencast mine

Open (golf) is always the Open or Open Championship, never the British Open

ophthalmic

opossum

opposition, the

or need not be used when explaining or amplifying - rather than "the NUT, or National Union of Teachers" say "the NUT (National Union of Teachers)" or, even better, "the National Union of Teachers" at first mention and then just "the NUT" or "the union"

orangutan one word

ordinance decree; **ordnance** military supplies; **Ordnance Survey** Britain's national mapping agency (ordnance because such work was originally undertaken by the army)

oriented, disoriented not orientated, disorientated

Orkney not the Orkney Isles or the Orkneys

Oo

Ottakar's bookshop taken over by Waterstone's

O2, the (cap O, not the number 0) is the name of the former Millennium Dome

Ötzi the Iceman Europe's oldest natural human mummy (dated to about 3300BC), found in the Alps in 1991

Ouija TM; the generic name most commonly used, though not very satisfactory, is talking board

outback (Australia)

outed, outing take care with these terms: if we say, for example, that a paedophile was outed, we are equating that with a gay person being outed; use exposed or revealed instead

outgrow, outgun, outmanoeuvre

outpatient St Thomas' hospital in south London boasts the following styles, all on signs within a few yards of each other: Out Patients, Out-Patients, Outpatients, and outpatients. Across London, Barts adds Out-patients and OUTPATIENTS to the eclectic mix. In a further development, the NHS has all but eradicated the apostrophe

outre no accent

outside not "outside of"

outward bound outdoor adventure or adventure training are safer terms: we have been sued twice for reporting that people have died on "outward bound" courses that were nothing to do with the Outward Bound Trust

over not overly

overestimate, overstate are frequently confused with underestimate or understate

overreact, override, overrule and most other words with the prefix "over" do not need a hyphen

Oxford comma *See Grammar & punctuation*

Oo

oxymoron does not just vaguely mean self-contradictory; an oxymoron is a figure of speech in which apparently contradictory terms are used in conjunction, such as bittersweet, "darkness visible" (Paradise Lost), "the living dead" (The Waste Land); one of Margaret Atwood's characters thought "interesting Canadian" was an oxymoron

Pp

66 My pet hate is the use of the word 'individual' instead of person. It's not the only usage to have been smelted in that least promising crucible of language: the police press conference. (We hear plenty these days about males and females, rather than men and women.) But it's the worst. It is bureaucratic, mechanical, dehumanising. It's a word designed to process people, not to recognise them. It has no place in journalism **99**

George Monbiot

Pp

pace Latin tag meaning "by the leave of", as a courteous nod to the views of a dissenting author, or "even acknowledging the existence of", not a clever way to say "such as"

Pacific Ocean

PacifiCorp part of ScottishPower

paean song of praise; **paeon** metrical foot of one long and three short syllables; **peon** peasant

page 1 etc but **Page 3 girl**

El País Spanish newspaper

palate roof of the mouth, sense of taste; **palette** used by an artist to mix paint; **pallet** hard bed, wooden frame moved by forklift truck

Palestine is best used for the occupied territories (the West Bank and Gaza); if referring to the whole area, including Israel, use "historic Palestine" (but Palestine for references to the area prior to 1948)

Palestinian Authority the authority, rather than PA, on second reference

palindrome A man, a plan, a canal. Panama!

Palme d'Or at the Cannes film festival

Palme, Olof (1927-86) Swedish prime minister who was assassinated in a Stockholm street (not Olaf)

panama hat

Pandora's box

panelled, panelling, panellist two Ls

panjandrum a pretentious or self-important person in authority

Panjshir valley of Afghanistan

pantyhose not pantihose

paparazzo plural paparazzi; named after a character in Federico (not Frederico) Fellini's 1960 film La Dolce Vita

Pp

paperboy, **papergirl** but **paper round**

papier-mache no accents

paraffin rather than kerosene

parallel, **paralleled**

Paralympic Games or just Paralympics

paraphernalia takes a singular verb: I save all the paraphernalia that accompanies every box set

parentheses *See Grammar & punctuation: brackets*

Parker Bowles, Camilla no hyphen

Parkinson's disease

Parkinson's law "Work expands so as to fill the time available for its completion"

parliament, **parliamentary** but cap up those parliaments referred to by their name in the relevant language, eg Bundestag, Duma, Folketing, Knesset

Parma ham but **parmesan cheese**

Parthenon marbles official name, recognised by both Britain and Greece, for the Elgin marbles

part-time

partwork a series of regularly published supplements or magazines

party lc in name of organisation, eg Monster Raving Loony party

Pashtuns (singular Pashtun; they speak Pashtu) make up about 40% of the Afghan population (called Pathans during the British Raj); a significant proportion of Pakistan's population is also Pashtun

passerby plural passersby

passive voice strive for active verbs, especially in headlines: compare "my hamster was eaten by Freddie Starr" with "Freddie Starr ate my hamster"

Pp

Passport Agency now part of the Identity and Passport Service

password

past in phrases such as the past few weeks, the past year

pâté with accents

Patent Office now the Intellectual Property Office, responsible for copyright, designs, patents and trademarks

patients are discharged from hospital, not released

payback, **payday**, **payoff**, **payout**, **paywall** all one word

peacekeeper, **peacetime**

Peak District

Pearl Harbor US placenames (but not buildings or organisations) take American English spellings

peccadillo plural peccadilloes

pedaller cyclist: **peddler** drug dealer; **pedlar** hawker

pedalo plural pedalos

pedro giménez white grape grown in South America; **pedro ximénez** white grape grown in Spain (and type of sherry)

peers in historical pieces should be given their titles only if they had received them at the time, ie Herbert Asquith's Liberal government and Margaret Thatcher's Tory government (not Lord Asquith's, Lady Thatcher's) - they had not yet been given peerages.

Avoid the construction "Lady Helena Kennedy": in this case we would write Lady Kennedy or Helena Kennedy, or - if you really think people will not recognise her from the title alone - Lady (Helena) Kennedy

peewit

peking duck

pendant noun, **pendent** adjective

Pp

peninsula noun, **peninsular** adjective

penknife

pensioners not "old age pensioners" or "OAPs"; older people is preferable to "elderly people" or (even worse) "the elderly".

While this term is useful in headlines, it should be avoided in text as a description of an individual. As one of our readers notes: "This usage defines older people by their non-participation in the workforce and immediately typifies them as dependants or drains on the public purse. Rupert Murdoch and Michael Caine are never described as 'pensioners' because they are perceived as still contributing to the economy, so does the term only apply to the little people?" Reporters should ask what job people used to do and then describe them as a retired banker/powerboat racer or former whatever (including homemaker)

peony flower

Pepsi-Cola TM; a brand of cola; the company is PepsiCo

per avoid; use English: "She earns £30,000 a year" is better than "per year". If you must use it, the Latin preposition is followed by another Latin word, eg per capita, not per head. Exception: miles per hour, which we write as mph

per cent % in headlines and copy

percentage rises seem to give us a lot of problems: an increase from 3% to 5% is a 2 percentage point increase or a 2-point increase, not a 2% increase; any sentence saying "such and such rose or fell by X%" should be considered and checked carefully

Pérez de Cuéllar, Javier Peruvian diplomat and former UN secretary general

performance-related pay

Performing Right Society not Rights; now known as PRS for Music

permissible

Peronists supporters of the nationalist/populist ideology of the late Argentinian president Juan Domingo Perón

personal equity plans were known as Peps

persons No! They are people, even if they are the luckiest persons in the world

Perspex TM

peshmerga Kurdish armed fighters (it means "those who face death")

phenomenon plural phenomena

Philippines inhabited by Filipinos (male) and Filipinas (female); adjective Filipino for both sexes, but Philippine for, say, a Philippine island or the Philippine president

Philips electronics company; **Phillips** auctioneers, screwdriver

philistine lc unless you are talking about the Old Testament Philistines

Phnom Penh

phone hacking no hyphen for the noun, but hyphenated when used adjectivally, eg the PCC responded with its usual vigour to the phone-hacking scandal

phoney not phony

phosphorus not phosphorous

photocall, photocopy, photofit, photojournalist but **photo-finish** and **photo opportunity**

pi the ratio of the circumference of a circle to its diameter, as every schoolgirl knows

picket noun (one who pickets), not picketer; picketed, picketing

piecework

pigeonhole verb or noun: I will not be pigeonholed as someone who puts everyone in a pigeonhole

Pigs should not be used as an acronym for Portugal, Ireland (or Italy), Greece and Spain in stories about eurozone countries whose economies are deemed more embattled than others

pigsty plural pigsties

Pilates fitness exercises

pill, the (contraceptive)

pillbox

Pimm's the most popular version is Pimm's No 1 cup, which has gin as its base (the others are or were No 2, whisky; No 3, brandy; No 4, rum; No 5, rye; and No 6, vodka)

pin or **pin number** (we realise pin stands for personal identification number), not Pin or PIN number

pinstripe suit, not pinstriped

pipebomb, pipeline

Pissarro, Camille (1830-1903) French impressionist painter; his son Lucien (1863-1944) was also an artist

pixelated an image divided into visible pixels, the basic unit of representation on a television or computer screen, or to display a person or object in pixels to disguise their identity; **pixilated** drunk

PKK Kurdistan Workers' party

placename

plane a higher plane, not a higher plain (unless literally)

planets take initial cap: Mercury, Venus, Earth, Mars, Jupiter, Saturn, Uranus, Neptune (note that Pluto is now classified as a dwarf planet, along with Ceres and Eris); the sun and the Earth's moon are lc, but named moons are capped up: Europa, Io, etc

planning not "forward planning"

Planning Inspectorate handles planning inquiries and appeals in England and Wales

Pp

plaster of paris

plateau plural plateaux

playwright although they write

Play-Doh TM but you can say play-dough

play down rather than "downplay"

playing the race card an overused phrase

play-off

PlayStation

plc not PLC

plea, **pledge** words used all the time by journalists (particularly when writing headlines), but only rarely by normal people; **pleaded** not pled

plebeian not plebian

plethora an excess, not just a lot

P&O

pocketbook, **pocketknife** but **pocket money**

poet laureate Carol Ann Duffy took over from Andrew Motion in 2009

poetry A suggested method is to separate the lines with spaces and a slash; italics are acceptable, though not essential:
I struck the board and cry'd, 'No more; / I will abroad.' / What, shall I ever sigh and pine? / My lines and life are free; free as the rode, / Loose as the winde, as large as store.

point-to-point

pointe (ballet); on pointe, not on point or en pointe

Pokémon

Polari a form of language used mostly by gay men and lesbians, derived in part from slang used by sailors, actors and prostitutes and popularised in the 1960s BBC radio comedy Round the

Pp

Horne by the characters Julian and Sandy. Example: "Vada the dolly eke on the bona omee ajax" (Look at the gorgeous face on that nice man over there); naff is an example of Polari that has passed into more general use, as are butch, camp and dizzy

Polaroid

pole position or **on pole** means starting from the front row in a motor race, so be careful if using metaphorically; "poll position" is a common error

police forces Metropolitan police (the Met after first mention), West Midlands police, New York police department (NYPD at second mention), etc; but note Police Service of Northern Ireland

police ranks PC on all references to police constable (never WPC), other ranks full out and initial cap at first reference; thereafter just surname

police units lc: anti-terrorist branch, flying squad, fraud squad, special branch, vice squad

policymaker, **policymaking**

politburo

political correctness a term to be avoided on the grounds that it is, in Polly Toynbee's words, "an empty rightwing smear designed only to elevate its user"

political language quotation marks should be used around partisan or questionable phrases such as "big society", "broken Britain" and "death tax"

political parties lc for word "party"; abbreviate if necessary (for example in parliamentary reporting) as C, Lab, Lib Dem (two words), SNP (Scottish National party, not "Scottish Nationalist party"), Plaid Cymru, SDLP (Social Democratic and Labour party), SF (Sinn Féin), UUP (Ulster Unionist party), DUP (Democratic Unionist party), Ukip (UK Independence party)

Pp

pollack (not pollock) fish

poncey not poncy

pond not a terribly witty way to refer to the Atlantic ("on the other side of the pond") which, in the words of one Guardian writer, is "smug, hackneyed, old-fashioned, inaccurate and generally crap"

poo but you might **pooh-pooh** something

pop art

pope, the and **papacy, pontiff**; not always necessary to give his name in full

poppadom

Portakabin, Portaloo TM; say portable building, portable toilets

portland cement, portland stone

Porthmadog not Portmadoc

Port of London authority PLA on second mention

postal workers not postmen

postcode

Postcomm UK postal services regulator; its full name (which you do not need to use) is Postal Services Commission

postgraduate no hyphen

Post-it TM

postmodern, postmodernist

postmortem one word, as adjective or noun

Post Office cap up the organisation, but you buy stamps in a post office or sub-post office

postwar but make it clear which war you are talking about

pound in text, £ only when figures are used (Britain saves the pound; Oliver saved £1); pound (weight) abbreviates to lb, eg 2lb

Pp

POV abbreviation for point of view

Pov term coined by a Guardian journalist to depict laboured attempts to produce synonyms by writers seeking what Fowler called "elegant variation" (and Orwell "inelegant variation"), often descending into cliche or absurdity. Thus Dalí becomes "the moustachioed surrealist" and Ireland "the cockatoo-shaped landmass". Pov, incidentally, stands for "popular orange vegetable". *You can try to decipher some Povs in our quiz at the end of this section*

PoW abbreviation for prisoner of war

Powergen

powerpop one word; musical genre defined by nostalgia for the 60s, in the form of chiming electric guitars and vocal harmonies. Its proponents often profess to being inspired by the Beatles and the Byrds, but are never as good as either

practice noun, **practise** verb

practising homosexual
Do not use this expression, or the equally grotesque "active homosexual"; where it is necessary to discuss someone's sex life, for example a story about gay clergy, it is possible to use other expressions, eg the Anglican church demands celibacy from gay clergy but permits the laity to have sexually active relationships

pre- redundant in such newly fashionable words as pre-booked, pre-reserved, pre-ordered, and even pre-rehearsed

precis singular and plural

predilection not predeliction

pre-eminent

prefab, prefabricated

premier should be used only when constitutionally correct (eg leaders of Australian states or Canadian provinces), therefore

Pp

not for Britain - do not use in headlines for British prime minister. The Chinese traditionally give their prime minister the title of premier, eg Premier Wen Jiabao. Bermuda also has a premier rather than a prime minister

premiere no accent

Premier League (no longer FA Premier League or Premiership) in England; in Scotland it was briefly the Premierleague, now the Scottish Premier League or more commonly SPL

premises of buildings and logic

premium bonds

prenuptial or (if you must) **prenup**

prepositions *See Grammar & punctuation*

prepubescent

pre-Raphaelite

presently means soon, not at present

president lc except in title: President Obama, but Barack Obama, the US president

press, the singular: eg the British press is a shining example to the rest of the world

Press Complaints Commission PCC on second mention

Press Gazette formerly UK Press Gazette

pressure use put pressure on or press to mean apply pressure, ie not "the Baggies pressured [or pressurised] the Wolves defence"

prestigious having prestige: nothing wrong with this, despite what wise old subeditors used to tell us

Pret a Manger food; **pret a porter** fashion

preteen

pretext by its nature false, so while you may think that Tony

Pp

Blair went to war on a pretext, it is tautologous to say he did so on a false one

prevaricate "to speak or act falsely or evasively with intent to deceive" (Collins); often confused with procrastinate, to put something off

preventive rather than preventative

prewar but make clear which war you are talking about

PricewaterhouseCoopers call it PwC after first mention; PwC Consulting, which for some reason was widely ridiculed for changing its name to Monday, was bought by IBM

prima donna plural prima donnas

prima facie not italicised

primary care trusts to be abolished as part of the latest NHS shakeup

primate another word for archbishop; primate of All England: archbishop of Canterbury; primate of England: archbishop of York; but "the primate" on second reference

primates higher members of the order Primates, essentially apes and humans

prime minister David Cameron, the prime minister; not prime minister David Cameron or the American English "prime minister Cameron"

primitive should not be used to describe tribal people *See stone age*

Prince Charles or **the Prince of Wales** at first mention; thereafter the prince

Prince's Trust

principal first in importance; **principle** standard of conduct

principality should not be used to describe Wales

prise apart open (not prize)

Pp

prisoners not inmates

prison officer not warder, a term that the Prison Officers' Association regards as "degrading, insulting and historically inaccurate" (the Home Office changed it from warder in 1922)

Prison Service but **immigration service** lc (it is properly called the Immigration and Nationality Directorate)

private finance initiative PFI on second mention

private member's bill

privy council but **privy counsellor**

prize Man Booker prize, Nobel prize, Whitbread prize, etc

prizefighter, **prizewinner** but **prize money**

proactive hideous jargon word - do not use with a hyphen. Or without one

probe a dental implement, not an inquiry or investigation

pro-choice not pro-abortion

procrastinate to delay or defer; often confused with prevaricate

Procter & Gamble not Proctor & Gamble

procurator fiscal Scottish public prosecutor; the Crown Office and Procurator Fiscal Service (COPFS), in Scotland, more wide-ranging than the Crown Prosecution Service in England and Wales, is responsible for the prosecution of crime, investigation of sudden or suspicious deaths, and investigation of complaints against the police

prodigal means wasteful or extravagant, not a returned wanderer; the confusion arises from the biblical parable of the prodigal son. A very common mistake, often used for example to describe a footballer who has re-signed for a former club

profile a noun, not a verb

program (computer); otherwise **programme**

prohibition lc for US prohibition (1920-33), a result of the 18th amendment of the US constitution

pro-life do not use to mean anti-abortion

Proms concerts; **proms** seafronts

prone face down; **supine** face up

proofreader, proofreading

propeller not propellor

prophecy noun, **prophesy** verb

pros and cons

prostate gland; **prostrate** lying face down

protege male and female, no accents

protest against, over or about not, for example, "protest the election result", which has appeared on our front page

Protestant

protester not protestor

proven proved is the past tense of prove; beware the creeping "proven", a term in Scottish law ("not proven") and in certain English idioms, eg "proven record"

province should not be used to describe Northern Ireland. Ulster is one of the four provinces of Ireland, comprising nine counties - six in Northern Ireland, and three in the Republic of Ireland (Cavan, Donegal and Monaghan)

proviso plural provisos

Ps and Qs

public schools are actually private schools, so that is what we should call them

publicly not publically

public-private partnership PPP on second mention

Pp

Puffa TM; say padded or quilted jacket

pundit self-appointed expert

purchase as a noun, perhaps, but the verb is buy

put athletics; **putt** golf

Pwllheli

pygmy plural pygmies, lc except for members of Equatorial African ethnic group

pyjamas not pajamas

pyrrhic victory

Quiz

Spot that synonym

Now you know what a Pov is, can you work out who or what these newspaper phrases refer to?

1. "The maverick old warhorse of the London left"
   - ○ Billy Bragg
   - ○ Billy the pitch-clearing hero of the 1923 FA Cup final
   - ○ Ken Livingstone
2. "The incorrigible, aristocratic puppet"
   - ○ Nick Clegg
   - ○ George Osborne
   - ○ Lord Charles
3. "The Christian emblem"
   - ○ Crucifix
   - ○ The pope
   - ○ The Bible
4. "Britain's newest double act"
   - ○ The Milibands
   - ○ Jedward
   - ○ Cameron and Clegg
5. "The north-west seaside town whose charms have faded in recent years"
   - ○ Southport
   - ○ Blackpool
   - ○ New Brighton
6. "The popular party drug"
   - ○ Mephedrone
   - ○ Ecstasy
   - ○ Cocaine
7. "The dominant roadside recovery operator"
   - ○ RAC
   - ○ AA
   - ○ Green Flag

8. "The famous, some might say infamous, chopped pork and ham product"
   ○ Pork pie
   ○ Spam
   ○ Sausage roll

9. "The world's largest atom smasher; the massive machine; the largest, most complex scientific instrument in the world" (all in one story)
   ○ The iPad
   ○ Large Hadron Collider
   ○ Large hammer

10. "The pointy veg"
    ○ Parsnip
    ○ Asparagus
    ○ Carrot

11. "The pint-sized chart queen"
    ○ Little Boots
    ○ Kylie Minogue
    ○ Pixie Lott

12. "Henry VIII's go-getting but beheaded second wife"
    ○ Catherine of Aragon
    ○ Anne Boleyn
    ○ Kathryn Howard

13. "The world's favourite natural sweetener"
    ○ Sugar
    ○ Honey
    ○ Cash

14. "The embattled carmaker"
    ○ Toyota
    ○ Ford
    ○ Vauxhall

15. "The esteemed organs"
    ○ Liver and heart
    ○ Hammond and Roland
    ○ New York Times and Wall Street Journal

Qq

66 English - or do we call it globish now? - is defaced by so many excrescences that one would need a lengthy essay even to start to tackle them. Here are three from the top of my head. First, mull. Until recently, one might have mulled over whether to include this. Now we simply mull it. Bring the over back pronto. Second, extraordinary: as used by the BBC's political editor, Nick Robinson, in every broadcast, and by desperate intro writers. Remember: if it wasn't extraordinary, it probably wouldn't be leading the news. Finally, train station. What's wrong with station, or perhaps railway station? Ah, you will say, what about bus stations? A modern term, I fancy. Didn't we used to call them bus depots or terminals, or does that add another layer of confusion? Suggestion: use station, by default, to mean trains; never, pace the Guardian style guide, say train station; spell out bus station if you must; best of all, let's adopt the nice Turkish word *otogar*. The Turks know how to do a proper bus terminal. Our linguistic confusion reflects the fact that our dilapidated, apologetic otogars are really just hangouts for drunks and the mentally deranged through which buses occasionally pass **99**

Stephen Moss

al-Qaida (it means "the base")

Qantas Australian airline

qat not kat or khat

QC without comma, eg Cherie Booth QC

QE2, **QM2** liners

QinetiQ arms company

Qom city in Iran; it is not compulsory to call it "the holy city of Qom"

Qualifications and Curriculum Authority QCA after first mention

quango plural quangos; stands for quasi-autonomous non-governmental organisation, but no need to spell out

quantum jump, quantum leap cliches best avoided in any area other than physics (unless you are referring to the cult 70s band Quantum Jump or the cult 90s TV series Quantum Leap)

quarterdeck, quartermaster

Québécois not Quebeckers

Queen, the if it is necessary to say so, she is Her Majesty or HM, never HRH

Queen's birthday honours list

Queen's Club in London

Queens' College, Cambridge

Queen's College, Oxford its official name is The Queen's College (named in honour of Queen Philippa in 1341)

Queen's Park the London tube station has an apostrophe

Queen's Park Scotland's oldest football club, winners of the Scottish Cup 10 times in the 19th century and twice runners-up in the FA Cup

Queens Park Rangers (no apostrophe) English football club

Qq

Queen's speech

Queen's University Belfast

queueing not queuing

quicklime, **quicksand**, **quicksilver**

quixotic

quiz a suspect is questioned, not quizzed (however tempting for headline purposes)

quizshow

Quorn TM

quotation marks *See Grammar & punctuation*

quotes
From the editor:

If a reader reads something in direct quotation marks in the Guardian he/she is entitled to believe that the reporter can vouch directly for the accuracy of the quote.

Copying quotes out of other newspapers without any form of attribution is simply bad journalism, never mind legally risky. If, where there are no libel issues, you're going to repeat quotes, then always say where they came from. It won't be much help in a legal action, but at least the reader can evaluate the reliability of the source. A quote in the Sunday Sport may - who knows - count for less than one from the Wall Street Journal.

If we're taking quotes from the radio or television it is our general policy to include an attribution. This matters less if it is a pooled interview or news conference that happens to be covered by, say, the BBC or Sky. If the quote comes from an exclusive interview on a radio or TV programme (eg, Today, Channel 4 News or Newsnight) we should always include an attribution.

Some further guidelines:

Take care with direct speech: our readers should be confident that words appearing in quotation marks accurately represent

Qq

the actual words uttered by the speaker, although ums and ahems can be removed and bad grammar improved. If you aren't sure of the exact wording, use indirect speech.

Where a lot of material has been left out, start off a new quote with: "He added: ... ", or signify this with an ellipsis.

Take particular care when extracting from printed material, for example a minister's resignation letter.

Avoid "that" quotes, ie The prosecutors maintained that "this was not a trial about freedom of the internet. Instead, a serious issue has been raised about the rights of the individual." There is no reason to introduce a complete direct quote of this kind with "that". It should be The prosecutors maintained: "This was not a trial ... " etc

Colons, rather than commas, should be used to introduce quotes, ie Guardian Style says: "Please use colons, not commas;" not Guardian Style says, "Please use ... " etc. We are writing a newspaper, not a novel.

Think about where the attribution goes, and avoid this kind of thing:

"Gordon Brown is a bully and a liar. I have had numerous complaints about his aggressive behaviour," said Mrs Pratt.

"The prime minister is completely out of control, and everyone inside No 10 knows it," added Andrew Rawnsley.

It's extremely annoying to get to the end of the second par and find out it is a different speaker, because it reads as a continuation of the words of Mrs Pratt.

As a general rule, and particularly with lengthy quotations, it is better to start with the attribution, so the reader does not have to engage in a series of mental double-takes trying to find out who is supposed to be saying what. It should be:

Mrs Pratt said: "Gordon Brown is a bully and a liar. I have had numerous complaints about his aggressive behaviour."

Andrew Rawnsley added: "The prime minister is completely out of control, and everyone inside No 10 knows it."

Avoid quoting words when it is unnecessary to do so, like

Qq

this: Benítez said he was "angry" that Liverpool were being written out of the title race.

Yes, maybe, quotation marks if he was "incandescent", or "spitting with rage" - but it is completely unnecessary to use quotation marks for mundane words and unexceptional quotes. They are even finding their way into headlines, which looks awful.

Similarly: MPs said they had not seen any evidence that Andy Coulson "knew that phone hacking was taking place". There is no need for the quotation marks, which are splattered like confetti across the paper and website every day but should be used only when it is necessary, in both copy and headlines.

Qur'an holy book of Islam (not Koran); regarded as the word of God, having been recited by the prophet Muhammad, so in the eyes of Muslims it is wrong to suggest that the prophet "wrote" the Qur'an

Qureia, Ahmed Palestinian politician, popularly known as Abu Ala (which means "father of Ala" - it is not a nom de guerre); he was prime minister of the Palestinian Authority until Fatah was defeated by Hamas in the parliamentary elections

Rr

66 An omnipresent and omnipotent figure now stalks the land - and our language. When it wants certain things the politicians must jump to it; when it doesn't like what it gets, we all know about it. I refer to the markets, that singular and all-knowing entity that must always be placated, at whatever cost. Or so the radio, the telly and the newspapers tell us. It's a nonsense of course: markets are merely a reflection of what investors - some clever, some dumb, some with attention spans no bigger than their BlackBerrys - think at any moment. And they can be badly wrong. Or did we not learn that lesson already? 99

Aditya Chakrabortty

Rr

race card as in "play the race card"; has become a cliche, especially at election times when someone is certain to be accused of it

racecard lists **racehorses** at a **racetrack**

race-fixing

RAC Foundation should be described on first mention as a pro-motoring thinktank

racial terminology
A person's race should only be included if relevant to the story. The words black and Asian should not be used as nouns, but as adjectives: black people rather than "blacks", an Asian woman rather than "an Asian", etc.

Say African-Caribbean rather than Afro-Caribbean. Use the word "immigrant" with great care, not only because it is often incorrectly used to describe people who were born in Britain, but also because it has been used negatively for so many years

rack one's brains for something; **rack and ruin; racked** by guilt, with pain, not wracked

rackets not racquets, except in club titles

Rada Royal Academy of Dramatic Art

Radio 1, Radio 2, Radio 3, Radio 4, 5 Live, 6 Music, BBC7

radiographer takes x-rays; **radiologist** reads them

Radio Telefís Éireann Irish public broadcasting corporation

radius plural radii

raft something Huck Finn and Jim were on when they floated down the river; do not say "a raft of measures", which has very rapidly become a cliche (particularly in political reporting)

Raid redundant array of independent disks (data storage)

railway station train station is acceptable, indeed more widely used nowadays, although it still sounds wrong to some readers (and writers)

Rr

Rainbows for girls from five (four in Northern Ireland) to seven, at which point they may become Brownies

raincoat, rainfall, rainproof

Ramadan month of fasting for Muslims

Ramsay, Gordon ex-footballing chef; note that England's World Cup-winning manager in 1966 was **Alf Ramsey**

Ramsey Street where good Neighbours become good friends

R&B whether you are listening to Bo Diddley or Beyoncé

Range Rover no hyphen

ranks for police and armed forces: spell out in full first time, then just use the surname

Rangers not Glasgow Rangers

rarefy, rarefied

rateable

Rawlplug TM

Ray-Ban TM; it's OK to call them Ray-Bans

re or re-?
Use re- (with hyphen) when followed by the vowels e or u (not pronounced as yu): eg re-entry, re-examine, re-urge. Use re (no hyphen) when followed by the vowels a, i, o or u (pronounced as yu), or any consonant: eg rearm, rearrange, reassemble, reiterate, reorder, reread, reuse, rebuild, reconsider. Exceptions (where confusion with another word would arise): re-cover/recover, re-form/reform, re-creation/recreation, re-sign/resign

realpolitik

rear admiral Rear Admiral Horatio Hornblower at first mention, thereafter Admiral Hornblower in leading articles, otherwise just Hornblower

received pronunciation (RP) a traditionally prestigious accent, associated with public schools and used by an estimated 3% of the population of England, also known as BBC English, Oxford English or the Queen's English; nothing to do with Standard English, which includes written as well as spoken language and can be (indeed, normally is) spoken with a regional accent

recent avoid: if the date is relevant, use it

recur not reoccur

Red Crescent, Red Cross

redbrick university the original six were Birmingham, Bristol, Leeds, Liverpool, Manchester and Sheffield

redshirts formally known as the United Front for Democracy Against Dictatorship (UDD), they were at the forefront of protests against the Thai government in 2010; their opponents, loyal to the Bangkok regime, were the yellowshirts

referendum plural referendums

reforestation not reafforestation

re-form to form again; **reform** to change for the better. We should not take the initiators' use of the word at its face value, particularly in cases where we believe no improvement is likely. The latest set of changes to education or the health service may, or may not, be reforms

refute this much abused word should be used only when an argument is disproved; otherwise contest, deny, rebut

regalia plural, of royalty; royal regalia is tautologous

regard with regard to, not with regards to (but of course you give your regards to Broadway)

Regent's Park in London

regime no accent

regional assemblies abolition of the eight bodies representing English regions outside London, along with the regional development agencies, was announced in 2010

register office not registry office – the first thing reporters used to be taught on local newspapers, although you still see the mistake

registrar general

regrettable

rein in not reign in

reinstate

religious right

Renaissance, the

reopen

repellant noun, **repellent** adjective: you fight repellent insects with an insect repellant

repertoire an individual's range of skills or roles;
repertory a selection of works that a theatre or dance company might perform

replaceable

report the Lawrence report, etc; use report on or inquiry into but not report into, ie not "a report into health problems"

reported speech *See Grammar & punctuation*

republicans lc (except for US and other political parties)

reread

residents has a rather old-fashioned feel to it, especially in the deadly form "local residents"; on the whole, better to call them local people

resistance, resistance fighters *See terrorism, terrorists*

restaurateur not restauranteur

résumé

retail prices index (RPI) prices not price, but normally no need to spell it out. No longer the official measure of inflation (that is

Rr

the consumer price index), but still used for uprating pensions and other state benefits

Rethink formerly the National Schizophrenia Fellowship

reticent unwilling to speak; do not confuse with reluctant, as in this example from the paper: "Like most graduates of limited financial means, Louise Clark was reticent about handing over a huge wad of dosh"

Reuters

the Rev at first mention, thereafter use courtesy title: eg the Rev Joan Smith, subsequently Ms Smith if honorific is needed; never say Reverend Smith, the Reverend Smith or Rev Smith

reveille

Revelation last book in the New Testament: not Revelations, a very common error; its full name is The Revelation of St John the Divine

Revenue & Customs acceptable shorthand for HM Revenue and Customs, formed in 2005 from a merger of the Inland Revenue and HM Customs and Excise

Rheims

rheumatoid arthritis not rheumatism or arthritis, but can be abbreviated to RA after first mention

Rhodes scholar

RIBA (not Riba) Royal Institute of British Architects

rice paddies tautologous, as *padi* is the Malay word for rice; so it should be paddy fields or simply paddies

Richter scale expresses the magnitude of an earthquake, but now largely superseded by the moment magnitude scale

rickety

ricochet, ricocheted, ricocheting

riffle to flick through a book, newspaper or magazine; often confused with **rifle**, to search or ransack and steal from, eg rifle goods from a shop

right, the right wing, rightwinger nouns; rightwing adjective

ringfence, **ringtone**

rivers lc, eg river Thames, Amazon river or just Thames, Amazon

riveted, **riveting**

RNIB Royal National Institute of Blind People (no longer "the Blind")

roadmap has become a cliche unless you are actually talking about a map

roadside

rob you rob a person or a bank, using force or the threat of violence; but you steal a car or a bag of money

Rock cap if referring to Gibraltar

rock'n'roll one word

role no accent

Rollerblade TM; say inline skates

rollercoaster one word

rollover noun (lottery rollover)

Rolls-Royce

Roman Catholic
The archbishop of Birmingham, Cardiff, Glasgow, Liverpool, St Andrew's, Southwark and Westminster: it is not normally necessary to say Roman Catholic (as there is no Anglican equivalent).

The Roman Catholic bishop of Aberdeen, Argyll, Lancaster, Plymouth, Portsmouth, Shrewsbury (for all of which there are Anglican bishops).

Unless obviously Roman Catholic from the context, say the Roman Catholic bishop of Brentwood, Clifton, Dunkeld,

Rr

Galloway, Hexham and Newcastle, Leeds, Menevia, Middlesbrough, Motherwell, Northampton, Nottingham, Paisley and Salford.

In a UK setting use Roman Catholic in describing Roman Catholic organisations and individuals and wherever an Anglican could argue ambiguity (eg "the Catholic church"). But Catholic is enough in most overseas contexts, eg Ireland, France, Italy, Latin America

Romania

Romany noun, adjective; Roma plural

Romeo cap up, whether referring to Juliet's boyfriend or using generically ("he's the office Romeo")

roofs plural of roof (not rooves, which has appeared in the paper)

Rooney, Coleen not Colleen

Roosevelt, Franklin Delano (FDR) US president 1933-45; **Roosevelt, Theodore** US president 1901-09

ro-ro roll-on, roll-off ferry

Rorschach test psychological test based on the interpretation of inkblots

rottweiler

roughshod

routeing or routing? They are routeing buses through the city centre after the routing of the protesters

Rovers Return, the (no apostrophe) Coronation Street's pub; it sells Newton & Ridley beer

Royal Academy of Arts usually known simply as the Royal Academy; members are known as Royal Academicians (RA)

Royal Air Force or RAF

Royal Ballet

Royal Botanic Garden (Edinburgh); **Royal Botanic Gardens** (London), also known as Kew Gardens or simply Kew

Royal College of Surgeons the college or the royal college is preferable to the RCS on subsequent mention

royal commission

Royal Courts of Justice

royal family

Royal Institute of International Affairs also known as Chatham House *See Chatham House rule*

Royal Logistic Corps not Logistics

Royal London hospital

Royal Mail for the company, not "the Royal Mail"

Royal Marines marines after first mention

Royal Navy or the navy

Royal Opera, **Royal Opera House**

royal parks

Royal Society of Arts RSA after first mention; its full name is Royal Society for the Encouragement of Arts, Manufactures and Commerce

RSPB, RSPCA do not normally need to be spelt out, but our readers outside the UK deserve a brief explanation of what they are

rubber strictly, a series of card games or sporting encounters, not an individual match; so if (say) Great Britain's tennis team lost the first three matches of a five-match Davis Cup tie, you would have a dead rubber (but it would be wrong to call the fourth or fifth matches "dead rubbers")

Rubens, Peter Paul (1577-1640) Flemish painter

Rubicon as in Clegg crossed his personal Rubicon

Rr

rugby league, rugby union

Rule, Britannia!

runoff, runup (nouns) no hyphen

rupee Indian currency; **rupiah** Indonesian currency

russian roulette

Ss

66 'Scientists claim' is a neon marker for rubbish journalism written by someone who doesn't understand the process of science. Scientists do experiments, they describe those experiments clearly, they describe the results, and then they explain how those results support a theory. Any meaningful explanation of a scientific claim needs to say what was done, what was measured, what the results were, and why they support a theory. When people write 'scientists claim', what they usually mean is: 'I don't understand this, I can't explain it, and yet weirdly, I seem to be writing about it in a national newspaper' **99**

Ben Goldacre

Ss

Saatchi brothers Maurice (now Lord Saatchi) and Charles (the one with the gallery) founded M&C Saatchi in 1994 after leaving Saatchi & Saatchi, the advertising agency best known for the slogan "Labour isn't working" in the 1979 general election campaign

saccharin noun, **saccharine** adjective

sacrilegious not sacreligious

Sad seasonal affective disorder

Sadler's Wells

al-Sadr, Moqtada creator of the Mahdi army, or as the magazine Red Pepper described it: "Moqtada al-Sadr's not-so-barmy army"

Safeway

Sahara no need to add "desert"

said normally preferable to added, commented, declared, pointed out, ejaculated, etc; you can avoid too many "saids", whether quoting someone or in reported speech, quite easily *See Grammar & punctuation: reported speech*

Sainsbury's for the stores; the company's name is J Sainsbury plc

Saint in running text should be spelt in full: Saint John, Saint Paul. For names of towns, churches, etc, abbreviate as St (no point) eg St Mirren, St Stephen's church. In French placenames a hyphen is needed, eg St-Nazaire, Ste-Suzanne, Stes-Maries-de-la-Mer

St Andrews no apostrophe for golf or university

St Catharine's College, Cambridge; **St Catherine's College, Oxford**

St James Park home of Exeter City; **St James' Park** home of Newcastle United; **St James's Park** royal park in London

St John Ambulance not St John's and no longer "Brigade"

St Katharine Docks London

Ss

St Martin-in-the-Fields London

Saint-Saëns, Camille (1835-1921) French composer

St Thomas' hospital in London; not St Thomas's

sake Japanese rice wine

saleable

Salvation Army not the Sally Army

salvo plural salvoes

Samaritans the organisation has dropped "the" from its name

sambuca

Samoa formerly known as Western Samoa; do not confuse with American Samoa

Sana'a capital of Yemen

sanatorium (not sanitarium or sanitorium) plural sanatoriums

Sane mental illness charity

San Sebastián

San Serriffe island nation profiled in the Guardian on 1 April 1977; **sans serif** typeface

San Siro stadium Milan

São Paulo Brazilian city, not Sao Paolo

Sars severe acute respiratory syndrome

SAS Special Air Service, but not normally necessary to spell it out; its naval equivalent is the SBS

Satan but **satanist, satanism**

satnav

Sats standard assessment tasks; SATs scholastic aptitude tests (in the US, where they are pronounced as individual letters)

Saumarez Smith, Charles secretary and chief executive of the Royal Society of Arts

Ss

Savile, Jimmy DJ who fixed it for generations of children

Savile Club, **Savile Row** in London

Saville theatre in London, once owned by the Beatles' manager Brian Epstein and used for concerts in the 60s (Jimi Hendrix played there); now the Odeon Covent Garden cinema

SBS Special Boat Service; not normally necessary to spell it out

Scalextric often erroneously called "Scalectrix"

Scandinavia Denmark, Norway and Sweden; with the addition of Finland and Iceland, they constitute the Nordic countries

scapegoat a noun, not (yet) a verb

sceptic *See climate change terminology*

schadenfreude

scherzo plural scherzos

schizophrenia, **schizophrenic** should be used only in a medical context, never to mean in two minds, contradictory, or erratic, which is wrong, as well as offensive to people diagnosed with this illness; schizophrenic is an adjective, not a noun. After many years we have largely eradicated misuse of this term, although as recently as 2010 a columnist contrived to accuse the Conservatives of "untreatable ideological schizophrenia"

Schoenberg, Arnold (1874-1951) Austrian-born composer

schoolboy, **schoolchildren**, **schoolgirl**, **schoolroom**, **schoolteacher**

schools if in full, like this: Alfred Salter primary school, Rotherhithe; King's school, Macclesfield; Eton college, etc; often the generic part will not be necessary, so: Alfred Salter primary; King's, Macclesfield; Eton, etc

school years year 2, year 10, key stage 1, etc

Schröder, Gerhard former German chancellor

Schwarzenegger, Arnold Arnie is acceptable in headlines

Ss

scientific measurements

Take care: m in scientific terms stands for milli (1mW is 1,000th of a watt), while M denotes mega (1MW is a million watts); in such circumstances it is wise not to bung in another m when you mean million, so write out, for example, 10 million C.

amps A, volts V, watts W, kilowatts kW, megawatts MW, milliwatts mW, joules J, kilojoules kJ

scientific names in italics, with the first name (denoting the genus) capped, the second (denoting the species) lc: *Escherichia coli*, *Quercus robur*. The name can be shortened by using the first initial: *E coli*, *Q robur* (but we do not use a full point after the initial)

scientific terms some silly cliches to avoid: you might find it difficult to hesitate for a nanosecond (the shortest measurable human hesitation is probably about 250 million nanoseconds, a quarter of a second); "astronomical sums" when talking about large sums of money is rather dated (the national debt in pounds surpassed the standard astronomical unit of 93 million [miles] 100 years ago)

ScotchTape TM; say sticky tape

scotch broth, scotch egg, scotch mist, scotch whisky but Scotch argus butterfly

Scotland

The following was written by a Scot who works for the Guardian and lives in London. Letters expressing similar sentiments come from across Britain (and, indeed, from around the world):

We don't carry much coverage of events in Scotland and to be honest, even as an expat, that suits me fine. But I do care very much that we acknowledge that Scotland is a separate nation and in many ways a separate country. It has different laws, education system (primary, higher and further), local government, national government, sport, school terms, weather, property market and selling system, bank holidays,

Ss

banks and money, churches, etc.

If we really want to be a national newspaper then we need to consider whether our stories apply only to England (and Wales) or Britain, or Scotland only. When we write about teachers' pay deals, we should point out that we mean teachers in England and Wales; Scottish teachers have separate pay and management structures and union. When we write about it being half-term, we should remember that it's known as mid-term in Scotland. When we write about bank holiday sunshine/rain, we should remember that in Scotland the weather was probably different and it possibly wasn't even a bank holiday.

When we write about the English cricket team, we should be careful not to refer to it as "we" and "us". When the Scottish Cup final is played, we should perhaps consider devoting more than a few paragraphs at the foot of a page to Rangers winning their 100th major trophy (if it had been Manchester United we'd have had pages and pages with Bobby Charlton's all-time fantasy first XI and a dissertation on why English clubs are the best in Europe). Andy Murray is Scottish, as well as British, rather than Scottish when he loses and British when he wins.

These daily oversights come across to a Scot as arrogance. They also undermine confidence in what the paper is telling the reader

Scotland Office not Scottish Office

Scott, Charles Prestwich (1846-1932) editor of the Manchester Guardian for 57 years and its owner from 1907 until his death (his uncle, John Edward Taylor, had founded the paper in 1821). Scott, who was editor when the first "Style-book of the Manchester Guardian" – forerunner of this book (*See Appendix 4*) – appeared in 1928, is most famous for his statement "comment is free, but facts are sacred." *See Appendix 1*

WP Crozier recalled of Scott: "Once, when an article in type was shown to him because a certain sentence expressed a doubtful judgment, he noticed that the English was slovenly,

Ss

amended it, and then, being drawn on from sentence to sentence and becoming more and more dissatisfied, he made innumerable minute corrections until at last, having made a complete mess of the proof, he looked up and said gently: 'Dear X; of course, he's not a trained subeditor.'"

Scott, Sir George Gilbert (1811-78) architect who designed the Albert Memorial and Midland Grand hotel at St Pancras station

Scott, Sir Giles Gilbert (1880-1960) grandson of the above, responsible for red telephone boxes, Bankside power station (now Tate Modern), Waterloo bridge, and the Anglican cathedral in Liverpool

Scottish government although its legal name remains Scottish executive

Scottish parliament its members are MSPs

scottish terrier not scotch or Scots; once known as Aberdeen terrier

scouse, scouser

Scouts not Boy Scouts (in the UK, at least); the organisation is the Scout Association

Scoville scale system that measures the heat level of chillies

Scrabble TM

Scram secure continuous remote alcohol monitor, as sported in 2010 by Lindsay Lohan

scratchcard, swipecard

SCSI capped up even though generally pronounced "scuzzy"; it stands for small computer system interface

Sea of Japan as generally known; but South Korea calls it the East Sea, and North Korea calls it the East Sea of Korea

seal pups not baby seals for the same reason we don't call lambs baby sheep

Ss

Séamus, Seán note accents in Irish Gaelic; sean without a fada means old

seaplane, seaport, seashore, seaside, seaweed but **sea change, sea level, sea sickness**

search engine optimisation (SEO)
How to increase traffic to your website by ensuring that your content shows up prominently in Google and other online search engines, for example by including in headlines key terms that people are most likely to search for. To help, you can monitor such things as hot topics on Google and what is trending on Twitter *See keywords*

seas, oceans uc, eg Black Sea, Caspian Sea, Pacific Ocean

seasons spring, summer, autumn, winter are lowercase

seatbelt

second hand on a watch, but **secondhand** goods

secretary general

Secret Intelligence Service official name of MI6; may also be abbreviated to SIS after first mention

section 28 1988 law, widely regarded as homophobic, that said local authorities "shall not intentionally promote homosexuality or publish material with the intention of promoting homosexuality" or "promote the teaching in any maintained school of the acceptability of homosexuality as a pretended family relationship"; it was repealed in Scotland in 2000 and the rest of the UK in 2003

Security Service better known as MI5

seize not sieze

self-control, self-defence, self-esteem, self-respect

Selfridges no apostrophe

sell-off

Ss

Sellotape TM; say sticky tape

semicolon *See Grammar & punctuation*

semtex no longer necessary to cap this

Senate (US)

senior abbreviate to Sr not Sen or Snr, eg George Bush Sr

September 11 (9/11 is acceptable)
The official death toll of the victims of the Islamist terrorists
who hijacked four aircraft on 11 September 2001 is 2,976. The
figure does not include the 19 hijackers. Of this total, 2,605 died
in the twin towers of the World Trade Centre or on the ground
in New York City (of whom approximately 1,600 have been
identified), 246 died on the four aeroplanes, and 125 were killed
in the attack on the Pentagon.

The hijackers were: Fayez Ahmed, Mohamed Atta, Ahmed al-
Ghamdi, Hamza al-Ghamdi, Saeed al-Ghamdi, Hani Hanjour,
Nawaf al-Hazmi, Salem al-Hazmi, Ahmed al-Haznawi, Khalid al-
Mihdhar, Majed Moqed, Ahmed al-Nami, Abdulaziz al-Omari,
Marwan al-Shehhi, Mohannad al-Shehri, Wael al-Shehri, Waleed
al-Shehri, Satam al-Suqami, Ziad Jarrah (though dozens of
permutations of their names have appeared in the paper, we
follow Reuters style as for most Arabic transliterations)

sequined not sequinned

Serb noun, **Serbian** adjective

sergeant major Sergeant Major Trevor Prescott on first mention,
subsequently Sgt Maj (not RSM or CSM) Prescott in leading
articles; elsewhere just surname

Serious Fraud Office SFO on second mention

Serious Organised Crime Agency Soca after first mention

serjeant at arms

services, the (armed forces)

settler should be confined to those Israeli Jews living in

Ss

settlements across the 1967 green line, ie in the occupied territories

set to
It is very tempting to use this, especially in headlines, when we think something might happen, but aren't all that sure; try to resist this temptation. It is even less excusable when we do know that something is going to happen: one of our readers counted no fewer than 16 uses of the phrase in the paper in two days; in almost every case, the words could have been replaced with "will", or by simply leaving out the "set", eg "the packs are set to come into force as part of the house-selling process".

The first readers' editor of the Guardian put it like this: "The expression 'set to', to mean about to, seems likely to ... is often used to refer to something that, though expected, is not absolutely certain to happen. It is a rascally expression which one of the readers who have learned to groan at the sight of it describes as an all-purpose term removing any precision of meaning from the sentence containing it"

sexing up is what happens in dodgy dossiers and not, we hope, our publications.

From the editor: "Guardian readers would rather we did give them the unvarnished truth - or our best stab at it. It seems obvious enough. But inside many journalists - this goes for desk editors as much as reporters - there is a little demon prompting us to make the story as strong and interesting as possible, if not more so. We drop a few excitable adjectives around the place. We overegg. We may even sex it up.

"Strong stories are good. So are interesting stories. But straight, accurate stories are even better. Readers who stick with us over any length of time would far rather judge what we write by our own Richter scale of news judgments and values than feel that we're measuring ourselves against the competition. Every time we flam a story up we disappoint somebody - usually a reader who thought the Guardian was different.

Ss

"We should be different. Of course we compete fiercely in the most competitive newspaper market in the world. Of course we want to sell as many copies as possible. We've all experienced peer pressure to write something as strongly as possible, if not more so. But our Scott Trust ownership relieves us of the necessity to drive remorselessly for circulation to the exclusion of all else. In other words, we don't need to sex things up, and we shouldn't"

sex offenders register no apostrophe

sexuality
From a reader: "Can I suggest your style guide should state that homosexual, gay, bisexual and heterosexual are primarily adjectives and that use of them as nouns should be avoided. It seems to me that this is both grammatically and politically preferable (politically because using them as nouns really does seem to define people by their sexuality). I would like to read that someone is 'homosexual', not 'a homosexual', or about 'gay people', not 'gays'. Lesbian is different as it is a noun which later began to be used adjectivally, not the other way round. As an example from Wednesday, the opening line 'Documents which showed that Lord Byron ... was a bisexual' rather than 'was bisexual' sounds both Daily Mail-esque and stylistically poor"

Sgt Pepper's Lonely Hearts Club Band 1967 album by a popular beat combo of the day; not Sergeant Pepper's Lonely Hearts Club Band

Shaanxi (capital Xi'an) and **Shanxi** (capital Taiyuan) are adjacent provinces in northern China

shakedown, shakeout, shakeup (nouns)

Shakespearean not Shakespearian

Shankill Road Belfast, not Shankhill

shantytown

Ss

shareholder

sharia law

sheepdog

sheikh

Shepherd Market Mayfair; **Shepherd's Bush** west London

Shetland rather than Shetland Isles or Shetlands, but note that the local authority is Shetland Islands council

Shia, **Sunni** two branches of Islam (note: not Shi'ite); plural Shia Muslims and Sunni Muslims, though Shias and Sunnis are fine if you are pushed for space

shiatsu massage; **shih-tzu** dog

shiitake mushrooms

ships not feminine: it ran aground, not she ran aground; no quotes, no italics; you sail in, not on, ships

shipbuilding, **shipmate**, **shipowner**, **shipyard**

shoo-in not shoe-in

shoot-out

shopkeeper

Shoreham-by-Sea not Shoreham on Sea

Short money payment to opposition parties to help them carry out their parliamentary functions, named after Ted Short, the Labour leader of the house who introduced it in 1975

shrank, **shrunk** shrank, not shrunk, is the past tense of shrink, except in the film title Honey, I Shrunk the Kids (and perhaps the occasional piece of wordplay based on it); shrunk is the past participle (the kids had shrunk) or what is sometimes known as the present perfect form (Honey, I've shrunk the kids)

Siamese twins conjoined twins, please

sickbed, **sicknote**, **sickroom** but **sick pay**

Ss

sickie

side-effects but **sidestreet**

siege not seige

Siena Tuscan city; **sienna** pigment

silicon computer chips; **silicone** breast implants – we have been known to confuse the two, as in "Silicone Valley"

Silkin, Jon (1930-97) English poet, not to be confused with his cousin John Silkin (1923-87), a Labour cabinet minister, as was John's brother Sam Silkin (1918-88)

sim card (it stands for subscriber identity module)

since *See as or since?*

Singaporean names in three parts, eg Lee Kuan Yew

Singin' in the Rain not Singing

single quotes in headlines (but sparingly), standfirsts, captions and web furniture

singles chart

singular or plural?
Corporate entities take the singular: eg The BBC has decided (not "have"). In subsequent references make sure the pronoun is singular: "It [not they] will press for an increase in the licence fee." Sporting teams and rock bands are the exception – England have an uphill task, Nirvana were overrated *See Grammar & punctuation: collective nouns*

sink past tense **sank**, past participle **sunk**: he sinks, he sank, he has sunk

Sinn Féin

siphon not syphon

sisyphean a futile or interminable task (Sisyphus had to spend eternity rolling a boulder up a hill only to have it roll down again ... and again)

Ss

six-day war between Israel and its neighbours in June 1967

size

Attempts to express the size of objects and places in terms of their relationship to double-decker buses, Olympic swimming pools, football pitches, the Isle of Wight, Wales and Belgium are cliched and unhelpful, which does not stop journalists engaging in them. The same applies to measuring quantities of, say, hotdogs served at the Cup final in terms of how many times they would stretch to the moon and back

ski, skied, skier, skiing, skis

skilful not skillful

skimmed milk not skim

skipper usually only of a trawler

Sky+

skyrocket No!

slavery was not abolished in 1807, as we sometimes say: slavery in Britain became illegal in 1772, the slave trade in the British empire was abolished in 1807, but slavery remained in the colonies until the Slavery Abolition Act 1833

slither slide; **sliver** small piece

Slovene is a language; **Slovenian** describes the people. Similarly Slovak, Slovakian

smartcard, smartphone

Smith & Wesson handguns

Smithsonian Institution not Institute

snowclone

A type of cliched phrase defined by the linguist Geoffrey Pullum as "a multi-use, customisable, instantly recognisable, timeworn, quoted or misquoted phrase or sentence that can be used in an entirely open array of different variants". The name

Ss

is derived from the cliche about how many words "Eskimos" are mistakenly said to have for snow. Examples of snowclones include "xxx [eg comedy] is the new yyy [eg rock'n'roll]", "you wait ages for a xxx [eg gold medal] and then yyy [eg three] come along at once", and so on. Such phrases are very popular with journalists searching for what Pullum calls "quick-fix ways of writing stuff without actually having to think out new descriptive vocabulary or construct new phrases and sentences"

snowplough

so-called overused: as a reader pointed out when we used the term "so-called friendly fire", the expression is "obviously ironic and really doesn't need such ham-fisted pointing out"

social grades

The NRS social grades (not classes), originally developed by the National Readership Survey and still widely used in stories about market research, are the familiar A (upper middle class), B (middle), C1 (lower middle), C2 (skilled working), D (semi- and unskilled) and E (at the lowest levels of subsistence); they are based on the occupation of the chief income earner of a household and are sometimes grouped into ABC1 (middle class) and C2DE (working class).

Since the 2001 census, the main UK social classification has been the National Statistics socio-economic classification (NS-SEC), grouping occupations by employment conditions and relations rather than skills. This has 17 categories, which can be broken down into eight (from higher managerial and professional occupations to never worked and long-term unemployed), or just three (higher, intermediate and lower occupations)

socialism, socialist lc unless name of a party, eg Socialist Workers party

social media are plural

social security benefits all lc, income support, working tax credit, etc

Ss

sod's law *See Murphy's law*

Sofía queen of Spain

soi-disant means self-styled, not so-called; these phrases should be used sparingly

soiree no accent

solar system *See planets*

solicitor general

Solzhenitsyn, Aleksandr (1918-2008) Russian novelist

Somalia adjective Somali; the people are Somalis, not Somalians

some should not be used before a figure: if you are not sure, about or approximately are better, and if you are, it sounds daft: "some 12 people have died from wasp stings this year alone" was a particularly silly example that found its way into the paper

Sotheby's

soundbite

sources
Anonymous sources should be used sparingly. We should - except in exceptional circumstances - avoid anonymous pejorative quotes. We should avoid misrepresenting the nature and number of sources, and we should do our best to give readers some clue as to the authority with which they speak. We should never, ever, betray a source

Southbank Centre on the South Bank in London

South Bank University

south south London, south-west England, the south-east, south Wales, etc

southern hemisphere

Southern Ocean not Antarctic Ocean

south pole

Ss

Southport Visiter newspaper, not to be confused with **the Visitor**, Morecambe

space hopper

spaghetti western

Spanish names and accents
Take care over use of the tilde, which can change the meaning: Los Años Dorados (the Spanish version of the sitcom The Golden Girls) means The Golden Years; leave out the tilde and Los Anos Dorados becomes The Golden Anuses.

The surname is normally the second last name, not the last, which is the mother's maiden name, eg the writer Federico García Lorca - known as García in Spain rather than Lorca - should be García Lorca on second mention. Note also that the female name Consuelo ends with an "o" not an "a".

In Spanish the natural stress of a word generally occurs on the second to last syllable. Words that deviate from this norm must carry a written accent mark, known as the *acento ortográfico*, to indicate where the stress falls. A guide to accents follows. If in doubt do an internet search (try the word with and without an accent) and look for reputable Spanish language sites, eg big newspapers.

Surnames ending -ez take an accent over the penultimate vowel, eg Benítez, Fernández, Giménez, Gómez, González, Gutiérrez, Hernández, Jiménez, López, Márquez, Martínez, Núñez, Ordóñez, Pérez, Quiñónez, Ramírez, Rodríguez, Sáez, Vásquez, Vázquez, Velázquez. Exception: Alvarez; note also that names ending -es do not take the accent, eg Martines, Rodrigues.

Other surnames Aristízabal, Beltrán, Cáceres, Calderón, Cañizares, Chevantón, Couñago, Cúper, Dalí, De la Peña, Díaz, Forlán, García, Gaudí, Miró, Muñoz, Olazábal, Pavón, Sáenz, Sáinz, Valdés, Valerón, Verón.

Forenames Adán, Alán, Andrés, César, Darío, Elías, Fabián, Ginés, Héctor, Hernán, Iñaki, Inés, Iván, Jesús, Joaquín,

Ss

José, Lucía, María, Martín, Matías, Máximo, Míchel, Raúl, Ramón, Róger, Rubén, Sebastián, Víctor. The forenames Ana, Angel, Alfredo, Alvaro, Cristina, Diego, Domingo, Emilio, Ernesto, Federico, Fernando, Ignacio, Jorge, Juan, Julio, Luis, Marta, Mario, Miguel, Pablo and Pedro do not usually take accents.

Placenames Asunción, Bogotá, Cádiz, Catalonia, Córdoba, La Coruña, Guantánamo Bay, Guipúzcoa, Jaén, Jérez, León, Medellín, Potosí, San Sebastián, Valparaíso.

Sports teams, etc América, Atlético, El Barça (FC Barcelona), Bernabéu, Bolívar, Cerro Porteño, Deportivo La Coruña, Huracán, Málaga, Peñarol.

Note: Spanish is an official language in Argentina, Bolivia, Chile, Colombia, Costa Rica, Cuba, Dominican Republic, Ecuador, El Salvador, Equatorial Guinea, Guatemala, Honduras, Mexico, Nicaragua, Panama, Paraguay, Peru, Puerto Rico, Spain, Uruguay and Venezuela

Spanish practices, Spanish customs
If you are talking about questionable trade union activities, restrictive practices might be a less offensive way to put it

span of years 2008-10; but between 2008 and 2010, not "between 2008-10" or from 2008 to 2010, not "from 2008-10"

spare-part surgery avoid this term

spark overused in headlines of the "rates rise sparks fury" variety

spastic the Spastics Society, which supports disabled people and in particular those with cerebral palsy, changed its name to Scope in 1994

Speaker, the (Commons) but deputy speaker (of whom there are several); Lord Speaker (Lords)

special often redundant

special branch

Ss

Special Immigration Appeals Commission Siac or the commission on second mention

spellchecker
If you use one, read through your work afterwards: a graphic on our front page was rendered nonsensical when a spellcheck turned the species *Aquila adalberti* into "alleyway adalberti", while *Prunella modularis* became "pronely modularise"; also note that most use American English spellings

spelled/spelt she spelled it out for him: "the word is spelt like this"

Spice Girls Victoria Beckham was Posh Spice; Melanie Brown was Scary Spice; Emma Bunton was Baby Spice; Melanie Chisholm was Sporty Spice; Geri Halliwell was Ginger Spice

spicy not spicey

Spider-Man for the cartoon and film character, but Spiderman (no hyphen) is the nickname of Alain Robert, a Frenchman who specialises in climbing skyscrapers without a safety net

spin doctor

spinster avoid this old-fashioned term, which has acquired a pejorative tone; say, if relevant, that someone is an unmarried woman

spiral, spiralling prices (and other things) can spiral down as well as up; try a less cliched word that doesn't suggest a circular movement

split infinitives *See Grammar & punctuation*

spoiled/spoilt she spoiled her son: in fact he was a spoilt brat

spokesman, spokeswoman a quote may be attributed to the organisation, eg "The AA said ... ", but if necessary say spokesman or spokeswoman rather than spokesperson (assuming they have actually spoken to you)

sponsorship try to avoid: we are under no obligation to carry

Ss

sponsors' names. So London Marathon, not Flora London Marathon, etc. When a competition is named after a sponsor, it is unavoidable: Friends Provident t20, etc

spoonful plural spoonfuls, not spoonsful

spree shopping or spending, not shooting: describing a series of murders as a "killing spree" sounds flippant

spring

square brackets are used for interpolated words in quotations, eg Mrs May said: "David [Cameron] has my full support"

square metres not the same as metres squared: eg 300m squared is 90,000 sq metres, which is very different to 300 sq metres; we often get this wrong

Square Mile rather old-fashioned term for City of London

squaw is regarded as offensive and should be avoided

SSSI site of special scientific interest

stadium plural stadiums

Stadium of Light home of Sunderland AFC; not to be confused with **Estádio da Luz** home of Benfica

staff are plural

stalactites cling to the ceiling; **stalagmites** grow from the ground

stalemate in chess, a stalemate is the end of the game, and cannot be broken or resolved; deadlock or impasse are more suitable for metaphorical use

Stalin, Joseph not Josef

stamp not stomp

standup adjective, as in a standup comedian performing standup comedy; and noun: a standup performing standup

Stansted

Starck, Philippe French designer

Ss

Starkey, Zak (not Zac) son of Ringo Starr; has played drums with, among others, Oasis and the Who

start up verb, **startup** noun (as in business startup);
star tup top-performing ram

state lc in all uses

statehouse office of the state governor in the US; one word except in New Jersey where it is the state house

state of the union address

stationary motionless; also used by some stationery shops to mean stationery; **stationery** writing materials; also used by some signwriters to mean stationary

STD or STI? STI (sexually transmitted infection) is a broader term than STD (sexually transmitted disease): you can have the infection without feeling ill or displaying any symptoms

steamboat, **steamhammer**, **steamship** but **steam engine**

Stelios Sir Stelios Haji-Ioannou, founder of easyJet; normally known as Stelios

sten gun

stentorian loud, sometimes confused with **stertorous**, a snoring sound

step change avoid, unless you are quoting someone; change is perfectly adequate

stepfamily, **stepfather**, **stepmother** etc, but **step-parents**. Don't confuse, say, a stepsister and half-sister, as we did when writing about Barack Obama's family

Stephen or Steven?
Stephen Baldwin, Stephen Chow (actors), Stephen Colbert (satirist), Stephen Crane (wrote The Red Badge of Courage), Stephen Foster (wrote Oh! Susanna), Stephen Fry (national treasure), Stephen Jay Gould (biologist), Stephen Hawking (physicist), Stephen King (novelist), Stephen Merchant (Ricky

Ss

Gervais collaborator).

Steven Gerrard (footballer), Steven Moffat (runs Doctor Who), Steven Spielberg (film director).

Steve Jobs (Apple founder)

sterling the pound; also sterling qualities

Stetson TM hat

sticky-back plastic

stiletto plural stilettos

still life plural **still lifes** not lives

stilton cheese

stimulus plural stimuli

Stock Exchange caps when referring to the London Stock Exchange; but lc in other countries, eg Hong Kong stock exchange

stock in trade

stock market

stolen generations Australian Aboriginal children forcibly removed from their families

stone age
The charity Survival says: "'Stone age' and 'primitive' have been used to describe tribal people since the colonial era, reinforcing the idea that they have not changed over time and that they are backward. This idea is both incorrect and very dangerous: incorrect because all societies adapt and change, and dangerous because it is often used to justify the persecution or forced 'development' of tribal people"

stony broke but **stony-hearted** (not stoney)

stopgap

storey plural storeys (buildings); **story** plural stories (tales)

straightforward

Ss

straitjacket

strait-laced

strait of Dover, **strait of Gibraltar**, **strait of Hormuz** not Strait, Straits or straits

straitened circumstances, **straitened times** not straightened, one of our most frequent errors

Strategic Rail Authority SRA on second mention

Stratford-on-Avon district council and parliamentary seat, although most other local organisations, such as the Royal Shakespeare Company, call this Warwickshire town Stratford-upon-Avon

stratum plural strata

Street-Porter, Janet

streetwise

stretchered off has a slight ring of Charles Buchan's Football Monthly; say carried off

strippergram

stumbling block

stumm not schtum

Sturm und Drang German literary movement

STV single transferable vote

stylebook but **style guide**

Subbuteo table football game in which players "flick to kick", named after the bird of prey *Falco subbuteo* (the hobby) and immortalised in the Undertones' My Perfect Cousin

subcommittee, subcontinent, sublet, subplot, subsection

subeditors, subs
Journalists who traditionally edit, check and cut copy, write headlines and other page furniture, and design pages; to which

Ss

can be added, in the digital age, an ever-widening range of multimedia and technical skills. In some countries, eg the US and Canada, they are known as copy editors.

WP Crozier said of CP Scott: "As a subeditor he got rid of the redundant and the turgid with the conscientiousness of a machine that presses the superfluous moisture out of yarn. The man who passed 'seaward journey to the great metropolis', and when the copy came back to him found written in firm blue pencil 'voyage to London', knew what sort of English 'CP' liked"

subjunctive *See Grammar & punctuation*

submachine gun

submarines are boats, not ships

subpoena, subpoenaed

sub-prime, sub-Saharan

suchlike

Sudan not the Sudan

sudoku

suffer little children nothing to do with suffering, this frequently misquoted or misunderstood phrase was used by Christ (Luke 18:16) to mean "allow the little children to come to me"; it is also the title of a song about the Moors murders on the first Smiths album

suicide
Say that someone killed him or herself rather than "committed suicide"; suicide has not been a crime in the UK for many years and this old-fashioned term can cause unnecessary further distress to families who have been bereaved in this way.

Journalists should exercise particular care in reporting suicide or issues involving suicide, bearing in mind the risk of encouraging others. This applies to presentation, including the use of pictures, and to describing the method of suicide. Any substances should be referred to in general rather than specific

Ss

terms. When appropriate, a helpline number (eg Samaritans) should be given. The feelings of relatives should also be carefully considered

summer

summer solstice the longest day of the year, but not the same as Midsummer Day (although we often seem to assume it is)

Super Bowl

supercasino, superinjunction

supermarkets Marks & Spencer or M&S, Morrisons, Safeway, Sainsbury's, Tesco (no wonder people get confused about apostrophes)

supermodel model is normally sufficient

supersede not supercede

supply days (parliament)

supreme court

Sure Start

surge prefer rise or increase, if that is the meaning; but surge is preferable to "upsurge"

Suriname (not Surinam) formerly Dutch Guiana

surrealism

svengali lc, although named after the sinister Svengali in George du Maurier's 1894 novel Trilby

swap not swop

swat flies; **swot** books

swath, swaths broad strip, eg cut a wide swath; **swathe, swathes** baby clothes, bandage, wrappings

swearwords
We are more liberal than any other newspaper, using language that most of our competitors would not. The statistics tell their

Ss

own story: the word "fuck" (and its variants) appeared 705 times in the Guardian in the 12 months to April 2010, with a further 269 mentions in the Observer. (The figures for other national newspapers were as follows: Independent 279, Independent on Sunday 74, Times 3, Sunday Times 2, all other papers 0.) The figures for the C-word, still regarded by many people as taboo, were: Guardian 49, Observer 20, Independent 8, Independent on Sunday 5, everyone else 0.

Even some readers who agree with Lenny Bruce that "take away the right to say fuck and you take away the right to say fuck the government" might feel that we sometimes use such words unnecessarily, although comments in response to Guardian Style's blogpost on the subject were overwhelmingly in support of our policy. The editor's guidelines are as follows:

First, remember the reader, and respect demands that we should not casually use words that are likely to offend.

Second, use such words only when absolutely necessary to the facts of a piece, or to portray a character in an article; there is almost never a case in which we need to use a swearword outside direct quotes.

Third, the stronger the swearword, the harder we ought to think about using it.

Finally, never use asterisks, or such silliness as b------, which are just a cop-out, as Charlotte Brontë recognised: "The practice of hinting by single letters those expletives with which profane and violent people are wont to garnish their discourse, strikes me as a proceeding which, however well meant, is weak and futile. I cannot tell what good it does - what feeling it spares - what horror it conceals"

swingeing

swinging 60s

synopsis plural synopses

syntax *See Grammar & punctuation*

Ss

synthesis, synthesise but **synthesizer**

systematic methodical; **systemic** relating to a system

Tt

66 My inner pedant screams whenever a device is advertised as having a 'massive memory' when technically it's storage. Random access memory (Ram) changes at the speed of light while processing data. Storage is where data sits quietly unchanged, waiting for a call from the processor. But it's a lost cause. Today's mobile phones, MP3 players, digital cameras and other devices store data on chips instead of disk drives, so things with embarrassingly small memories (Ram) can be described as having massive memories (storage). Well, Flash memory chips remember things, don't they? They do. I'll shut up now **99**

Jack Schofield

Tt

-t ending for past participle: the cakes were burnt, the word was misspelt. But earned, not earnt

T (not tee) as in it suited her to a T, he had it down to a T

tableau plural tableaux

table d'hote

tabloid refers to longstanding redtops such as the Sun and Daily Mirror, rather than the more recent breed of shrunken broadsheets; tabloids are sometimes accused of writing in tabloidese

tactics singular and plural

tad is a tad overused

Taiwanese names as with Hong Kong and Korean names, these are in two parts with a hyphen, eg Lee Teng-hui (Lee after first mention)

Tajikistan the adjective is Tajik

takeoff noun, **take off** verb

Takeover Panel

Taliban plural (it means students; the singular is Talib)

talkshow mainly American English; the British English version is chatshow

TalkSport although the radio station's brand is talkSPORT

Tamiflu trade name of oseltamivir, an antiviral drug that slows the spread of the influenza virus between cells in the body. Do not call it a vaccine - it treats, but does not pre-empt

tam o'shanter woollen cap

Tampax TM; say tampon

Tangier not Tangiers

Tannoy TM; say public address system or just PA

taoiseach the Irish prime minister

Tt

targeted, **targeting**

tariff

Tarmac a company; **tarmac** formerly used to make pavements, roads and runways (we now walk and drive on asphalt)

tarot cards

Taser TM; the generic term is stun gun

taskforce

Tate the original London gallery in Millbank, now known as Tate Britain, houses British art from the 16th century; Tate Modern, at Southwark, south London, Tate Liverpool and Tate St Ives, in Cornwall, all house modern art

Tavener, Sir John English composer (born 1944) of such works as The Protecting Veil; **Taverner, John** English composer (c1490-1545) of masses and other vocal works

tax avoidance is legal; **tax evasion** is illegal

taxi, **taxiing** of aircraft

Tbilisi capital of Georgia

Tchaikovsky

teabag, **teacup**, **tealeaves**, **teapot**, **teaspoon** all one word

team-mate

teams sports teams take plural verbs: Wednesday were relegated again, Australia have won by an innings, etc; but note that in a business context, they are singular like other companies, eg Manchester United reported its biggest loss to date

Tea Party movement named after the Boston Tea Party protest of 1773

teargas

Teasmade TM; say teamaker

Technicolor TM

Tt

teddy boys (1950s) took their name from their Edwardian style of clothing

Teesside

teetotaller

Teflon TM; say non-stick pan

telephone numbers should be hyphenated after three or four-figure area codes, but not five-figure area codes: 020-3353 2000, 0161-832 7200; 01892 456789, 01227 123456; treat mobile phone numbers as having five-figure area codes: 07911 654321

Teletubbies Tinky Winky (purple), Laa-Laa (yellow), Dipsy (green), and Po (red)

temazepam

temperatures thus: 30C (85F) - ie celsius, with fahrenheit in brackets on first mention; but be extremely wary when converting temperature changes, eg an average temperature change of 2C was wrongly converted to 36F in an article about a heatwave (although a temperature of 2C is about the same as 36F, a temperature change of 2C corresponds to a change of about 4F)

Ten Commandments not 10

tending one's flock, the sick, etc (not "tending to")

tendinitis not tendonitis

tenpin bowling

tenses *See Grammar & punctuation*

Terfel, Bryn Welsh opera singer; for some reason we often describe him as a tenor, but he is a bass baritone

Terminal 5 (Heathrow) may be abbreviated to T5 after first mention

terraced houses

terracotta but Terracotta Warriors

Tt

terra firma

Terrence Higgins Trust

terrorism, terrorists

A terrorist act is directed against victims chosen either randomly or as symbols of what is being opposed (eg workers in the World Trade Centre, tourists in Bali, London commuters). It is designed to create a state of terror in the minds of a particular group of people or the public as a whole for political or social ends. Although most terrorist acts are violent, you can be a terrorist without being overtly violent (eg poisoning a water supply or gassing people on the underground).

Does having a good cause make a difference? The UN says no: "Criminal acts calculated to provoke a state of terror in the general public are in any circumstances unjustifiable, whatever the considerations of a political, philosophical, ideological, racial, ethnic, religious or other nature that may be invoked to justify them."

Whatever one's political sympathies, suicide bombers, the 9/11 attackers and most paramilitary groups can all reasonably be regarded as terrorists (or at least groups some of whose members perpetrate terrorist acts).

Nonetheless we need to be very careful about using the term: it is still a subjective judgment - one person's terrorist may be another person's freedom fighter, and there are former "terrorists" holding elected office in many parts of the world. Some critics suggest that, for the Guardian, all terrorists are militants - unless their victims are British. Others may point to what they regard as "state terrorism".

Often, alternatives such as militants, radicals, separatists, etc, may be more appropriate and less controversial, but this is a difficult area: references to the "resistance", for example, imply more sympathy to a cause than calling such fighters "insurgents". The most important thing is that, in news reporting, we are not seen - because of the language we use - to

Tt

be taking sides.

Note that the phrase "war on terror" should always appear in quotes, whether used by us or (more likely) quoting someone else

Tesco not Tesco's

Tessa tax-exempt special savings account, replaced by Isa

Test (cricket and rugby) the third Test, etc

testament, **testimony** the former is sometimes misused for the latter, eg "it's a testament to her skill that … "

Tetra Pak TM

Texan a person; the adjective is **Texas**: Texas Ranger, Texas oilwells, Texas tea etc

textbook

thalidomide

that *See Grammar & punctuation*

the
Leaving "the" out often reads like jargon: say the conference agreed to do something, not "conference agreed"; the government has to do, not "government has to"; the Super League (rugby), not "Super League".

Avoid the "prime minister David Cameron" syndrome: do not use constructions such as "prime minister David Cameron said … ". Prominent figures can just be named, with their function at second mention: "David Cameron said last night" (first mention); "the prime minister said" (subsequent mentions). If it is thought necessary to explain who someone is, write "Arsène Wenger, the Arsenal manager, said" or "the Arsenal manager, Arsène Wenger, said". In such cases the commas around the name indicate there is only one person in the position, so write "the prime minister, David Cameron, said" (only one person in the job), but "the former Tory prime minister John Major said" (there have been many).

Tt

lc for newspapers (the Guardian), magazines (the New Statesman), pubs (the Coach and Horses), bands (the Not Sensibles, the The), nicknames (the Hulk, the Red Baron), and sports grounds (the Oval).

uc for books (The Lord of the Rings), films (The Matrix), poems (The Waste Land), television shows (The West Wing), and some placenames (The Hague)

theatre normally lc in name, eg Adelphi theatre, Crucible theatre (or just Adelphi, Crucible); initial cap if Theatre comes first, eg Theatre Royal, Stratford East

Théâtre de Complicité is now known simply as Complicite, with no accent

theatregoer

theirs no apostrophe

then the then prime minister, etc (no hyphen)

thermonuclear one word

Thermos TM; say vacuum flask

Thessaloniki not Salonica or Salonika

thinktank one word

Third Reich

third way

third world meaning not the west (first) or the Soviet Union (second), so today an outdated (as well as objectionable) term; use developing countries or developing nations

this and that that was then, but this is now; this looks forward, that looks back: so the man showing his son and heir the lands lying in front of them says: "One day, son, all this will be yours." Then he points behind him to the house and says: "But that remains mine"

thoroughbred, thoroughgoing

Tt

threefold, threescore

3G third generation mobile telephony

three-line whip

throe, throw you might make a last throw of the dice, but if you are in your last throes, your situation is considerably more serious

thunderstorm one word

Tiananmen Square Beijing

Tianjin not Tientsin

tidewater

tikka masala

timebomb, timescale, timeshare

times 1am, 6.30pm, etc; 10 o'clock last night but 10pm yesterday; half past two, a quarter to three, 10 to 11, etc; 2hr 5min 6sec, etc; for 24-hour clock, 00.47, 23.59; noon, midnight (not 12 noon, 12 midnight or 12am, 12pm).

The week starts on Mondays, but stories published on Sunday refer to the following week as "this week" and the six days preceding that Sunday as "last week". Writers must put the date in brackets when there might be ambiguity. Never start a story "last week" *See yesterday*

Timor-Leste formerly East Timor

tinfoil

tipi not tepee or teepee

tipoff one word as a noun

Tipp-Ex TM; use correction fluid (not that many people do any more)

tipping point another example of jargon that has quickly become hackneyed through overuse

Tt

Tirol

titbit not tidbit

titles
Do not italicise or put in quotes titles of books, films, TV programmes, paintings, songs, albums or anything else. Words in titles take initial caps except for a, and, at, for, from, in, of, the, to, with (except in initial position or after a colon): A Tale of Two Cities, Happy End of the World, Shakespeare in Love, Superman: The Early Years, I'm in Love with the Girl on a Certain Manchester Megastore Checkout Desk, etc. Exception: the Review and the Observer, which still italicise titles *See italics*

T-junction

toby jug inexplicably capped up in the paper at least twice

to-do as in "what a to-do!"

told the Guardian is used far too often: it should normally be replaced by "said" and reserved for occasions when it genuinely adds interest or authority to a story (if someone got an exclusive interview with, say, Osama bin Laden)

Tolkien, JRR (1892-1973) British author and philologist, notable for writing The Lord of the Rings and not spelling his name "Tolkein"

tomato plural tomatoes

tonnage is measured in tons (units of volume), not tonnes (units of mass) - derived from the number of tuns (large barrels) a vessel could hold; registered tonnage is the total internal capacity of a vessel, displacement tonnage is its actual weight, equal to the weight of water it displaces

tonne not ton (with the above exception): the metric tonne is 1,000kg (2,205lb), the British ton is 2,240lb, and the US ton is 2,000lb; usually there is no need to convert

top 10, top 40 etc

Tt

Topman, **Topshop**

Torah, the

tornado plural tornadoes (storm); **Tornado** plural Tornados (aircraft)

tortuous a tortuous road is one that winds or twists; **torturous** a torturous experience is one that involves pain or suffering

Tory party (but Conservative party is more SEO friendly)

total
Avoid starting court stories with variations on the formula "three men were jailed for a total of 19 years", a statistic that conveys no meaningful information (in this case, they had been given sentences of nine, six and four years). The only time this might be justified is when one person is given a series of life sentences, and "he was jailed for a total of 650 years" at least conveys how serious the crimes were

Tote, the

totalled two Ls

touchscreen

Tourette syndrome

Toussaint, Allen US blues musician; **Toussaint, Jean** US jazz musician; **Toussaint L'Ouverture, Pierre Dominique** (1743-1803) leader of Haiti's slave revolt of 1791 and subsequent fight for independence, which was granted in 1801

town councillor, **town hall**

townie not townee

Townshend, Pete one of the two members of the Who who didn't die before he got old (the other is Roger Daltrey)

trademarks (TM)
Take care: use a generic alternative unless there is a very good reason not to, eg ballpoint pen, not biro (unless it really is a Biro,

Tt

in which case it takes a cap B); say photocopy rather than Xerox, etc; you will save our lawyers, and those of Portakabin and various other companies, a lot of time and trouble

trade union, **trade unionist** but **Trades Union Congress** and **trades union council**

tragic people do not need to be told that an accident is "tragic"

train a number of things in a string – such as animals, railway carriages or wagons. In railway terms it is hauled by a locomotive or engine, with which it is not synonymous. Many thanks to a reader for this entry

transatlantic

Transnistria separatist region that declared its independence from Moldova in 1990, but has not been recognised by the international community; also known as Trans-Dniester

Transport for London TfL on second mention

Trans-Siberian railway

Travellers capped: they are recognised as an ethnic group under the Race Relations Act; note **new age travellers** (lc)

Treasury, the (officially HM Treasury)

treaties lc, eg peace of Westphalia (1648), treaty of Versailles (1919)

Trekkers how to refer to Star Trek fans unless you want to make fun of them, in which case they are Trekkies

trenchcoat

tricolour French and Irish

trillion a thousand billion (1 followed by 12 noughts), abbreviate like this: $25tn

Trinity College, Cambridge not to be confused with **Trinity Hall, Cambridge**

Trinity College Dublin

Tt

trip-hop

Trips trade-related intellectual property rights

Trojan horse

trooper soldier in a cavalry regiment; **trouper** member of a troupe, or dependable worker ("the night team are real troupers")

trooping the colour (no "of")

tropic of cancer, **tropic of capricorn**

the Troubles (Northern Ireland)

try to never "try and", eg I will try to do something about this misuse of language

tsar not czar

tsetse fly

T-shirt not tee-shirt

tsunami wave caused by an undersea earthquake; not the same thing as a tidal wave

tube, the lc (London Underground is the name of the company); individual lines thus: Jubilee line, Northern line, etc; the underground

TUC Trades Union Congress, so TUC Congress is tautological; the reference should be to the TUC conference

Tupperware TM

turgid does not mean apathetic or sluggish - that's torpid - but swollen, congested, or (when used of language) pompous or bombastic

turkish delight

Turkmenistan adjective Turkmen; its citizens are Turkmen, singular Turkman

Turkomans (singular noun and adjective is Turkoman) are a

Tt

formerly nomadic central Asian people who now form a minority in Iraq; they speak Turkmen

turned the subeditor turned stylebook guru Amelia Hodsdon said ... (no hyphens)

turnover (noun) in business; **turn over** (verb) in bed

21st century but hyphenate if adjectival: newspapers of the 21st century, 21st-century newspapers

Tutankhamun

Twenty20 cricket

twitchers birdwatchers or birders are preferable terms

Twitter users, also known as tweeters (and sometimes Twitterers, but not tweeps, please), spend much of their time sending tweets, also known as tweeting or Twittering; the editors of Guardian Style tweet @guardianstyle

twofold

tying

Uu

66 When I was at school, a teacher once wrote in my margin 'some interesting spelling in an otherwise uninteresting essay'. It distresses me to admit that, even though I knew she was being arch, the message nevertheless penetrated my subconscious that spelling mistakes spice things up a bit 99

Zoe Williams

Uu

uber no accent if you are saying something like uber-hip (although uber in this sense is uber-used), use the umlaut if you are quoting German

U-boat

uc strictly the abbreviation for UPPERCASE but more generally used to mean initial capital letters

Ucas Universities and Colleges Admissions Service

Uighur, Uighurs the Uighur people, particularly of the Xinjiang region in China

UK or Britain in copy and headlines for the United Kingdom of Great Britain and Northern Ireland (but note Great Britain comprises just England, Scotland and Wales)

Ukraine no "the"; adjective Ukrainian

ukulele not ukelele

Ulan Bator capital of Mongolia

Ulster avoid if possible but acceptable in headlines to mean Northern Ireland, which in fact comprises six of the nine counties of the province of Ulster

Uluru formerly known as Ayers Rock

Umist the former University of Manchester Institute of Science and Technology merged with the University of Manchester in 2004

umlaut
In German placenames, ae, oe and ue should almost always be rendered ä, ö, ü. Family names, however, for the most part became petrified many years ago and there is no way of working out whether the -e form or the umlaut should be used; you just have to find out for each individual

umm-ed and ahh-ed

UN United Nations

UNAids

Uu

Unesco United Nations Educational, Scientific and Cultural Organisation

UN general assembly

UNHCR United Nations high commissioner for refugees; not commission (although the name stands for both the high commissioner and the refugee agency s/he fronts)

Unicef United Nations Children's Fund

UN secretary general

UN security council

unbiased

uncharted not unchartered

unchristian

under- words with this prefix are normally one word, eg underachieve, underact, underage, undercover, underdeveloped, undermanned, underprivileged, undersea, undersecretary, undersigned, undervalue, underweight

underestimate, understate take care that you don't mean overestimate or overstate. We often get this wrong - a typical example from the paper: "Qian's contribution to China's space and missile programme cannot be underestimated" (the writer meant the opposite)

underground, the but London Underground for name of company

under way not underway

uneducated "with no formal education" may be more accurate

unfollow, unfriend is what you do to people you don't like on, respectively, Twitter and Facebook

uninterested means not taking an interest; not synonymous with **disinterested**, which means unbiased, objective

union lc when debating the future of "the union" (England and Scotland)

Uu

union flag not union jack and not capitalised

unionists (Northern Ireland) lc except in the name of a party, eg Democratic Unionist party

unique one of a kind, so cannot be qualified as "absolutely unique", "very unique", etc

Unite the UK's biggest trade union, formed in 2007 by the merger of Amicus and the Transport and General Workers' Union

United Kingdom England, Wales, Scotland and Northern Ireland; no need to write in full: say Britain or the UK

United Reformed Church not United Reform Church, as pointed out on a wearisomely regular basis in the corrections column

universities cap up, eg Sheffield University, Johns Hopkins University, Free University of Berlin

University College London no comma; UCL after first mention

University of the Arts London comprises Camberwell College of Arts, Central Saint Martins College of Art and Design, Chelsea College of Art and Design, London College of Communication, London College of Fashion, and Wimbledon College of Art

Unknown Soldier, tomb of the

unmistakable

until not "up until"

unveiled pictures are, as are cars sometimes, but these days almost everything seems to be - so the government "unveiled a raft of new policies" (two cliches and a redundant "new" in six words) or a company "unveiled record profits". There is nothing wrong with announcing, reporting, presenting or publishing

upbeat, upfront, upgrade, upstage, uptight

upcoming the coining and, even worse, use of such jargon words is likely to make many otherwise liberal, enlightened readers (and editors) wonder if there is not after all a case to bring back

Uu

capital, or at least corporal, punishment for crimes against the English language; an editor once told his staff: "If I read upcoming in the Wall Street Journal again, I shall be downcoming and somebody will be outgoing"

upmarket not the American English upscale

up to date but in an up-to-date fashion

US for United States, not USA: no need to spell out, even at first mention; do not call it America, although its people are Americans *See America*

USAid

used he used to do something, not "he did use to do something" and certainly not "he did used to do something" (double imperfect); a column said "high street shops did, it's true, used to be more varied" - something like "high street shops certainly used to be more varied" would have been better

user-generated content

utopian

U-turn

Uzbekistan the adjective is Uzbek

Vv

❝ People can sometimes become very unreasonable. Vasily Grossman, in Life and Fate, his account of life in the gulag, records this meeting with a released prisoner: 'He had been a proofreader on a newspaper and had spent seven years in the camps for missing a misprint in a leading article - the typesetter had got one letter wrong in Stalin's name.' Well, of course, names are important ❞

Ian Mayes

v for versus, not vs: England v Australia, Rochdale v Sheffield Wednesday, etc

V for the organisation, call it "V, the National Young Volunteers Service" at first mention

V&A abbreviation for Victoria and Albert Museum

Vajpayee, Atal Bihari former prime minister of India

Val d'Isère

Valentine's Day

valley lc, eg Thames valley, Ruhr valley, the Welsh valleys, valley girl (California)

Valium TM; a brand of diazepam

Valparaíso

Valuation Office Agency (VOA after first mention) an executive agency of HM Revenue & Customs, it compiles business rating and council tax valuation lists for England and Wales but not Scotland, where the job is done by the Scottish Assessors

ValuJet Atlanta-based budget airline now called AirTran

Vanessa-Mae violinist

van Gogh, Vincent (1853-90) Dutch artist; note that as with other Dutch names it is Van Gogh when just the surname is used (a Van Gogh masterpiece) but van Gogh with the forename (a masterpiece by Vincent van Gogh)

Van Rompuy, Herman president of the European council

Vanuatu formerly New Hebrides

vapour but **vaporise**

Vargas Llosa, Mario Peruvian writer and politician, born 1936; his son Álvaro is also a writer

Vaseline TM; call it petroleum jelly

VAT value added tax; no need to spell it out

Vv

Vaughan or Vaughn?

Frankie Vaughan (late singer), Johnny Vaughan (broadcaster), Michael Vaughan (cricketer), Sarah Vaughan (late singer).

Matthew Vaughn (film producer), Robert Vaughn, Vince Vaughn (actors)

VE Day 8 May 1945; **VJ Day** 15 August 1945

Vehicle Inspectorate

Velázquez, Diego (1599-1660) Spanish painter

Velcro TM

veld not veldt

venal open to bribery; **venial** easily forgiven

venerable worthy of reverence, not just old

venetian blind

veranda not verandah

verdicts recorded by coroners, returned by inquest juries

Verkhovna Rada (supreme council) Ukraine's parliament

vermilion

verruca not verucca

very usually very redundant. Mark Twain wrote: "Substitute 'damn' every time you're inclined to write 'very'. Your editor will delete it and the writing will be just as it should be"

Vespa scooters; **Vesta** curries

veterinary

veto, vetoed, vetoes, vetoing

Viagra TM; the generic is sildenafil citrate

vicar a cleric of the Anglican church (which also has rectors and curates, etc), not of any other denomination.

A priest writes: "A vicar is a person who is the incumbent of a parish, and the term is a job description in the same way that

Vv

editor is a job description. All editors are journalists but not all journalists are editors. In the same way, all vicars are priests, but not all priests are vicars. Some priests are chaplains; some (like me) are forensic social workers; some are retired; some are shopworkers; some are police officers"

vice-chair, **vice-chancellor**, **vice-president**

vice versa

vichyssoise

videogame

videotape noun and verb, although normally shorten to video or tape (the two are interchangeable – Did you video that programme? No, I taped something else)

vie, **vying**

Vientiane capital of Laos

Villa-Lobos, Heitor (1887-1959) Brazilian composer

virtuoso plural virtuosos

virus not the same as a bacterium, but we often confuse the two; if in doubt, consult the science desk

vis-a-vis no accent

vocal cords not chords

Vodafone

voiceover

volcano plural volcanoes

volcanology not vulcanology

vortex plural vortices

voting systems lc, but may be abbreviated after first mention, eg first past the post (FPTP), alternative vote (AV), single transferable vote (STV)

vuvuzela not vuvuzuela

Ww

66 I like new coinings. Consider their inventive legacy, from boycott to Wendy and back to Frisbee. Style guides should not suppress them and will not, however many readers initially splutter. Otherwise, clarity is the lodestar and surely the most convincing reason for grammatical rules. I also greatly dislike the word 'refurbish' and admit with shame that my proudest Guardian word-moment was getting 'wainwright' as a common noun into a piece about the Waggoners' Memorial at Sledmere in the East Riding 99

Martin Wainwright

Ww

wacky not whacky

wagon not waggon

Wags wives and girlfriends (generally of footballers: the term was popularised during the 2006 World Cup, although Fabio Capello initially banned them from joining the 2010 team in South Africa); the singular is Wag. Regarded by many as sexist, although variations include Habs (husbands and boyfriends)

Wahhabism branch of Islam practised by followers of the teachings of Muhammad ibn Abd-al-Wahhab (1703-92)

wah-wah pedal

waive, **waiver** the relinquishing of a claim or right; **waver** to hesitate

wake "in the wake of" is overused; nothing wrong with "as a result of" or simply "after"

Wales avoid the word principality, and do not use as a unit of measurement ("50 times the size of Wales") *See size*

Wales Office not Welsh Office

walking stick

Walkman TM; plural Walkmans not Walkmen

Wallpaper* magazine (note asterisk)

Wall's ice-cream, sausages

Wal-Mart owner of Asda

Wap (wireless application protocol) phones

war crime, war dance, war game, war zone but **warhead, warhorse, warlord, warpath, warship, wartime**

"war on terror" always in quotes

wars first world war, second world war (do not say "before the war" or "after the war" without making it clear which war you mean)

hundred years war (it actually lasted 116 years, from 1337 to 1453)
war of Jenkins' ear (1739-48)
civil war (England), American civil war, Spanish civil war
Crimean/Boer/Korean/Vietnam war
six-day war
Gulf war (1991), Iraq war (2003)

Was (Not Was) US rock band featuring Don Was and David Was (no relation)

Waste Land, The poem by TS Eliot (not The Wasteland)

washing-up liquid

washout noun, **wash out** verb

watchdog, watchmaker, watchword

watercolour, watercourse, watermark, waterproof, waterskiing, waterworks

Waterford Wedgwood glass and china (not Wedgewood)

water polo

Waterstone's bookseller

Watford Gap service area on the M1 in Northamptonshire, near the village of Watford, 80 miles north of London; nothing to do with the Hertfordshire town of Watford, 60 miles away, with which it is sometimes confused by lazy writers who think using such phrases as "anyone north of the Watford Gap" is a witty way to depict the unwashed northern hordes

wayzgoose traditional term for a printer's works outing

web, webpage, website, world wide web

web 2.0

websites addresses can be broken at a sensible point within the name if you need to turn a line

Weee directive (note three Es) EU scheme to encourage recycling of waste electrical and electronic equipment

Ww

weight in kilograms with imperial conversion, eg 65kg (10st 2lb)

Weight Watchers TM

welch (not welsh) to fail to honour an obligation

Welch Regiment, **Royal Welch Fusiliers**

welfare state

wellbeing

well-known as with famous, if someone or something is well-known, it should not be necessary to say so

wellnigh

Welsh assembly comprises the national assembly for Wales (the representative body with 60 assembly members - AMs - meeting in the Senedd) and the Welsh assembly government (led by the first minister, and a distinct body from the national assembly since 2006)

welsh dresser, **welsh rarebit**

Welsh, Irvine Scottish author

Welsh spellings (eg F for the V sound in English, dd for the th sound): prefer Welsh spellings such as Caernarfon and Conwy to old-fashioned anglicised versions (Caernarvon, Conway) - although there are exceptions, such as Cardiff not Caerdydd

wendy house

Wen Jiabao succeeded Zhu Rongji as Chinese premier (prime minister) in 2003; Wen at second mention (except in leading articles, where he is Mr Wen)

west, **western**, **the west**, **western Europe**

western (cowboy film)

West Bank

West Bank barrier should always be called a barrier when referred to in its totality, as it is in places a steel and barbed-wire

Ww

fence and in others an eight-metre-high concrete wall; if referring to a particular section of it then calling it a fence or a wall may be appropriate. It can also be described as a "separation barrier/fence/wall" or "security barrier/fence/wall", according to the nature of the article

west coast mainline

West Country

Western Isles

West Lothian question asks why MPs from Scotland, Wales and Northern Ireland are able to vote on policies that will apply in England but, because of devolution, will not apply in their own constituencies

West Midlands

Westminster Abbey

West Nile virus

Weyerhaeuser US pulp and paper company

what is a phrase that, while occasionally helpful to add emphasis, has become overused to the point of tedium; examples from the paper include:

"Beckham repaid the committed public support with what was a man-of-the-match performance ... "

"Principal among Schofield's 19 recommendations in what is a wide-ranging report ... "

What is clear is that these would be improved by what would be the simple step of removing the offending phrase

wheelchair
Say (if relevant) that someone uses a wheelchair, not that they are "in a wheelchair" or "wheelchair-bound" – stigmatising and offensive, as well as inaccurate

whence means where from, so don't write "from whence"

whereabouts singular: her whereabouts is not known

Ww

which *See Grammar & punctuation*

Which? the magazine, and the organisation that publishes it (formerly the Consumers' Association)

while not whilst

whisky but Irish and US **whiskey** and plural **whiskies** for both

whistleblower

white lc in racial context

white paper

white-van man

Whitsuntide, Whit Sunday

whiz, whiz-kid not whizz or wiz

whodunnit

who or whom? *See Grammar & punctuation*

wicketkeeper

Widdecombe, Ann former Tory cabinet minister who, briefly, became a Guardian agony aunt

wide awake

Wiesel, Elie Holocaust survivor and author; he was awarded the Nobel peace prize in 1986, and female status in a particularly crass Guardian error

Wi-Fi TM; the generic term is wireless computer network

Wii Nintendo games machine

wiki website that allows multiple users to edit its content, hence WikiLeaks, Wikipedia

wild west

Willans, Geoffrey (not Williams or Willians, as have appeared in the paper) author of the Molesworth books, illustrated by Ronald Searle, as any fule kno

Ww

Wimpey houses; **Wimpy** burgers

windfarm one word

Windermere not Lake Windermere; note that Windermere is also the name of the town

Windows Phone 7 not Windows 7 Phone

wines normally lc, whether taking their name from a region (eg beaujolais, bordeaux, burgundy, chablis, champagne) or a grape variety (eg cabernet sauvignon, chardonnay, merlot, muscadet).

The regions themselves are capped up – so one might drink a burgundy from Burgundy, or a muscadet from the Loire valley – as are wines of individual chateaux, eg I enjoyed a glass of Cos d'Estournel 1970

wing commander in leading articles, abbreviate on second mention to Wing Cdr; Wing Commander Barry Johnson, subsequently Wing Cdr Johnson; otherwise just Johnson

Winnie-the-Pooh in the original AA Milne books, although the "bear of little brain" has lost the hyphens in his Disney incarnation

winter

winter of discontent overused

wipeout noun, **wipe out** verb

Wirral not "the Wirral", unless referring specifically to the Wirral peninsula

wishlist

wisteria not wistaria

witchcraft but **witch-doctor**, **witch-hunt**

with (not "together with")

withhold

witness not eyewitness, except for the Eyewitness picture spread in the Guardian

wits' end

woeful

Wolfram Alpha

woman, **women** are nouns, not adjectives, so say female president, female MPs etc rather than "woman president", "women MPs"

womenswear but the magazine is Women's Wear Daily

Woolies the defunct shopping chain more formally known as Woolworths; **woollies** jumpers

Worcestershire sauce not Worcester

working class noun, **working-class** adjective

working tax credit replaced the working families tax credit

World Bank

world championship

World Cup, **World Cup final** football, cricket or rugby

World Food Programme may be abbreviated to WFP after first mention

World Health Organisation WHO on second mention

world heritage site

World Series
It is a myth that this baseball event got its name from the New York World: originally known as the World's Championship Series, it had nothing to do with the newspaper. It has become tedious every time the World Series comes round to see its name cited as an example of American arrogance

World Trade Centre, **Ground Zero** but the **twin towers**

worldview

worldwide often redundant, eg "it has automotive plants in 30 countries worldwide" (as opposed to galaxy-wide?)

Ww

world wide web

wounds combatants in battle are wounded, not injured

wrack seaweed; **racked** with guilt and shame, not wracked; **rack and ruin**

wrest as in wresting back, rather than wrestling back, your title

wriggle room not wiggle room

wrinklies patronising, unfunny way to refer to elderly people; do not use

wrongfoot (verb) as in I was wrongfooted by the question

wuss

WWE World Wrestling Entertainment, formerly the World Wrestling Federation (thank you, Patrick)

WWF formerly the World Wide Fund for Nature (or, in the US, World Wildlife Fund)

Xx

❝ Is there much point in being grumpy when one sees 'disinterested' or 'ironic' being misused in print, or hears 'like' deployed as a form of punctuation in conversation? Usage and meaning are always evolving, so mourn the loss and get over it. Personally, I would like it to become a criminal offence for anyone under 59 to use the word 'unprecedented' when they usually mean 'not lately'. But let's be positive. News reports, in the FT as well as the Sun, would read better if journalists used the present tense instead of the past imperfect. 'Is happening', not 'was happening'. Simple, but effective ❞

Michael White

Xbox

xenophobe, xenophobia, xenophobic

Xerox TM; say photocopy

Xhosa South African ethnic group and language

Xi'an city in China where the Terracotta Warriors are located

Xmas Christmas is preferable unless you are writing a headline, up against a deadline, and desperate (or quoting Slade's Merry Xmas Everybody)

x-ray

Yy

66 The critics' "you" makes me want to poke out my own eyes so I can no longer read: 'You want to get up and dance to this song;' 'This scene puts you in mind of the opening scene in A Bout de Souffle;' 'The apricot crumble will make you think of sun-dappled evenings punting down the Cam.' I somehow doubt it will. It's as if the critic either has so little faith in his judgment that he refuses to take responsibility for it and instead puts it on the reader, or else has so much faith in his judgment that he assumes everyone will have the same reaction as him. Either is nauseatingly pretentious. It's rare that one needs to encourage a journalist to use the first person pronoun more frequently but in these instances I think longingly of the letter 'I' 99

Hadley Freeman

y or ie?

As a general rule: -y is an English suffix, whose function is to create an adjective (usually from a noun, eg creamy); -ie was originally a Scottish suffix, whose function is to add the meaning of "diminutive" (usually from a noun, eg beastie). So in most cases, where there is dispute over whether a noun takes a -y or an -ie ending, the correct answer is -ie: she's a girly girl, but she's no helpless girlie. Think also scrunchie, beanie, nightie, meanie ... There are exceptions (a hippy, an indie band), but where specific examples are not given, use -ie for nouns and -y for adjectives

Yahoo (the company) no exclamation mark

Yangtze river; not Yangtse

Yar'Adua, Umaru president of Nigeria from 2007, when he succeeded Olusegun Obasanjo, until his death in May 2010

year write 2010, not "the year 2010"; for a span of years use hyphen thus: 2009-10, not 2009/10. If you need to say it aloud – for example, in a podcast – say "twenty-ten" not "two thousand and ten"

year 1, **year 10** etc (schools)

yearbook

Yekaterinburg

Yellow Pages TM

Yemen not "the Yemen"

yes campaign, **no campaign** not Yes or "yes" campaign

yesterday
Give some thought to where you place the time element in a story: do not automatically put it at the start ("David Cameron yesterday insisted ... "), a style satirised by the subeditor turned bestselling author Bill Bryson, who wrote: "Anyone not acquainted with journalists could be forgiven for assuming that they must talk something like this: I last night went to bed early

Yy

because I this morning had to catch an early flight."

Constructions such as "the two sides were today to consider", as we have been known to say, sound ugly and artificial. As with headlines, try reading out loud to find the most natural arrangement.

A relatively recent complication is that we have millions of readers in different time zones around the world, for whom yesterday, today and tomorrow will not necessarily mean the same thing. Some websites, such as the BBC, have dropped references to the date or time at the start of a story; others, such as the Los Angeles Times, give the day an event took place ("on Monday" rather than "yesterday"). We favour a flexible approach, where "yesterday" is appropriate for the newspapers, which are most likely to be read in the UK first thing in the morning, but not for the website, which may be read at any time, anywhere in the world

yoghurt

yo-yo toy; **Yo-Yo Ma** cellist

York Minster

Yorkshire North Yorkshire, South Yorkshire, West Yorkshire but east Yorkshire

Yorkshire dales but North York Moors national park

yorkshire pudding, **yorkshire terrier**

Yorkshire Ripper

Young, Lady
Lady Young of Hornsey, a former actor (she appeared in the TV series Metal Mickey), artist and academic.

Lady Young of Old Scone, former chief executive of the Environment Agency and the Care Quality Commission, appointed chancellor of Cranfield University in 2010.

Lady Young of Farnworth, a former Tory leader of the Lords and staunch defender of section 28, died in 2002

Yy

young turks

The Young Visiters (not Visitors) novel by the Victorian child author Daisy Ashford, filmed by the BBC in 2003

yours no apostrophe

YouTube

yuan Chinese currency; we don't call it renminbi

Yu-Gi-Oh! trading card game

yuletide

Zz

66 Few things disappoint me more than an intelligent, literate person actively choosing to write in a sloppy fashion. I don't care how busy you are - if you don't have time to punctuate, move away from the keyboard. At the next election, I'm voting for the party which promises to make textspeak illegal and correct capitalisation mandatory. (Going by their current literature, I'm fairly confident this won't be the BNP.) I long to live in a world where omitting full stops from the ends of sentences is deemed a social faux pas akin to walking around with your penis hanging out of your trousers **99**

Ariane Sherine

Zz

al-Zaidi, Muntazer Iraqi journalist who served a jail sentence for throwing his shoes at the then US president, George W Bush

Zanu-PF Zimbabwean political party led by Robert Mugabe, the country's president, which in 2008 reached a power-sharing agreement with the opposition Movement for Democratic Change (MDC), led by Morgan Tsvangirai, who became prime minister

Zapatero, José Luis Rodríguez Spanish politician, elected prime minister in 2004, and re-elected four years later

-ze endings: use -se, even if this upsets your (American) spellchecker, eg emphasise, realise; but capsize, synthesizer

zeitgeist

Zellweger, Renée

zero plural zeros; but zeroes in on

Zeta-Jones, Catherine

zeugma
A figure of speech in which, typically, a single verb is used to yoke together two or more parts of a sentence with different meanings. Some examples:
"The queen takes counsel and tea" (Pope).
"Mr Pickwick took his hat and his leave" (Dickens).
And more recently: "The following year, in Sing Your Worries Away, she played a stripper, taking off her clothes and her sister" (Ronald Bergan, in a 2010 Guardian obituary of June Havoc, Gypsy Rose Lee's sister)

zhoosh
An example of gay slang (*see Polari*), used in the fashion industry and on US television shows such as Will and Grace and Queer Eye for the Straight Guy; it has various shades of meaning: (noun) clothing, ornamentation; (verb) zhoosh your hair, zhoosh yourself up; zhooshy (adjective) showy

Zhu Rongji Chinese premier (prime minister) from 1998 to 2003, when he was succeeded by Wen Jiabao

Zz

zigzag no hyphen

Zimmer TM; if it's not a Zimmer frame, call it a walking frame

Zionist refers to someone who believes in the right for a Jewish national home to exist within historic Palestine; someone who wants the borders of that entity to be expanded is not an "ultra-Zionist" but might be described as a hardliner, hawk or rightwinger

zloty Polish unit of currency

zoos lc: London zoo, San Diego zoo, etc

Answers

Spot that synonym

The answers to our Pov quiz on pages 240 and 241:

1. Ken Livingstone
2. Lord Charles
3. Crucifix
4. Cameron and Clegg
5. Blackpool
6. Mephedrone
7. AA
8. Spam
9. Large Hadron Collider
10. Asparagus
11. Little Boots
12. Anne Boleyn
13. Sugar
14. Toyota
15. New York Times and Wall Street Journal

66 I am about to - or I am going to - die; either expression is used **99**

Last words of the 17th-century French Jesuit grammarian Dominique Bouhours

66 The life of a journalist is poor, nasty, brutish and short. So is his style **99**

Stella Gibbons

References

- Amis, Kingsley: The King's English, A Guide to Modern Usage (HarperCollins, 1997)
- Baker, Paul: Fantabulosa, A Dictionary of Polari and Gay Slang (Continuum, 2002)
- Bauer, Laurie and Trudgill, Peter (eds): Language Myths (Penguin, 1998)
- Bierce, Ambrose: The Devil's Dictionary (Neal Publishing Company, 1911; reprinted by Dover Publications, 1993)
- Bryson, Bill: Mother Tongue (Penguin, 1991)
- Bryson, Bill: Troublesome Words (Viking, 3rd edition, 2001)
- Burchfield, RW: The New Fowler's Modern English Usage (OUP, revised 3rd edition, 1998)
- Collins English Dictionary (HarperCollins, 30th anniversary edition, 2010)
- Crystal, David: The Cambridge Encyclopedia of English (Cambridge University Press, 1995)
- Crystal, David: Who Cares About English Usage? (Penguin, 2nd edition, 2000)
- Crystal, David: Fight for English: How Language Pundits Ate, Shot and Left (OUP, 2006)
- Crystal, David: Language and the Internet (Cambridge University Press, 2nd edition, 2006)
- David Crystal's blog http://david-crystal.blogspot.com/
- The Economist Style Guide (Profile Books, 2005)
- Fowler's Modern English Usage (Oxford, 1965, revised by E Gowers)
- Hammond, JL: CP Scott (G Bell and Sons, 1934)
- Hicks, Wynford: Writing for Journalists (Routledge, 2nd edition, 1998)
- Hicks, Wynford and Holmes, Tim: Subediting for Journalists (Routledge, 2002)
- Huddlestone, Rodney: Introduction to the Grammar of English (Cambridge University Press, 1984)

- Miller, Casey and Swift, Kate: The Handbook of Non-Sexist Writing (The Women's Press, 1980)
- onlinestylebooks.com
- Oxford English Dictionary online: http://dictionary.oed.com
- Palmer, FR: The English Verb (Longman, 2nd edition, 1987)
- Poole, Steven: Unspeak (Little, Brown, 2006)
- Quirk, R; Greenbaum, S; Leech, G; Svartvik, J: A Comprehensive Grammar of the English Language (Longman, 1985)
- Pinker, Steven: The Language Instinct (Penguin, 1994)
- Pinker, Steven: Words and Rules (Phoenix, 1999)
- Siegal, Alan M and Connolly, William G: The New York Times Manual of Style and Usage (Times Books, 1999)

Appendix 1

CP Scott's essay published in the Manchester Guardian on the centenary of the paper's first issue

A hundred years is a long time; it is a long time even in the life of a newspaper, and to look back on it is to take in not only a vast development in the thing itself, but a great slice in the life of the nation, in the progress and adjustment of the world.

In the general development the newspaper, as an institution, has played its part, and no small part, and the particular newspaper with which I personally am concerned has also played its part, it is to be hoped, not without some usefulness. I have had my share in it for a little more than fifty years; I have been its responsible editor for only a few months short of its last half-century; I remember vividly its fiftieth birthday; I now have the happiness to share in the celebration of its hundredth. I can therefore speak of it with a certain intimacy of acquaintance. I have myself been part of it and entered into its inner courts. That is perhaps a reason why, on this occasion, I should write in my own name, as in some sort a spectator, rather than in the name of the paper as a member of its working staff.

In all living things there must be a certain unity, a principle of vitality and growth. It is so with a newspaper, and the more complete and clear this unity the more vigorous and fruitful the growth. I ask myself what the paper stood for when first I knew it, what it has stood for since and stands for now. A newspaper has two sides to it. It is a business, like any other, and has to pay in the material sense in order to live. But it is much more than a business; it is an institution; it reflects and it influences the life of a whole community; it may affect even wider destinies. It is, in its way, an instrument of government. It plays on the minds and consciences of men. It may educate, stimulate, assist, or it may do the opposite. It has, therefore, a moral as well as a material existence, and its character and influence are in the main determined by the balance of these two forces. It may make profit or power its first object, or it may conceive itself as fulfilling a higher and more exacting function.

I think I may honestly say that, from the day of its foundation, there has not been much doubt as to which way the balance tipped as far as regards the conduct of the paper whose fine tradition I inherited and which I have had the honour to serve through all my working life. Had it not been so, personally, I could not have served it. Character is a subtle affair, and has many shades and sides to it. It is not a thing to be much talked about, but rather to be felt. It is the slow deposit of past actions and ideals. It is for each man his most precious possession, and so it is for that latest growth of time the newspaper. Fundamentally it implies honesty, cleanness, courage, fairness, a sense of duty to the reader and the community. A newspaper is of necessity something of a monopoly, and its first duty is to shun the temptations of monopoly. Its primary office is the gathering of news. At the peril of its soul it must see that the supply is not tainted. Neither in what it gives, nor in what it does not give, nor in the mode of presentation must the unclouded face of truth suffer wrong. Comment is free, but facts are sacred. "Propaganda," so called, by this means is hateful. The voice of opponents no less than that of friends has a right to be heard. Comment also is justly subject to a self-imposed restraint. It is well to be frank; it is even better to be fair. This is an ideal. Achievement in such matters is hardly given to man. We can but try, ask pardon for shortcomings, and there leave the matter.

But, granted a sufficiency of grace, to what further conquests may we look, what purpose serve, what task envisage? It is a large question, and cannot be fully answered. We are faced with a new and enormous power and a growing one. Whither is the young giant tending? What gifts does he bring? How will he exercise his privilege and powers? What influence will he exercise on the minds of men and on our public life? It cannot be pretended that an assured and entirely satisfactory answer can be given to such questions. Experience is in some respects disquieting. The development has not been all in the direction which we should most desire.

One of the virtues, perhaps almost the chief virtue, of a newspaper is its independence. Whatever its position or character, at least it should have a soul of its own. But the tendency of newspapers, as of other businesses, in these days is towards amalgamation. In proportion, as the function of a newspaper has developed and its organisation expanded, so have its costs increased. The smaller newspapers have had a hard struggle; many of them have disappeared. In their place we have great organisations controlling a whole series of publications of various kinds and even of differing or opposing politics. The process may be inevitable, but clearly there are drawbacks. As organisation grows personality may tend to disappear. It is much to control one newspaper well; it is perhaps beyond the reach of any man, or any body of men, to control half a dozen with equal success. It is possible to exaggerate the danger, for the public is not undiscerning. It recognises the authentic voices of conscience and conviction when it finds them, and it has a shrewd intuition of what to accept and what to discount.

This is a matter which in the end must settle itself, and those who cherish the older ideal of a newspaper need not be dismayed. They have only to make their papers good enough in order to win, as well as to merit, success, and the resources of a newspaper are not wholly measured in pounds, shillings, and pence. Of course the thing can only be done by competence all round, and by that spirit of co-operation right through the working staff which only a common ideal can inspire.

There are people who think you can run a newspaper about as easily as you can poke a fire, and that knowledge, training, and aptitude are superfluous endowments. There have even been experiments on this assumption, and they have not met with success. There must be competence, to start with, on the business side, just as there must be in any large undertaking, but it is a mistake to suppose that the business side of a paper should dominate, as sometimes happens, not without distressing consequences.

A newspaper, to be of value, should be a unity, and every part of it should equally understand and respond to the purposes and ideals which animate it. Between its two sides there should be a happy marriage, and editor and business manager should march hand in hand, the first, be it well understood, just an inch or two in advance. Of the staff much the same thing may be said. They should be a friendly company. They need not, of course, agree on every point, but they should share in the general purpose and inheritance. A paper is built up upon their common and successive labours, and their work should never be task work, never merely dictated. They should be like a racing boat's crew, pulling well together, each man doing his best because he likes it, and with a common and glorious goal.

That is the path of self-respect and pleasure; it is also the path of success. And what a work it is! How multiform, how responsive to every need and every incident of life! What illimitable possibilities of achievement and of excellence! People talk of "journalese" as though a journalist were of necessity a pretentious and sloppy writer; he may be, on the contrary, and very often is, one of the best in the world. At least he should not be content to be much less. And then the developments. Every year, almost every day, may see growth and fresh accomplishments, and with a paper that is really alive, it not only may, but does. Let anyone take a file of this paper, or for that matter any one of half a dozen other papers, and compare its whole make-up and leading features today with what they were five years ago, ten years ago, twenty years ago, and he will realise how large has been the growth, how considerable the achievement. And this is what makes the work of a newspaper worthy and interesting. It has so many sides, it touches life at so many points, at every one there is such possibility on improvement and excellence. To the man, whatever his place on the paper, whether on the editorial or business, or even what may be regarded as the mechanical side – this also vitally important in its place – nothing should satisfy short of the best, and the best must always seem a little ahead of the actual. It is here that ability counts and that character counts, and it is on these that a newspaper, like every great undertaking, if it is to be worthy of its power and duty, must rely.

CP Scott, Editor, Thursday May 5, 1921

Appendix 2

(incorporating the Press Complaints
Commission code of practice)

Summary

*"A newspaper's primary office is the gathering of news. At the
peril of its soul it must see that the supply is not tainted."*

The most important currency of the Guardian is trust. This is as
true today as when CP Scott marked the centenary of the
founding of the newspaper with his famous essay on journalism
in 1921.

The purpose of this code is, above all, to protect and foster
the bond of trust between the Guardian (in print and online)
and its readers, and therefore to protect the integrity of the
paper and of the editorial content it carries.

As a set of guidelines this will not form part of a journalist's
contract of employment, nor will it form part, for either
editorial management or journalists, of disciplinary,
promotional or recruitment procedures. However, by observing
the code, journalists working for the Guardian will be protecting
not only the paper but also the independence, standing and
reputation of themselves and their colleagues. It is important
that freelancers working for the Guardian also abide by these
guidelines while on assignment for the paper.

Press Complaints Commission code of practice

The Guardian — in common with most other papers in Britain —
considers the PCC's code of practice to be a sound statement of
ethical behaviour for journalists. It is written into our terms of
employment that staff should adhere to the code of practice. It
is published below so that all editorial staff can familiarise
themselves with it.

1 Professional practice

Anonymous quotations

We recognise that people will often speak more honestly if they are allowed to speak anonymously. The use of non-attributed quotes can therefore often assist the reader towards a truer understanding of a subject than if a journalist confined him/herself to quoting bland on-the-record quotes. But if used lazily or indiscriminately anonymous quotes become a menace.

We should be honest about our sources, even if we can't name them.

The New York Times policy on pejorative quotes is worth bearing in mind: "The vivid language of direct quotation confers an unfair advantage on a speaker or writer who hides behind the newspaper, and turns of phrase are valueless to a reader who cannot assess the source."

There may be exceptional circumstances when anonymous pejorative quotes may be used, but they will be rare – and only after consultation with the senior editor of the day. In the absence of specific approval we should paraphrase anonymous pejorative quotes.

Children

Special care should be taken when dealing with children (under the age of 16). Heads of departments must be informed when children have been photographed or interviewed without parental consent. *(See PCC code, section 6)*

Copy approval

The general rule is that no one should be given the right to copy approval. In certain circumstances we may allow people to see copy or quotes but we are not required to alter copy. We should avoid offering copy approval as a method of securing interviews or co-operation.

Direct quotations

Should not be changed to alter their context or meaning.

Errors

It is the policy of the Guardian to correct significant errors as soon as possible. Journalists have a duty to co-operate frankly and openly with the readers' editor and to report errors to him. All complaints should be brought to the attention of a department head, the managing editor or the readers' editor. All journalists should read both the daily and weekly columns.

Fairness

"The voice of opponents no less than of friends has a right to be heard ... It is well be to be frank; it is even better to be fair." (CP Scott, 1921)

The more serious the criticism or allegations we are reporting the greater the obligation to allow the subject the opportunity to respond.

Grief

People should be treated with sensitivity during periods of grief and trauma. (*See PCC code, section 5*)

Language

Respect for the reader demands that we should not casually use words that are likely to offend. Use swearwords only when absolutely necessary to the facts of a piece, or to portray a character in an article; there is almost never a case in which we need to use a swearword outside direct quotes. The stronger the swearword, the harder we ought to think about using it. Avoid using in headlines, pullquotes and standfirsts and never use asterisks, which are just a cop-out.

Legal

Our libel and contempt laws are complex, and constantly

developing. The consequences of losing actions can be expensive and damaging for our reputation. Staff should a) familiarise themselves with the current state of the law and seek training if they feel unconfident about aspects of it; b) consult our in-house legal department or night lawyers about specific concerns on stories; c) read the regular legal bulletins about active cases and injunctions emailed by the legal department.

Payment
In general, the Guardian does not pay for stories, except from bona fide freelance sources. The editor or his deputies must approve rare exceptions.

PCC and libel judgments
Judgments by the PCC and the outcome of defamation actions relating to the Guardian should be reported promptly.

Photographs
Digitally enhanced or altered images, montages and illustrations should be clearly labelled as such.

Plagiarism
Staff must not reproduce other people's material without attribution. The source of published material obtained from another organisation should be acknowledged, including quotes taken from other newspaper articles. Bylines should be carried only on material that is substantially the work of the bylined journalist. If an article contains a significant amount of agency copy then the agency should be credited.

Privacy
In keeping with both the PCC Code and the Human Rights Act we believe in respecting people's privacy. We should avoid intrusions into people's privacy unless there is a clear public

interest in doing so. Caution should be exercised about reporting and publishing identifying details, such as street names and numbers, that may enable others to intrude on the privacy or safety of people who have become the subject of media coverage.

Race

In general, we do not publish someone's race or ethnic background or religion unless that information is pertinent to the story. We do not report the race of criminal suspects unless their ethnic background is part of a description that seeks to identify them or is an important part of the story (for example, if the crime was a hate crime).

Sources

Sources promised confidentiality must be protected at all costs. However, where possible, the sources of information should be identified as specifically as possible.

Subterfuge

Journalists should generally identify themselves as Guardian employees when working on a story. There may be instances involving stories of exceptional public interest where this does not apply, but this needs the approval of a head of department.

Suicide

Journalists are asked to exercise particular care in reporting suicide or issues involving suicide, bearing in mind the risk of encouraging others. This should be borne in mind both in presentation, including the use of pictures, and in describing the method of suicide. Any substances should be referred to in general rather than specific terms if possible. When appropriate a helpline number should be given (eg Samaritans 08457 909090). The feelings of relatives should also be carefully considered.

2 Personal behaviour and conflicts of interest

The Guardian values its reputation for independence and integrity. Journalists clearly have lives, interests, hobbies, convictions and beliefs outside their work on the paper. Nothing in the following guidelines is intended to restrict any of that. It is intended to ensure that outside interests do not come into conflict with the life of the paper in a way that either compromises the Guardian's editorial integrity or falls short of the sort of transparency that our readers would expect. The code is intended to apply to all active outside interests which, should they remain undeclared and become known, would cause a fair-minded reader to question the value of a contribution to the paper by the journalist involved.

These are guidelines rather than one-size-fits-all rules. If you are employed as a columnist – with your views openly on display – you may have more latitude than a staff reporter, who would be expected to bring qualities of objectivity to their work. (The Washington Post's code has some sound advice: "Reporters should make every effort to remain in the audience, to stay off the stage, to report the news, not to make the news.") If in doubt, consult a head of department, the managing or deputy editors, or the editor himself.

Commercial products
No Guardian journalist or freelance primarily associated with the Guardian should endorse commercial products unless with the express permission of their head of department or managing editor.

Confidentiality
Desk editors with access to personal information relating to other members of staff are required to treat such information as confidential, and not disclose it to anyone except in the course of discharging formal responsibilities.

Conflicts of interest

Guardian staff journalists should be sensitive to the possibility that activities outside work (including holding office or being otherwise actively involved in organisations, companies or political parties) could be perceived as having a bearing on – or as coming into conflict with – the integrity of our journalism. Staff should be transparent about any outside personal, philosophical or financial interests that might conflict with their professional performance of duties at the Guardian, or could be perceived to do so.

Declarations of interest

1. It is always necessary to declare an interest when the journalist is writing about something with which he or she has a significant connection. This applies to both staff journalists and freelances writing for the Guardian. The declaration should be to a head of department or editor during preparation. Full transparency may mean that the declaration should appear in the paper or on the website as well.

2. A connection does not have to be a formal one before it is necessary to declare it. Acting in an advisory capacity in the preparation of a report for an organisation, for example, would require a declaration every time the journalist wrote an article referring to it.

3. Some connections are obvious and represent the reason why the writer has been asked to contribute to the paper. These should always be stated at the end of the writer's contribution even if he or she contributes regularly, so long as the writer is writing about his or her area of interest.

4. Generally speaking a journalist should not write about or quote a relative or partner in a piece, even if the relative or partner is an expert in the field in question. If, for any reason, an exception is made to this rule, the connection should be made clear.

5. Commissioning editors should ensure that freelances asked

to write for the Guardian are aware of these rules and make any necessary declaration.

Declarations of corporate interest

The Guardian is part of a wider group of media companies. We should be careful to acknowledge that relationship in stories. Anyone writing a story concerning Guardian-related businesses should seek comments and/or confirmation in the normal way. Staff should familiarise themselves with the companies and interests we have.

Financial reporting

For many years the Guardian's business desk has maintained a register of personal shares. All staff are expected to list all shares that they own, any transactions in those shares and any other investments which they believe ought to be properly disclosed because of a potential conflict of interest. While it is acceptable for financial members to own shares, it is not acceptable for them to be market traders on a regular basis. It is most important that the register is kept and that all information is up to date. The attention of Guardian journalists is also drawn to section 13 of the PCC code of practice (below) and to the PCC's best-practice guidelines on financial journalism, which can also be found in the "code advice" section of the PCC website.

The code: prohibits the use of financial information for the profit of journalists or their associates; imposes restrictions on journalists writing about shares in which they or their close families have a significant interest without internal disclosure; stops journalists dealing in shares about which they have written recently or intend to write in the near future; requires that financial journalists take care not to publish inaccurate material and to distinguish between comment, conjecture and fact. This is particularly important for any journalists making investment recommendations to readers about whether to buy, sell or hold shares.

Freelance work

As a general rule avoid freelance writing for house magazines of particular businesses or causes if the contribution could be interpreted as an endorsement of the concern. If in doubt consult your head or department.

Freebies

1. Staff should not use their position to obtain private benefit for themselves or others.
2. The Guardian and its staff will not allow any payment, gift or other advantage to undermine accuracy, fairness or independence. Any attempts to induce favourable editorial treatment through the offer of gifts or favours should be reported to the editor. Where relevant the Guardian will disclose these payments, gifts or other advantages.
3. We should make it clear when an airline, hotel or other interest has borne the cost of transporting or accommodating a journalist. Acceptance of any such offer is conditional on the Guardian being free to assign and report or not report any resulting story as it sees fit.
4. Except in some areas of travel writing it should never need to be the case that the journalist's partner, family or friends are included in any free arrangement. When a partner, family member or friend accompanies the journalist on a trip, the additional costs should generally be paid for by the journalist or person accompanying the journalist.
5. Staff should not be influenced by commercial considerations – including the interests of advertisers – in the preparation of material for the paper.
6. Gifts other than those of an insignificant value (say, less than £25) should be politely returned or may be entered for the annual raffle of such items for charity, "the sleaze raffle".

Guardian connections

Staff members should not use their positions at the Guardian to seek any benefit or advantage in personal business, financial or commercial transactions not afforded to the public generally. Staff should not use Guardian stationery in connection with non-Guardian matters or cite a connection with the paper to resolve consumer grievances, get quicker service or seek discounts or deals.

Outside engagements or duties

The Guardian accepts the journalist's right to a private life and the right to take part in civic society. However, staff should inform their immediate editor if, in their capacity as an employee of the Guardian, they intend to:

1. Give evidence to any court.
2. Chair public forums or seminars arranged by professional conference organisers or commercial organisations.
3. Undertake any outside employment likely to conflict with their professional duties at the Guardian.
4. Chair public or political forums or appear on platforms.
5. Make representations or give evidence to any official body in connection with material that has been published in the Guardian.

Relationships

Staff members should not write about, photograph or make news judgments about any individual related by blood or marriage or with whom the staff member has a close personal, financial or romantic relationship. A staff member who is placed in a circumstance in which the potential for this kind of conflict exists should advise his or her department head.

Press Complaints Commission code of practice

The Press Complaints Commission is charged with enforcing the following Code of Practice which was framed by the newspaper and periodical industry and was ratified by the PCC in September 2009.

The editors' code

All members of the press have a duty to maintain the highest professional standards. The code, which includes this preamble and the public interest exceptions below, sets the benchmark for those ethical standards, protecting both the rights of the individual and the public's right to know. It is the cornerstone of the system of self-regulation to which the industry has made a binding commitment.

It is essential that an agreed code be honoured not only to the letter but in the full spirit. It should not be interpreted so narrowly as to compromise its commitment to respect the rights of the individual, nor so broadly that it constitutes an unnecessary interference with freedom of expression or prevents publication in the public interest.

It is the responsibility of editors and publishers to apply the code to editorial material in both printed and online versions of publications. They should take care to ensure it is observed rigorously by all editorial staff and external contributors, including non-journalists, in printed and online versions of publications.

Editors should co-operate swiftly with the PCC in the resolution of complaints. Any publication judged to have breached the code must print the adjudication in full and with due prominence, including headline reference to the PCC.

1 Accuracy
i)   The press must take care not to publish inaccurate, misleading or distorted information, including pictures.

ii) A significant inaccuracy, misleading statement or distortion once recognised must be corrected, promptly and with due prominence, and - where appropriate - an apology published.

iii) The Press, whilst free to be partisan, must distinguish clearly between comment, conjecture and fact.

iv) A publication must report fairly and accurately the outcome of an action for defamation to which it has been a party, unless an agreed settlement states otherwise, or an agreed statement is published.

2 Opportunity to reply

A fair opportunity for reply to inaccuracies must be given when reasonably called for.

3 * Privacy

i) Everyone is entitled to respect for his or her private and family life, home, health and correspondence, including digital communications.

ii) Editors will be expected to justify intrusions into any individual's private life without consent. Account will be taken of the complainant's own public disclosures of information.

iii) It is unacceptable to photograph individuals in private places without their consent.

Note - Private places are public or private property where there is a reasonable expectation of privacy.

4 * Harassment

i) Journalists must not engage in intimidation, harassment or persistent pursuit.

ii) They must not persist in questioning, telephoning, pursuing or photographing individuals once asked to desist; nor remain on their property when asked to leave and must not follow them. If requested, they must identify themselves and whom they represent.

iii) Editors must ensure these principles are observed by those working for them and take care not to use non-compliant material from other sources.

5 Intrusion into grief or shock

i) In cases involving personal grief or shock, enquiries and approaches must be made with sympathy and discretion and publication handled sensitively. This should not restrict the right to report legal proceedings, such as inquests.

ii) * When reporting suicide, care should be taken to avoid excessive detail about the method used.

6 * Children

i) Young people should be free to complete their time at school without unnecessary intrusion.

ii) A child under 16 must not be interviewed or photographed on issues involving their own or another child's welfare unless a custodial parent or similarly responsible adult consents.

iii) Pupils must not be approached or photographed at school without the permission of the school authorities.

iv) Minors must not be paid for material involving children's welfare, nor parents or guardians for material about their children or wards, unless it is clearly in the child's interest.

v) Editors must not use the fame, notoriety or position of a parent or guardian as sole justification for publishing details of a child's private life.

7 * Children in sex cases

1. The press must not, even if legally free to do so, identify children under 16 who are victims or witnesses in cases involving sex offences.

2. In any press report of a case involving a sexual offence against a child –

i) The child must not be identified.

ii) The adult may be identified.

iii) The word "incest" must not be used where a child victim might be identified.

iv) Care must be taken that nothing in the report implies the relationship between the accused and the child.

8 * Hospitals

i) Journalists must identify themselves and obtain permission from a responsible executive before entering non-public areas of hospitals or similar institutions to pursue enquiries.

ii) The restrictions on intruding into privacy are particularly relevant to enquiries about individuals in hospitals or similar institutions.

9 * Reporting of Crime

i) Relatives or friends of persons convicted or accused of crime should not generally be identified without their consent, unless they are genuinely relevant to the story.

ii) Particular regard should be paid to the potentially vulnerable position of children who witness, or are victims of, crime. This should not restrict the right to report legal proceedings.

10 * Clandestine devices and subterfuge

i) The press must not seek to obtain or publish material acquired by using hidden cameras or clandestine listening devices; or by intercepting private or mobile telephone calls, messages or emails; or by the unauthorised removal of documents or photographs; or by accessing digitally-held private information without consent.

ii) Engaging in misrepresentation or subterfuge, including by agents or intermediaries, can generally be justified only in the public interest and then only when the material cannot be obtained by other means.

11 Victims of sexual assault

The press must not identify victims of sexual assault or publish material likely to contribute to such identification unless there is adequate justification and they are legally free to do so.

12 Discrimination

i) The press must avoid prejudicial or pejorative reference to an individual's race, colour, religion, gender, sexual orientation or to any physical or mental illness or disability.

ii) Details of an individual's race, colour, religion, sexual orientation, physical or mental illness or disability must be avoided unless genuinely relevant to the story.

13 Financial journalism

i) Even where the law does not prohibit it, journalists must not use for their own profit financial information they receive in advance of its general publication, nor should they pass such information to others.

ii) They must not write about shares or securities in whose performance they know that they or their close families have a significant financial interest without disclosing the interest to the editor or financial editor.

iii) They must not buy or sell, either directly or through nominees or agents, shares or securities about which they have written recently or about which they intend to write in the near future.

14 Confidential sources

Journalists have a moral obligation to protect confidential sources of information.

15 Witness payments in criminal trials

i) No payment or offer of payment to a witness - or any person who may reasonably be expected to be called as a witness - should be made in any case once proceedings are active as defined by the Contempt of Court Act 1981.

This prohibition lasts until the suspect has been freed unconditionally by police without charge or bail or the proceedings are otherwise discontinued; or has entered a guilty plea to the court; or, in the event of a not guilty plea, the court has announced its verdict.

ii) * Where proceedings are not yet active but are likely and foreseeable, editors must not make or offer payment to any person who may reasonably be expected to be called as a witness, unless the information concerned ought demonstrably to be published in the public interest and there is an overriding need to make or promise payment for this to be done; and all reasonable steps have been taken to ensure no financial dealings influence the evidence those witnesses give. In no circumstances should such payment be conditional on the outcome of a trial.

iii) * Any payment or offer of payment made to a person later cited to give evidence in proceedings must be disclosed to the prosecution and defence. The witness must be advised of this requirement.

16 * Payment to criminals

i) Payment or offers of payment for stories, pictures or information, which seek to exploit a particular crime or to glorify or glamorise crime in general, must not be made directly or via agents to convicted or confessed criminals or to their associates - who may include family, friends and colleagues.

ii) Editors invoking the public interest to justify payment or offers would need to demonstrate that there was good reason to believe the public interest would be served. If, despite payment, no public interest emerged, then the material should not be published.

The public interest

There may be exceptions to the clauses marked * where they can be demonstrated to be in the public interest.

1. The public interest includes, but is not confined to:
   i)   Detecting or exposing crime or serious impropriety.
   ii) Protecting public health and safety.
   iii) Preventing the public from being misled by an action or statement of an individual or organisation.
2. There is a public interest in freedom of expression itself.
3. Whenever the public interest is invoked, the PCC will require editors to demonstrate fully that they reasonably believed that publication, or journalistic activity undertaken with a view to publication, would be in the public interest.
4. The PCC will consider the extent to which material is already in the public domain, or will become so.
5. In cases involving children under 16, editors must demonstrate an exceptional public interest to override the normally paramount interest of the child.

Appendix 3

Social media guidelines used at
guardian.co.uk

Social media and participation

As editorial sites increasingly turn to social media tools and
techniques to add interactivity or amplify their content in the
wider web, it has become crucial for publishers and web
practitioners to understand the potential and the pitfalls of
social media approaches. Here are a few pointers the Guardian
uses to inform its own social media activity.

Social media facilitates participation by and with readers,
which can add both *breadth* and *depth* to content. It can also be
effective in turning a one-day story, article or blogpost into a
conversation that lasts much longer.

As social media revolves around interactivity, the distinction
between "us" (writing "above the line") and "them"
(commenting "below the line") is becoming blurred. Sites that
are successful at using social media have in many cases become
so through thinking of the site as a platform for conversation
about interesting or timely issues and ideas.

Social media have inspired content publishers to participate
in conversations about things they are passionate about or
specialists in, though making this work relies on editors,
journalists and other content creators knowing how to
participate effectively and appropriately. This can mean
developing new skills to do with listening and facilitating
constructive conversations as well as knowing how to conduct
themselves in the face of sometimes feisty exchanges.

There's also a recognition that communities and
conversations need nurturing after they begin – it's no longer
enough to simply press "publish" on a piece of content and then
walk away. Content creators often need to put in as much work
after launch as before.

A crucial part of the "site-as-platform" approach is to
embrace, rather than replace, existing social activities or
external sites, such as Twitter, Flickr and Facebook. By
encouraging people to use applications they're comfortable
with to discuss, promote, extend and share content, it's possible

to extend reach and impact, without forcing people to change their existing online behaviours or site loyalties.

There's a growing recognition that in social media, we need to consider both *quantity* and *quality* of interactions. On editorial sites, constructive, enlightening conversations by and with loyal site users may well be more desirable than a mass of low-value interactions by drive-by commenters.

Content creators can also use social media tools and techniques to change the way they tell stories – or rather, to change their relationship with readers and work with them to tell stories together. In a genuinely social media company, the role of the journalist becomes more important, not less.

If you think about a blog as being an unfolding exploration of a particular context, issue or situation, bloggers and journalists can become curators of contexts – interactive storytellers, trusted guides and interpreters of fact and experience.

The art of curation is central to this activity. In web journalism, this means aggregation of content and contextually appropriate resources that help deepen understanding of an issue, plus links to relevant sources or further reading, which help place content in a web of relevance and discovery. Links and resources may be curated from your own site (ie here's how we've covered this story over time) or around the web (ie here's what other sites are saying about this issue).

The aim is to develop a relationship of trust with readers who will have confidence in your suggested further reading, but continue to view you as the main source for information – the first stop on a web journey, rather than the last.

Active resource and information curation and presentation is a significant part of good web content management, helping content to be truly *of* the web, not just *on* it. Combined with active, engaged and well-managed participation plus a clever approach to making the most of user activity, content sites will have a firm foundation to succeed in using social media to extend and enhance their editorial activities.

There are lots of tools and skills you can adopt to get social media working for you and your particular content, but becoming a really social media organisation means thinking in a different way. Here are five simple things you can start doing today without any special tools or skills, all of which will help social media to help you.

1. Commission, write, edit and curate with the web in mind. Consider how a story will live after it is published online or off. Link internally and externally, provide source material or further reading or action points.

2. Anticipate and plan for likely interaction. How would you like people to respond? Are you soliciting experiences, or asking them to share opinions and insights and ideas, or looking for data or further knowledge about a subject? Sometimes you need to invite particular kinds of contribution rather than just hoping the readers intuit what you're looking for. Planning for likely interaction also means keeping an eye on conversations, especially on topics that may provoke robust conversation.

3. Participate and encourage participation. Keep an eye on conversations you start and get involved where relevant. Respond when you can, especially if people are asking questions or making interesting points. Get the ball rolling by participating yourself: invite or encourage particular perspectives and tease out interesting kernels into new ideas and conversational threads. Plan the participatory behaviour you'd like to see.

4. Recognise and reward quality participation. Give attention and praise to contributions that are constructive or interesting. When someone makes a good point, say so (to them, in public, not just to other people in the office). Recommend comments, point to them, link to them, highlight them in print or in regular roundups online. Ditto loyal or constructive users. Don't reward negative behaviour with attention.

5. Keep it up. The hardest thing of all! Try to build social media activity into your daily editorial routines, even if it's just running Twitter in the background and checking in on active comment threads once in a while.

Putting external links in content

If your article contains reference to a website, service or application, it should be linked, at least once, as high as possible within the body text of the article. If your article contains a typed web address, or references a specific page on the web, it should be made into a link.

Add links within the body text when making reference to previously covered stories or topics. Make frequent contextual navigation links within blog posts (e.g. "Last week everyone was in a tizz about Madonna's bandage look ... ") - allow people to move through a story or topic by showing them what came before or inspired the post. Related links can also be added as further resources.

There is no perfect phrase or method to use when creating a link, but there are some simple things worth bearing in mind.

1. Add links to content where it is relevant and adds value to the reader.
2. As a rule of thumb, the first link in a blogpost or article will gain the most attention, so make sure it's also the most relevant one for your article.
3. Link only to pages/resources that are truly relevant or useful. Using too many links will make text difficult to read, and may cause deflation in the value (perceived importance) of all your existing links.
4. Link text should be able to be read and understood out of context and regardless of the fact that it's a link. Don't say "click here". Describe what's on the destination page or what will happen when a user clicks (eg "full directions are available for visitors" or "find out how to get here").

5. Longer text works better than linking a single word. Obviously, there are exceptions, but linking a number of words has the dual benefits of making it easier to click on than a single word, and also being more descriptive.

Some blogging tips

1. Post regularly. Establish a rhythm. As a rough guide you should be looking to post a minimum of four or five times a week. That said, the likes of Roy Greenslade and Jemima Kiss often post that many times a day.
2. Vary the content and length of your posts. Sometimes your pieces will be 800 words of opinion, original reporting or issue exploration. Sometimes they will be two lines with a couple of links. Combine reporting, observations and commentary with round-ups of what the blogosphere is saying, links to external pieces and video clips you like. Try to be thought-provoking rather than simply provocative. You can rant from time to time, but mix up the tone. No one likes a constant grouch.
3. Think about – and be ready for – the reaction you're likely to inspire. Get involved in the discussion "below the line". When people take the time to respond to your blog it's nice if you pop back into your blog, even if it is just to thank people for posting.
4. Link, link, link. Not just to big media sites but to content sites, rivals, other blogs and so on.
5. Find and acknowledge subject experts. Find the best blogs and Twitter users covering your area of interest. Follow and link to them often.

Glossary

Above/below the line content directly commissioned and/or sanctioned by an editorial organisation v comments added to a content object by site users

Blog (n) an unfolding exploration of a particular context, issue or event. A collection of articles, the body of work. (v) the act of publishing to same

Blogger (n) person who publishes or writes blogposts which make up a blog

Blogpost (n) a single entry or article in a blog cf newspaper (blog) v article (blogpost)

Commenter (n) person who adds comments to a blogpost

Link text the clickable words that form a hyperlink to another web page or resource

Social media an ever-expanding set of technologies and techniques which encourage engagement with and conversation around a topic, object or community online

Thread (n) conversation that follows a blogpost, contributed to by commenters and (hopefully) the original blogger

Trolling the online art of interacting in a way intended to needle, disrupt or upset proceedings. Trolls thrive on attention. Best ignored

Appendix 4

Selected pages from the 1928 Style Book
of the Manchester Guardian

NOTE.

The Authors' and Printers' Dictionary is founded on the Oxford Dictionary, and is in general agreement with the practice of the "Manchester Guardian." Below are the principal differences:—

All words ending with "ize" in both dictionaries are spelled in the "M.G." with an "s," as specialise.

Compounds are made of many words which are generally printed as one, as re-arrange, cod-fish, corn-crake, base-ball, head-quarters, life-boat, race-course, schoolmaster. Also sergeant-major, Attorney-General, Lord-Advocate, colour-sergeant, &c. These are not to be followed.

Capital letters are sometimes oddly placed, as County palatine, County court, Monroe doctrine, Court leet. All these words should have a capital letter.

Commas and full-points are placed outside quotation marks. Only colons and semi-colons should be so placed.

Very many contractions are given, but the practice of the "M.G." is to make only usual contractions and to be sparing of them. Signatures, however, should always be followed.

LEADERS.

No small caps to be used. Quotation marks to be put down the side when the quoted words extend to three lines or more. Figures are not to be used below 100, except in statistics and subjects of a similar nature, also dates.

PARLIAMENTARY.

Names and titles of speakers to be in capitals, as the Marquis of SALISBURY, the CHANCELLOR of the EXCHEQUER, Mr. HODGE (Lab.—Gorton), Mr. LEACH (L.—Colne Valley), &c. Where a person is only mentioned as having spoken, the name to be in lower-case, as—"Mr. Lee also spoke." "The noble Earl," "his Lordship," the gallant Admiral, the Archbishop, the Bishop, capital letters, but "the right rev. prelate, the hon. member lower case. A capital L for the Leader of the House and the party leaders. Interjections to be printed thus:—At the end of a sentence: (Hear, hear.) (Cheers and "Hear, hear.") (Oh, oh.) (Laughter, and a Member: "Question.") No dash before these. In a sentence: —(Hear, hear)— —(cheers)— —("Oh, oh," and "Hear, hear")— —(Oh, oh)—. Act, bill, Lobby, Division Lobby, Strangers' Gallery, &c.; Front Bench (meaning the persons who sit on it), the Chair (meaning the Speaker), House, Chamber, Committee-room, Chief Whip, Whip, Clerks, Sergeant-at-Arms, the mace, bar, front bench, the chair, the throne, the woolsack, whip (a circular), first reading, second reading, third reading, committee stage, report, royal assent. Insurance Bill, Part II., section 3, subsection 1, clause 4. Estimates, Budget.

IRISH FREE STATE PARLIAMENT.

Oireachtas. Legislature; Dail Eireann, Chamber of Deputies; Seanad Eireann, Senate; Cumann na nGaedheal, Government; Clan Eireann, Constitutional Republicans; Sinn Fein, Extreme Republicans; Fianna Fail, De Valera's party.

LETTERS TO THE EDITOR.

Orders as to leads to be strictly followed. The contractions inst., ult., and prox. are barred—the month must be substituted. Subjoined are specimens of signatures, addresses, and dates:—

of the League of Nations would be easy.— Yours, &c.,   F. LLEWELLYN-JONES. Mold, November 12.

this difficult but most necessary and vital task.—Yours, &c.,
 W. ARTHUR WESTLEY, Chairman
 Oldham Branch English Church
 Union.
 St. John's Vicarage, Oldham,
 November 17.

previous negotiations with their representatives.—Yours, &c.,
 ALFRED H. COX, Medical Secretary
 British Medical Association.
British Medical Association House,
 Tavistock Square, London, W.C. 1,
 December 9.

[As incorporation is not at present feasible, certainly it would be desirable to see what can be done by arrangement.—ED. "GUARD."] Editorial note.

The first specimen is a common form of signature. The second shows a signature in three lines, with address and date in two. The third has the signature in two lines and the address and date in three. In the first case there should be not less than four ems between &c. and the signature. Similarly, signatures to the other two should not be indented less than three and four ems to the left, all signatures being indented one em on the right, and addresses and dates one em on the left for the first line.

BOOK REVIEWS.

Full-headed articles take six leads, the others four. "London" before publishers' names is omitted from paragraph notices, but provincial publishers have the names of their towns prefixed, as—Derby: Bemrose and Sons. Signatures to full-headed reviews may be a separate line, but all the others must be in line with the matter where possible. Set in bourgeois. Examples:

COLLECTED POEMS. By Alfred Noyes. Vol. IV. London· Blackwood and Sons. Pp. xi. 300. 7s. 6d. net.

a day which never quite fades into the common.   A. DE S.

The most obvious merit of CROMWELL A CHARACTER STUDY, by John Drinkwater (Hodder and Stoughton, pp. 226, 2s. 6d. net), is a style which, in spite of occasional lapses,

PROPER NAMES.

Christian names should not be contracted, but contractions in signatures must be followed. Names beginning with Mac to be printed as their owners write them— MacFarlane, Macfarlane, or McFarlane. Foreign names beginning with de and von to be printed—M. de la Bere, De la Bere, Baron von der Goltz. Von der Goltz. Prefixes as follows:—M., Mme., Mlle.; Herr, Frau. Frl. (Fräulein); Señor, Señora (Spanish); Senhor, Senhora (Portuguese); Gospodin, Gospozha (Russian); Signor, Signora (Italian).

DIVISION OF WORDS.

Never divide a group of letters representing a single sound, and do not divide words at the second letter if it can be avoided. The part of the word left at the end of a line should suggest the part commencing the next line. A few words generally misdivided: Catholi-cism, fanati-cism, atmosphere, episco-pal, cor-re-spon-dence, archæology, taut-ology, topog-raphy, prob-able. Care should be taken in dividing words, as the correcting of a wrong division entails the resetting of two lines.

8

THE POSSESSIVE CASE.

Use the 's wherever possible. Singular, Jones, Jones's; plural, Joneses, Joneses'. Other examples:—Three weeks' vacation, an hour's work, Smith's and Robinson's families. Where the s is silent it should be omitted, as in conscience' sake.

PREFIXES.

Words beginning re, pre, inter, pro, &c. are usually better without a hyphen, but it is not possible to omit it in many cases. Pre-exist, re-elect, pre-Neolithic, pre-war, mis-hit, are examples.

MUSIC.

Do not quote titles of works which consist of musical terms only, as Sonata in E minor, Op. 10, or are merely descriptive, as Chanson d'Amour. Where titles consist of musical and other words, the non-musical alone should be quoted: the "Tannhäuser" Overture, the "Kreutzer" Sonata, "Symphonie Pathétique," "Drink to me only with thine eyes" (where a title is obviously taken from the first line it should be kept down). "The Pipes of Pan" are other examples. Sub-titles thus: Presto non troppo, Allegro molto moderato, Adagio, Andante. Overture, sonata, symphony, &c. to be l.c. when used apart from the full title.

MONEY.

No full point after the pounds in sums of money, as £30 2s. 6d. Do not use 0d. if there are no pence, or 0s. if there are no pence and shillings. (This does not apply to tabular matter.) Such combinations as £2½ millions are not allowed—£2,500,000. Foreign money should be printed thus:— £E1,000, £T1,000 Rs.1,23,000 (one lac 23,000 rupees), Brazilian 1$000 (one milreis), schilling (Austrian), kroner (Danish and Norwegian), kronor (Swedish), piastre (Turkey), peseta (Spain), escudo (Portugal), yen (Japan), lira (Italy), drachma (Greece), tael (China), Reichsmark, Rm. (Germany), franc (France). The dollar sign should always be used with figures in American money.

FINANCIAL.

Bank rate, Bank return, Consols, bank-note.

account, bears, bulls, settlement.

debenture-holder, debenture-stock holder, shareholder, policy-holder, bondholder, ex dividend, ex all, ex bonus, &c.

Money market, Mining market, Foreign market, American Railroad market, &c.

Street, Three per Cents, 5s. in the pound (not £).

FIGURES.

Spell single figures. This rule does not apply where there is a quantity or where figures and words would be intermixed (as 10, two, 20, nine), or sums of money or the numeration of paragraphs, sections, or sentences. Figures commencing a sentence to be spelled out, also indefinite and round numbers, as "about twenty years ago," "fifty miles away," &c. Numerals must be caps. or l.c. according as the words with which they are connected are caps. or l.c., as Book IV., chap. iv. Figures should not be used with capitalised words, as Chapter 6, but chapter 6. Biblical numeration to be as these: I. Kings xiv. 37, Psalm xix. Time of day: One to twelve o'clock (no figures with "o'clock"), and 2 10 a.m. or p.m. (always figures with a.m. and p.m.). Combinations of figures and letters are not allowed, except in dates and ages, as 1st June (never June 1st), 1st inst., and "in his 51st year." Single figures should be spelled out—"aged two years," "in his second year." Related figures and words, as streets and their numbers, districts and numbers (S.W. 1), &c., to be printed in one line wherever possible.

CRICKET.

No-ball, cover-point, long-on, long-slip, short-slip, mid-on, wicket-keeper, lbw. In tables nb, lb, c, b, st, run out. Spell out the number of wickets—Jones took ten wickets for 50 runs. Smith hit four sixes —not 6's. Team, side, eleven—not XI.

FOOTBALL.

Points and goals in reports to be spelt out. United won by two goals to one; Swinton won by ten points to three. Centre forward, right wing forward, half-back, full-back, right half-back, goalkeeper, off-side, penalty line, goal line, touch line, midfield, cup-tie.

HOUSE SERVANTS.

Cook general, housemaid, kitchen-maid, housemaid waitress, between-maid, house parlour-maid, nursery-maid, children's maid.

A AND AN.—A European, a ewe, a hospital, a humble, a unanimous, a uniform, a union, a universal, a unique. An heirloom, an heroic, an historical, an historic, an hotel, an honourable, an hour.

NOR AND OR.—Neither one nor the other; neither Peter nor Paul. Either one or the other; either Peter or Paul. If there is a further comparison, or or nor should be repeated.

Titles of sermons, lectures, &c. to be kept down after the first word, as "The place of man in nature," also titles of songs, &c. which are obviously only the first line or part of it, as "Curfew shall not ring to-night."

Verdicts of juries, if summarised, not to be quoted—The jury returned a verdict of found drowned.

Do not hyphen "well known" in "This man is well known," and in similar cases.

Names of houses, &c. beginning "The" to be as The Firs (not quoted).

London Letter paragraphs must not be passed by the readers unless they have been initialled.

When a compositor cannot decipher a word, it is better to put in a blank than a word that is obviously wrong.

11

Correspondence paragraphs must not be quoted.

Where " and " joins three or more words together, as in "black, white, and green," names of companies, &c., the comma before " and " should not be omitted. Where firm names are in cps. or s.c. an " & " should be used, except when it occurs at the end of a line; then it should be l.c.

Mineral oils are sold per ton—not tun. Olive oils and fish oils are per tun.

Authors' or editorial corrections should not be made from uncorrected proofs. They should be sent to the Reading Department for transference to the revise.

Split infinitives should be avoided—that is, the separation of the verb from its preposition. "To run swiftly" or "swiftly to run" is correct; not "to swiftly run."

Verse, part of an article, should be set in smaller type than the body, and in cases where lines turn over or are full out there must be no general indention. All lines of an equal number of syllables are usually indented alike. It is advisable in doubtful cases to follow copy.

Théâtre Français
Thérèse
thesis, pl. theses
Thirty-nine Articles
thoroughbred
thoroughgoing
thrashed out—not threshed
threescore
Throne-room
Tibet
" Times " (the)—not " The
Times "
time-table
tinplate
title-deed
tithe rent charge
title-rôle
Toc H (Talbot House)
Tolstoy, Count Leo
tonic sol-fa
Tootal Broadhurst Lee Co.
topmast
torpedo-boat, torpedo-boat
destroyer
toward—not towards
town-planning
trade-mark
trade unions
Trade Unions Congress
tram-car, tram-lines
tranquillity
transatlantic
transferrer
Transubstantiation
treasure-trove
tricolour
trousers—not trouser or
trowsers
Tuileries
turkey-red
twentieth century — not
20th
tyre (of wheel)
Ukraine, Ukrainian
Ulster King of Arms
ult.—not ultimo
underestimate
Under Secretary (political)
United States (singular
number)
University Extension
unmistakable
upstairs
up to date, an up-to-date
newspaper
veld—not veldt
Velazquez

Ven.   Archdeacon—not
Venerable
Vénisélos, Eleutherios
Vice Admiral
vice chairman
Vice Chancellor
vice president
villain, villainous
viz.—" namely " preferred
Vote on Account
Wallace, Alfred Russel
wagon
wainscoted, wainscoting
walking-stick
Walküre
wallpaper
Ward, Mrs. Humphry
washhouse
water-closet
water-colour
watering-place
watermark
waterworks
Wedgwood ware
weekday
Welch Regiment, Royal
Welch Fusiliers, Welsh
Guards
wellbeing
wellnigh
west coast
Wei-Hai-Wei
West End (London)
Western Counties
Whip (person), whip (cir-
cular)
whisky, whiskies
" Whitaker's Almanack "
White Paper (Parliamen-
tary)
Whit Monday
Whittingehame   (Lord
Balfour's seat)
whooping-cough
wideawake, widespread
wigeon—not widgeon
Wilhelmshafen (not haven)
winsey (cloth)
woeful
women's suffrage
woolsack—House of Lords
workmanlike
Wormwood Scrubs
X-rays
Yudenitch—not Judenitch
zigzag